CRIMMIGRATION LAW

CÉSAR CUAUHTÉMOC GARCÍA HERNÁNDEZ

Printed in the United States of America.

17 16 15 5 4 3 2 1

ISBN: 978-1-62722-387-4
e-ISBN: 978-1-62722-388-1

Library of Congress Cataloging-in-Publication Data
García Hernández, César Cuauhtémoc, author.
  Crimmigration Law: a legal guide/César Cuauhtémoc García Hernández
    pages cm
  Includes bibliographical references and index.
  ISBN 978-1-62722-387-4 (alk. paper)
  1. Emigration and immigration law--United States--Criminal provisions.
I. Title.
  KF4819.G37 2015
  345.73'0237--dc23

                                                                  2015016265

Discounts are available for books ordered in bulk. Special consideration is given to state bars, CLE programs, and other barrelated organizations. Inquire at Book Publishing, ABA Publishing, American Bar Association, 321 N. Clark Street, Chicago, Illinois 60654-7598.

www.ShopABA.org

To Margaret, without whom this book would not exist.

ACKNOWLEDGMENTS

The thoughts and research laid out in the following pages have been simmering for many years. In that time, I have been blessed by the support of several institutions and countless individuals. While it is impossible to recognize all the invaluable assistance I have received, I would be remiss not to mention a handful without whom this project would not have been possible. The many lawyers, judges, journalists, policy analysts, and activists who have read my blog, crImmigration.com, since its launch in January 2009 have pushed me to deepen my understanding and sharpen my analysis of the issues addressed in these pages. Linus Chan, Ingrid V. Eagly, Mark Noferi, Stephen Lee, and Yolanda Vázquez have been steadfast sounding boards for many years. Their insights are reflected throughout this book. The students in my Crimmigration Law seminar at the University of Denver and Capital University have given me the opportunity to think deeply about how to disentangle this material. Without them, I wouldn't have known how to start. On a related note, my many fabulous colleagues at Denver and Capital have encouraged my attempts to train a generation of crimmigration lawyers. Lastly, I cannot overstate the importance that my two brothers—Raúl García and Carlos Moctezuma García—have had on this book. Their crimmigration law practice (where I remain of counsel) keeps me up-to-date, their counsel keeps me grounded, and their life's work keeps me inspired.

CONTENTS

The law embodies the story of a nation's development through many centuries, and it cannot be dealt with as if it contained only the axioms and corollaries of a book of mathematics. In order to know what it is, we must know what it has been, and what it tends to become.

—Oliver Wendell Holmes, Jr., *The Common Law*

CHAPTER 1
Introduction

At its most basic, "crimmigration" law describes the convergence of two distinct bodies of law: criminal law and procedure with immigration law and procedure. For most of the nation's history, these operated almost entirely free of the other. Criminal law and procedure was thought to be the province of prosecutors, criminal defense attorneys, and the state and federal judges who oversee criminal prosecutions every day. Immigration law, in contrast, was confined to immigration courts housed within the executive branch of the federal government and staffed by immigration attorneys, immigration judges, and prosecutors employed for many years by the Immigration and Naturalization Service (INS) and now the Department of Homeland Security (DHS) or Department of Justice.

That division has undeniably become a historical relic. The world of criminal courthouses has collided with the world of immigration courthouses. The substantive criminal law that defines what constitutes a state or federal crime has increasingly come to turn on a person's immigration status. Criminal procedure norms embodied in court rules and

constitutional amendments have made special allowances for immigration law enforcement concerns and the citizenship status of defendants.
Meanwhile, immigration law now frequently turns to a migrant's criminal history to dictate whether imprisonment is merited while the government decides whether to mete out immigration law's greatest sanction,
deportation, and its close cousin, exclusion from the United States.

These developments are unquestionably significant to the migrants
whose liberty and ability to live in the United States are at stake. But they
are also immensely important to the attorneys who have taken on the
weighty task of defending migrants facing criminal prosecution or placed
in "removal" proceedings, the modern technical term for what used to be
called "deportation" and "exclusion" proceedings. These changes to the
practice of criminal law and immigration law are just as relevant to the
prosecutor whose interest is "that justice shall be done," as the Supreme
Court says is their duty.[1] No matter the side on which an attorney falls,
sound representation requires understanding the consequences at stake
for the parties—the individuals that defense attorneys represent and the
communities in whose name prosecutors appear before courts.

With those attorneys in mind, this book lays out crimmigration law's
contours. It tracks the legal developments that have created crimmigration law and explains the many ways in which the stark line that once
appeared to keep criminal law firmly divided from immigration law has
melted away. In doing so, it highlights crimmigration law's most salient
features—its ability to substantially raise the stakes of criminal prosecutions by dramatically expanding the list of crimes that can result in removal from the United States, its willingness to freely rely on crimes that
apply only to migrants, and its vast dependence on detention as a means
of policing immigration law.

What Is "Crimmigration" Law?

As with any area of law, understanding crimmigration law doctrine requires
first identifying a working definition of what the term "crimmigration"
means. Unlike criminal law or immigration law, there is no ready-made

---

1. Berger v. United States, 295 U.S. 78, 88 (1935).

interpretation. This is a new area of law that largely emerged in the last
three decades and evolves daily, sometimes in radical and unpredictable
directions. That is not to say, however, that it is a term devoid of meaning.
Generally, "crimmigration law" refers to the intersection of criminal law
and procedure with immigration law and procedure. This broad outline
can be filled by the details of three trends that have dominated the evolution that criminal law and immigration law have undergone in recent
years: criminal convictions now lead to immigration law consequences
ever more often; violations of immigration law are increasingly punished
through the criminal justice system; and law enforcement tactics traditionally viewed as parts of one or the other area of law have crossed into
the other making enforcement of immigration law resemble criminal law
enforcement and turning criminal law enforcement into a semblance of
immigration law enforcement. The end result, Juliet Stumpf wrote in the
2006 article that for the first time provided a conceptual framework for
crimmigration law, is that the line between criminal law and immigration
law "has grown indistinct" such that today "immigration law and the
criminal justice system are merely nominally separate."[2]

This book is organized so as to follow the three trends that characterize crimmigration law's development. It begins in Part 1 by addressing
the many ways in which migrants are subjected to "removal" proceedings (a term that includes deportation and exclusion from the United
States) as a result of having been involved in criminal activity. In Part 2,
it then turns to a discussion of features of criminal prosecutions in state
and federal courts that are unique to noncitizens—either because they
involve substantive criminal offenses or procedural devices that apply
only to noncitizens or that have a special focus on noncitizens. Lastly, in
Part 3, the book addresses the increasingly overlapping and codependent
enforcement tactics utilized in the criminal and immigration contexts.
Some of the enforcement initiatives to be addressed—for example, Secure
Communities and the 287(g) programs—are unique to crimmigration
law, while others—in particular detention—operate under exceptional
authority allowing them to take uniquely expansive forms.

---

2. Juliet Stumpf, *The Crimmigration Crisis*, 56 AM. U. L. REV. 367 (2006).

Crimmigration Law's Legal Lineage

Though its moniker as a "nation of immigrants" is rooted in an accurate—though exaggerated—version of history, the United States is also a nation that has long been accustomed to excluding migrants deemed undesirable. As far back as 1788, the Continental Congress urged states to enact laws to prevent the arrival of "convicted malefactors from foreign countries."[3] Several states did so within a few years. Throughout this era, the states retained the power to regulate immigration, and, with a few exceptions in the late 1700s, the federal government kept its focus on other matters. As the country expanded over the course of the next seventy-five years, many other states followed their founding predecessors by also limiting the entry of criminals.[4]

By the time the federal government returned its attention to immigration law in the closing decades of the nineteenth century, it too had developed a special eye for crime. The Page Act of 1875, the law that marks the modern beginning of the federal government's regulation of immigration, prohibited the entry of convicted felons.[5] Sixteen years later, Congress introduced into immigration law a provision that remains a source of much confusion to lawyers and judges—exclusion on the basis of having committed a "crime involving moral turpitude."[6] Another predecessor of today's immigration law provisions that turn on criminal involvement was adopted in 1922—that year Congress decided that narcotics offenses justified deportation.[7]

Despite immigration law's early reliance on criminal law to decide upon whom to allow to enter into or remain in the United States, the Supreme Court made clear that deportation was not to be considered a form of punishment. It was, instead, the Court announced in *Fong Yue Ting v. United States*, nothing more than "the removal of an alien out of the country simply because his presence is deemed inconsistent with the public welfare, and

---

3. New York v. Miln, 36 U.S. 102, 112 (1837).
4. *See* Gerald L. Neuman, *The Lost Century of American Immigration Law (1776–1875)*, 93 COLUM. L. REV. 1833, 1841–46 (1993).
5. *See* Act of March 3, 1875, ch. 141, § 5, 18 Stat. 477.
6. *See* Immigration Act of March 3, 1891, ch. 551, § 1, 26 Stat. 1084, 1084.
7. Act of May 26, 1922, ch. 202, Pub. L. No. 227, 42 Stat. 596; *see* Matter of V-, 1 I. & N. Dec. 293, 295 (B.I.A. 1942) (applying this provision to exclusion proceedings).

without any punishment being imposed or contemplated."[8] The Court has yet to show much inclination to reconsider this position. At most, it indicated in a 1954 opinion, *Galvan v. Press*, that "were we writing on a clean slate" it might hold the Constitution's Ex Post Facto Clause—the constitutional provision that in most situations prohibits legislatures from criminalizing conduct that already occurred—applicable to deportation. But, as the Court added, "the slate is not clean."[9] It is instead filled with repeated judicial declarations that immigration law is a form of civil law and more than a century's worth of legislative reliance on this fundamental characterization. Because immigration law is deemed civil, most of the constitutional procedures required for criminal prosecutions do not apply. When it comes to immigration court proceedings, there is no Fifth Amendment privilege against self-incrimination, Sixth Amendment right to counsel, and only a limited Fourth Amendment prohibition against unreasonable searches and seizures.

Practice Pointer

For more than a century, the Supreme Court has repeated that the process of admitting and deporting people from the United States is civil rather than criminal. As a result of immigration law's civil characterization, a host of constitutional provisions that apply to criminal proceedings either do not apply or apply in a much more limited fashion:

- *Fourth Amendment*: The Fourth Amendment's prohibitions against arbitrary arrest and unreasonable searches are largely inapplicable in removal proceedings. Evidence obtained through law enforcement actions that would normally violate the Fourth Amendment if introduced in a criminal prosecution can be admitted in removal proceedings to show that a person is removable from the United States. The Supreme Court has identified two exceptions for egregious or widespread constitutional violations, but these have been interpreted exceedingly narrowly.
- *Fifth Amendment*: The Fifth Amendment ensures that no one shall be prosecuted multiple times for the same offense (the Double Jeopardy Clause), protects defendants from being forced to incriminate themselves (the privilege against

(continued)

---

8. Fong Yue Ting v. United States, 149 U.S. 698, 709 (1893).
9. Galvan v. Press, 347 U.S. 522, 531 (1954).

self-incrimination), and guarantees basic due process protections (Due Process Clause). The Double Jeopardy Clause does not bar the same activity serving as the basis of a criminal prosecution and immigration prosecution. The privilege against self-incrimination prevents migrants from being forced to admit information that could result in criminal prosecution, but it does not keep immigration judges from making adverse inferences about a migrant's immigration status. Similarly, though the Due Process Clause ensures that migrants receive a hearing at which they are provided the opportunity to be heard, it does not require a hearing before a judicial officer (thus immigration judges are actually part of the Executive Branch).

- *Sixth Amendment*: None of the guarantees that the Sixth Amendment provides—the right to counsel, including appointed counsel; the right to a jury trial; the right to a speedy trial; or the right to confront adverse witnesses—are applicable to removal proceedings. The Fifth Amendment Due Process Clause protects versions of some of these rights but almost always to a lesser extent than the Sixth Amendment.

Likewise, the Federal Rules of Evidence and Federal Rules of Criminal Procedure do not apply to removal proceedings.

Even though the Supreme Court has long made clear that the constitutional protections afforded to criminal defendants do not apply in immigration court, immigration has nonetheless appeared within criminal proceedings since the late nineteenth century. The Chinese Exclusion Act of 1882—a law infamous for using explicitly race-based criteria to identify people prohibited from entering the United States—punished by up to one year of imprisonment anyone who helped a Chinese person enter the United States without authorization.[10] An amendment enacted a decade later required all Chinese laborers in the United States to get a certificate of residence from the government indicating their lawful presence. Crucially, they could only receive this certificate if they obtained the affidavit of at least one white witness attesting to the Chinese applicant's residence. Congress, the Supreme Court surmised in an 1893 decision, might have imposed the white witness requirement after having grown tired of the "suspicious nature" of

---

10. Act of May 6, 1882 (Chinese Exclusion Act), ch. 126, §§ 7, 11, 22 Stat. 58, 60–61 (*repealed by* Chinese Exclusion Repeal Act of 1943, ch. 344, 57 Stat. 600).

testimony provided by Chinese witnesses in the past "arising from the loose notions entertained by the witnesses of the obligation of an oath."[11]

Though its exclusive application to Chinese migrants, its punishment method, and the white witness requirement were all significant, the Chinese Exclusion Act played an important role in crimmigration law's history due to a fourth provision—one that granted executive branch officials the power to determine whether a particular person was subject to imprisonment as a punitive sanction for committing a crime. There was no room for the standard criminal procedure that usually precedes imprisonment—presentation before a neutral judge in which the prosecution is required to prove critical facts beyond a reasonable doubt. Four Chinese men challenged that process claiming that if they were going to be imprisoned it could come only after receiving the benefits of a criminal trial. In *Wong Wing v. United States*, the Court agreed. Punitive imprisonment is permitted for having done nothing more than failed to comply with immigration laws, the Court concluded, but only if the defendant's guilt is established by a criminal proceeding.[12] Roughly thirty years later, Congress did just this, making unauthorized entry a federal crime punishable by up to a year in prison. That same statute also authorized as much as two years imprisonment for people who enter the United States without authorization after having previously been deported.[13] Both crimes remain on the books today, though punishable by up to six months imprisonment for a first time unauthorized entry conviction and twenty years imprisonment for first time unauthorized reentry conviction.[14]

This early interaction between criminal law and procedure and immigration law and procedure might suggest that crimmigration law developed in the late nineteenth or early twentieth century. It did not for one principal reason: the government did not use these powers very much. In the ninety-two years between 1892 and 1984, all of 14,287 people were excluded from the United States due to a criminal conviction or

---

11. *See Fong Yue Ting*, 149 U.S. at 727, 730 (quoting Chae Chan Ping v. United States, 130 U.S. 581, 598 (1889)).
12. Wong Wing v. United States, 163 U.S. 228, 235 (1896).
13. *See* Act of March 4, 1929, ch. 690, §§ 1-2, 45 Stat. 1551, 1551.
14. *See* INA §§ 275(c), 276(b).

narcotics violation (categories that the federal government reported separately). Another 56,669 were deported for these reasons between 1908 and 1980. Combined 70,956 people were removed on the basis of a conviction in the eight or nine decades preceding the mid-1980s. All that changed dramatically within a few years such that in fiscal year 2013 alone U.S. Immigration and Customs Enforcement (ICE) reported having removed 216,810 people with a criminal conviction on their record.[15] In other words, criminal activity appears to have affected the ability of more than three times as many people to live in the United States in 2013 than throughout most of the twentieth century combined.

A second reason why crimmigration law did not take hold until the late 1900s is that immigration law enforcement was of a wholly different character than traditional criminal policing. For example, detention of migrants facing removal, the form of punishment that most emblematizes criminal law enforcement, was the exception during the century leading up to the 1990s. Indeed, from the 1950s until the 1980s, the INS had a policy of not using detention except in unusual circumstances. Like immigration officials' reliance on criminal activity the use of detention to police immigration law increased substantially in a matter of years. By 2001, over 200,000 people were being detained each year while they waited to learn whether they would be allowed to remain in the United States. The immigration detention population has continued to grow steadily since then. In fiscal year 2011, for example, 429,247 people were detained pending immigration proceedings. Meanwhile, Congress now requires that ICE pay for a minimum of 34,000 beds per night, almost guaranteeing that the historically anomalous annual detention populations of recent years will not become a momentary blip.[16]

---

15. See U.S. IMMIGRATION & NATURALIZATION SERV., 1996 STATISTICAL YEARBOOK OF THE IMMIGRATION AND NATURALIZATION SERVICE 175 tbl.60 (1997) (providing exclusion data for 1892–1984); id. at 183 tbl.65 (providing deportation data for 1908–1980); U.S. DEP'T OF HOMELAND SECURITY, IMMIGRATION & CUSTOMS ENFORCEMENT, ICE IMMIGRATION REMOVALS: FY 2013 ERO ANNUAL REPORT 3 (2013) (providing 2013 statistics).

16. See DORIS MEISSNER ET AL., IMMIGRATION ENFORCEMENT IN THE UNITED STATES: THE RISE OF A FORMIDABLE MACHINERY 126 fig.30 (2013) (providing 2001 data); U.S. DEP'T OF HOMELAND SEC., IMMIGRATION ENFORCEMENT ACTIONS: 2011 ANNUAL REPORT 5 tbl.4 (2012) (providing FY 2011 data). For the 34,000 bed mandate, see e.g., H.R. 3547, Consolidated Appropriations Act, 2014, Div. F, U.S. Immigration and Customs Enforcement.

Crimmigration Law's Three Heads

Neither history nor statistics can explain crimmigration law's multiple parts. The number of people removed due to having committed a crime has grown because the number of crimes that can result in immigration problems has expanded. Similarly, the number of people in immigration detention has multiplied because Congress has boosted immigration officials' legal power to detain and provided them with the money to do so. At the same time, the number of people prosecuted for immigration-related crimes has increased because the criminal justice system has become a central feature in the way some states and the federal government seek to control immigration. Each of these trends developed over the years in a series of legislative or policy amendments. All are equally significant to the creation of crimmigration law.

Crimmigration's first part, removing migrants on the basis of criminal activity, expanded steadily throughout the 1980s and 1990s. Building off the statutory provision enacted in 1922 that authorized deportation upon conviction for a narcotics offense, Congress targeted migrant drug offenders with vigor during the last decades of the twentieth century. The Anti-Drug Abuse Act of 1986, for example, replaced a narrow reference to opiate addiction in the list of crimes that could lead to deportation with a wide-ranging provision authorizing deportation upon conviction of any state, federal, or foreign country's offense relating to a controlled substance. This provision, often described as the "controlled substance offense" basis of removal, remains a part of the Immigration and Nationality Act (INA) and makes frequent appearances in immigration court proceedings because of its broad language.[17]

More groundbreaking than that statutory shift was an immigration law amendment that came two years later in the Anti-Drug Abuse Act of 1988. That public law added the term "aggravated felony" to the INA and in the process changed the severity of the consequences meted out on migrants convicted of criminal activity as well as the practice of immigration law. Amended repeatedly over the next decade and a half, the aggravated felony provision now encompasses twenty types of crimes ranging

---

17. INA § 237(a)(2)(B)(i); *see* Anti-Drug Abuse Act of 1986, Pub. L. No. 99-570, § 1751, 100 Stat. 3207 (amending INA § 212(a)(23), 8 U.S.C. § 1182(a)(23)).

from murder to altering a passport. Despite its name, some state misdemeanors come within its purview.[18]

While more and more crimes were becoming possible bases of removal, Congress also found time to raise the stakes of immigration-related activity in criminal courtrooms while federal prosecutors boosted resources devoted to pursuing immigration-related criminal activity, crimmigration law's second branch. The decades-old crime of unauthorized reentry became much more consequential in 1988 when Congress raised the maximum sentence to fifteen years imprisonment for anyone convicted of unauthorized reentry after having been convicted of an aggravated felony. The maximum sentence currently stands at twenty years imprisonment. Repeated convictions for unlawful entry, meanwhile, may be punished by as much as two years in a federal prison. Document fraud offenses also became more heavily punished. In 1986, Congress increased the penalty for possession or use of a false immigration document to two years imprisonment.[19] A decade later Congress even authorized courts to strip individuals of any property used to commit passport fraud.[20]

During the 1980s, Congress also added new immigration-related crimes to the federal penal code. The Immigration Reform and Control Act of 1986 that famously provided legalization paths for millions of unauthorized migrants also made it a federal crime to hire unauthorized workers and increased the penalty for knowingly or recklessly smuggling people into the United States. Another statute enacted that year criminalized

---

18. INA § 101(a)(43); see Anti-Drug Abuse Act of 1988, Pub. L. No. 100-690, § 7342, 102 Stat. 4181, 4469–70 (amending INA § 101(a), 8 U.S.C. 1101(a)); Guerrero-Perez v. INS, 242 F.3d 727, 737 (7th Cir. 2001) (concluding that the term "aggravated felony" can include misdemeanors).

19. INA § 276(b)(2) (providing the current maximum punishment for unauthorized reentry); INA § 275(a)(3) (providing the current maximum penalty for unauthorized entry); see Anti-Drug Abuse Act of 1988, Pub. L. No. 100-690, § 7345, 102 Stat. 4181, 4469–70 (raising the maximum sentence to fifteen years); Immigration Marriage Fraud Amendments of 1986, Pub. L. No. 99-639, § 2(d), 100 Stat. 3537, 3542 (criminalizing marriage fraud); Immigration Reform and Control Act of 1986 [hereinafter IRCA], Pub. L. No. 99-603, § 103, 100 Stat. 3359, 3360 (amending 18 U.S.C. § 1546) (increasing the document fraud penalty).

20. Illegal Immigration Reform and Immigrant Responsibility Act of 1996 [hereinafter IIRIRA], Pub. L. No. 104-208, § 217, 110 Stat. 3009, 3009-571 (codified at 18 U.S.C. § 982(a)(6)(A) (2012)).

marrying solely for the purpose of obtaining an immigration benefit. Ten years later Congress created a host of crimes as part of the mammoth Illegal Immigration Reform and Immigrant Responsibility Act (IIRIRA). Falsely claiming to be a United States citizen, voting in a federal election, and participating in the false preparation of an immigration application were suddenly criminalized.[21]

It did not take long for federal prosecutors to put these new powers into use. Arrests for immigration crimes doubled from 1994 to 1998, doubled again from 1998 to 2004, and yet again from 2004 to 2008.[22] Indeed, arrests for immigration crimes grew faster than any other type of federal crime from 2006 to 2010.[23] This trend shows no sign of abating. In 2010 a full 46 percent of individuals arrested and booked by the United States Marshals Service for suspicion of any federal crime found themselves in that predicament because of an immigration offense.[24] This has had a profound impact on federal criminal law practice. While just over 5 percent of the criminal cases appearing in federal courts in 1993 listed an immigration crime as the most serious offense, that percentage jumped to 13.4 percent in 1997 and 18.2 percent in 2001, well above the proportion of the population that was not a United States citizen.[25] Immigration prosecutions and convictions now make up one of the two most frequently pursued types of crime in the federal court system, competing with drug offenses for the top spot.[26] Not surprisingly, federal prosecutors spend an enormous amount of time on immigration cases. Almost 45 percent of matters concluded in 2010 involved an immigration crime; the next most consuming category, drug crimes, appeared in just shy of 20 percent of cases.[27]

---

21. IRCA § 101, 100 Stat. 3359, 3360 (codified at INA § 274A, 8 U.S.C. § 1324a (2012)) (criminalizing employment of unauthorized migrants); *id.* at 112 (regarding smuggling); IIRIRA, §§ 213, 215, 216, 110 Stat. 3009, 3009-571 (codified at INA § 274C(e), 8 U.S.C. § 1324c(e) (2012), 18 U.S.C. § 1015(e) (2012), 18 U.S.C. 611(a) (2012)).

22. MARK MOTIVANS, FEDERAL JUSTICE STATISTICS, 2010, at 4 (Dec. 2013).

23. *Id.* at 2.

24. *Id.* at 3.

25. ADMIN. OFFICE OF THE U.S. COURTS, JUDICIAL BUS. 1997 ANNUAL REPORT 188 tbl.D-2, 198 (providing 1993 and 1997 data); ADMIN. OFFICE OF THE U.S. COURTS, JUDICIAL BUSINESS 2005 ANNUAL REPORT 11, 225, 227 tbl.D-2 (providing 2001 data).

26. *See* Motivans, *supra* note 22, at 17 fig.9, 22 tbl.13.

27. *Id.* at 12 tbl.6.

Not to be outdone, several states have also turned to their traditional criminal law systems to target individuals who violate federal immigration law. Over 100 state laws were enacted between 2010 and 2012 dealing with state and local law enforcement powers regarding immigration.[28] Most prominently, Arizona's Senate Bill 1070—which critics called the "show me your papers" law—relied quite heavily on the state's criminal law enforcement authority. One provision, for example, made it a misdemeanor to fail to register with the federal government as required by federal law.[29] Another part of the statute criminalized unauthorized migrants searching for work in public places, usually sidewalks.[30] A third section permitted warrantless arrests by police officers if they developed probable cause that a person committed an offense that would allow removal from the United States.[31] The Supreme Court struck down all three provisions. It did so, however, not because states are necessarily prohibited from regulating immigration through their criminal processes, but on the much narrower basis that Arizona's legislation treaded on ground in which Congress had already legislated. The Constitution's Supremacy Clause, therefore, led the Court to conclude that federal law trumped state law in these instances. It does not, however, prohibit the state from requiring its police officers to ask ICE about the immigration status of a person lawfully detained. As a result, that provision survived a constitutional challenge.[32]

Crimmigration law's third feature, the intermingling of law enforcement tactics, also expanded quite significantly beginning in the 1980s. The lax procedural protections of immigration proceedings began to appear in criminal investigations and prosecutions, while the heavy-handed enforcement strategies that characterize criminal law policing made their way into investigations of possible immigration law violations. Though the Fourth and Fifth Amendments formally apply to immigration law,

28. *2012 Immigration-Related Laws and Resolutions in the States (Jan. 1-Dec. 31, 2012)*, NAT'L CONFERENCE OF STATE LEGISLATURES tbl.1 (Jan. 2013), http://www.ncsl.org/issues-research/immig/2012-immigration-related-laws-jan-december-2012.aspx.

29. Ariz. Rev. Stat. § 13-1509(a), *held unconstitutional by* Arizona v. United States, 132 S. Ct. 2492, 2503 (2012).

30. *Id.* § 13-2928(c), *held unconstitutional by Arizona*, 132 S. Ct. at 2505.

31. *Id.* § 13-3883, *held unconstitutional by Arizona*, 132 S. Ct. at 2507.

32. *Id.* § 11-1051(b), *upheld by Arizona*, 132 S. Ct. at 2510.

they have historically done so in a much more limited fashion than is true of criminal proceedings. Similarly, courts have consistently held that the Sixth Amendment has no relevance to immigration law, but it is a cornerstone of criminal procedure.

In recent years immigration law's posture toward Fourth, Fifth, and Sixth Amendment rights has bled into criminal law. The Supreme Court has long held that the Fourth Amendment applies quite crudely under immigration law. The exclusionary rule, for example—the powerful incentive to police officers to comply with the Fourth Amendment lest they risk losing the ability to use evidence against the defendant—does not apply to ordinary constitutional transgressions. Rather, it applies only to "egregious" or "widespread" Fourth Amendment violations.[33] In some instances, police officers investigating traditional criminal activity have flouted the Fourth Amendment but been able to use the unconstitutionally obtained evidence in immigration court.[34]

In a similar vein, the Fifth Amendment Due Process Clause has historically applied more loosely to immigration court than criminal court proceedings. Immigration judges, for example, regularly address multiple respondents at once. In contrast, Federal Rule of Criminal Procedure 11(b) requires a judge presiding over a plea hearing to address each defendant "personally in open court" to ensure that the defendant understands the nature of the charges against her and the consequences of pleading guilty or nolo contendere. This obligation is rooted in the Due Process Clause's requirement that a plea be knowing and voluntary.[35] Despite Rule 11(b)'s seemingly clear mandate, criminal proceedings involving immigration crimes have come to resemble the en masse style of immigration court proceedings. Under Operation Streamline, federal judges throughout the country now address large groups of defendants—sometimes as many as 100—simultaneously.

Likewise, the Sixth Amendment right to counsel, which has never been applied to immigration proceedings but has been called a cornerstone

---

33. INS v. Lopez-Mendoza, 468 U.S. 1032, 1051–52 (1984); *see* Oliva-Ramos v. Attorney General, 694 F.3d 259, 272 (3d Cir. 2012).

34. *See* Puc-Ruiz v. Holder, 629 F.3d 771, 775–80 (8th Cir. 2010).

35. *See* McCarthy v. United States, 394 U.S. 459, 467 (1969).

of fair criminal proceedings, has surfaced in a more superficial iteration in immigration-related criminal proceedings. The Supreme Court's 2010 decision in *Padilla v. Kentucky*[36] broke new ground by clarifying that criminal defendants' constitutional guarantee of effective assistance of counsel includes receiving accurate advice about the immigration consequences of conviction. In an interesting and important twist, however, the *Padilla* Court actually adopted a two-part test that waters down the prevailing ineffective assistance framework, itself long criticized as too weak to actually help defendants.

While this has been happening in criminal courtrooms, immigration officials have busied themselves adopting some of the tactics of criminal policing. Since receiving statutory authorization to carry firearms in 1990, immigration law enforcement agents have increasingly resembled police agencies charged with investigating crime. ICE now has law enforcement units that resemble SWAT teams, including military-style uniforms and powerful weapons, and regularly restrains detainees using handcuffs and shackles. ICE counts among its inventory armored personnel carriers while its border-focused twin agency, U.S. Customs and Border Protection (CBP), owns drone aircraft more commonly associated with the Defense Department.

Most palpably, immigration officials have devoted enormous energy and money to boosting ICE's detention capacity. In recent years ICE has been able—indeed, required by a directive in funding legislation—to pay for a minimum of 34,000 beds each night to hold people suspected of having violated some INA provision.[37] Though ICE takes pains to describe them as "detention centers" or "service processing centers"—anything but a jail or prison—most of these beds are located in facilities that are in many ways indistinguishable from jails or prisons. Barbed-wire fencing surrounds them, movement by detainees and visitors is severely restricted, and they tend to be located in remote locations far removed from legal services. Guards, meanwhile, constantly watch detainees, physical abuse is rampant, and medical care remains lamentable. Many others are

---

36. 559 U.S. 356 (2010).
37. Consolidated Appropriations Act, H.R. 3547, Div. F, Security, Enforcement, and Investigations, U.S. Immigration and Customs Enforcement, Salaries and Expenses (2014).

actually kept in jails or prisons that ICE simply pays to house its detainees. All at a cost that has exceeded $2 billion annually in recent years.

This detention population does not account for everyone confined due
to crimmigration law's rise. Of all individuals awaiting trial on federal
criminal charges of any type, those alleged to have committed an immigration offense are most likely to wait inside a federal prison or contracted
facility. Immigration defendants made up fully 45 percent of federal defendants detained prior to their case coming to some resolution in 2010. Even
people accused of having committed a violent crime were less likely to be
detained while their cases made their way through the district courts.[38] Migrants make up a significantly lower but still remarkable percentage of the
population imprisoned after conviction for a federal crime—23.6 percent
in 2009, and hovering near there as far back as 2001. The vast majority
of these (roughly 70 percent) were imprisoned upon conviction for an immigration crime. By comparison, approximately four-tenths of 1 percent of
noncitizen federal prisoners were convicted of a violent crime.[39]

Crimmigration Law Entities
To carry out all of this, crimmigration law depends on an array of public
and private entities. The federal government's Department of Homeland
Security is most obviously a key actor, but so too are other governmental
units. In particular, state and local governments are hugely important in
crimmigration law enforcement both because of their size and because
their role is frequently overlooked in discussions of traditional immigration law. This section briefly maps the various entities involved in crimmigration law.

State and local law enforcement play an enormous role in crimmigration law. The vast majority of police officers in the United States are employed by a city, county, or state government, thus the bulk of police work
is in the hands of these officials. Likewise, state and county prosecutors
pursue most criminal prosecutions. There were 20.4 million criminal

---

38. *See* Motivans, *supra* note 22, at 16 & tbl.9.
39. *See* MARC R. ROSENBLUM & WILLIAM A. KANDEL, CONG. RES. SERV., INTERIOR
IMMIGRATION ENFORCEMENT: PROGRAMS TARGETING CRIMINAL ALIENS 7 tbl.2 & 8 tbl.3
(Dec. 20, 2012).

cases lodged in state trial courts in 2010, a far cry from the 77,287 cases filed in federal district courts that year.[40] Each of the roughly three-quarters of a million state and local police officers stationed throughout the country is responsible for investigating criminal activity and bringing alleged perpetrators to the attention of prosecutors.[41] Any one of these investigations can lead to a criminal prosecution and conviction that creates immigration law problems for people who lack United States citizenship. These police officers, therefore, play an important role in implementing crimmigration law.

State and local prosecutors, of course, are not obligated to pursue any particular investigation brought to their attention by police officers. They can decline to prosecute for almost any reason. Perhaps they believe the facts don't support the charge. Maybe they agree to drop a charge in favor of a guilty plea to an alternative offense. And sometimes they might even refuse to move forward with a criminal case because they have better ways of spending the office's resources. There is no legal impediment to exercising prosecutorial discretion in these ways. As the Supreme Court explained in 1978 and has repeated since then, "the decision whether or not to prosecute . . . generally rests entirely in [the prosecutor's] discretion."[42] Indeed, though clear data don't exist, it appears that prosecutors choose not to pursue about a third of felonies and a tenth of misdemeanor cases.[43] All of these decisions affect the criminal and immigration law consequences defendants without U.S. citizenship face, thus state and local prosecutors, like police officers, have a significant impact on crimmigration law.

State court judges play a similarly important role. Not only do they oversee state criminal prosecutions, but since 2010 they have increasingly been called upon to determine whether defendants receive the type of advice about potential immigration consequences of conviction that is constitutionally

40. ROBERT C. LA FOUNTAIN ET AL., EXAMINING THE WORK OF STATE COURTS: AN ANALYSIS OF 2010 STATE COURT CASELOADS 3 (2012); ADMINISTRATIVE OFFICE OF THE U.S. COURTS, FEDERAL JUDICIAL CASELOAD STATISTICS: MARCH 31, 2010, tbl.D (2010).
41. BRIAN A. REAVES, CENSUS OF STATE AND LOCAL LAW ENFORCEMENT AGENCIES, 2008, at 1 (2011).
42. Bordenkircher v. Hayes, 434 U.S. 357, 364 (1978).
43. Josh Bowers, *Punishing the Innocent*, 156 U. PA. L. REV. 1117, 1129 (2008).

required. The Sixth Amendment right to counsel, the Supreme Court recognized that year, obligates defense attorneys to determine whether a client is clearly going to face immigration consequences if convicted and advise accordingly. State trial court judges now carry the majority of the work of ensuring that defense attorneys provide this type of advice prior to accepting a plea. They also review post-conviction relief applications to determine whether a conviction was entered in compliance with this Sixth Amendment obligation. As chapter 5 explains, neither is an easy task.

Federal law enforcement officers, prosecutors, and judges perform much the same function as their state and local counterparts. There are about 120,000 federal law enforcement officers empowered to arrest suspects.[44] Though more than half a million fewer than the number of state or local police officers, they are much more directly plugged into the crimmigration pipeline. Roughly half of federal officers, it turns out, are employed by DHS. The department's CBP, for example, is charged with regulating cross-border movement of people and goods. DHS's other principal immigration law enforcement agency, ICE, identifies and arrests people suspected of violating civil or criminal immigration law. As a whole, DHS was responsible for bringing 54 percent of defendants to the attention of federal prosecutors in 2010.[45] In turn, those prosecutors—ninety-three U.S. attorneys and approximately 6,000 assistant U.S. attorneys that they employ—are responsible for litigating most of the federal government's trial work, including prosecuting allegations of federal immigration crimes in federal district courts. While being prosecuted for a federal crime many individuals are subject to pretrial detention under the control of the U.S. Marshals Service, a division of the Department of Justice. Upon conviction, federal prisoners are transferred into the custody of the Justice Department's Federal Bureau of Prisons. A convicted individual can appeal to the federal court of appeals in which the district court is located.

While awaiting removal proceedings, ICE holds migrants in immigration detention centers, though county governments or private prison corporations frequently operate these facilities. DHS attorneys prosecute these cases in one of the nation's fifty-seven immigration courts.

44. BRIAN A. REAVES, FEDERAL LAW ENFORCEMENT OFFICERS, 2008, at 1 (2012).
45. See Motivans, supra note 22, at 12 & tbl.5.

Immigration judges presiding over those cases then decide whether a migrant is entitled to remain in the United States and members of the Board
of Immigration Appeals (BIA or Board) review those decisions when
the losing party appeals.[46] Despite being called "courts" and "judges,"
neither the immigration courts nor the immigration judges who oversee
hearings there are part of the judicial branch. Instead, these are Justice
Department tribunals run by Justice Department officials. Even the BIA
members who hear appeals are Justice Department employees. A migrant
who loses at the BIA can appeal to the federal courts at which point federal judges become involved. Interestingly enough, appeals go directly to
the court of appeals, the federal court system's intermediate layer rather
than to the federal district courts.[47] In most circumstances, immigration
courts and the BIA are obligated to abide by precedential circuit court
decisions issued by the circuit court from which the case arises.

A Note on Labels

Before proceeding, it is worth taking a moment to describe the various
terms used throughout the book. There is a great deal of controversy
over the most appropriate term to use to describe people who are not
United States citizens and who have violated immigration law. Political
conservatives tend to favor some variation of "illegal alien," while liber-
als adopt the more sanguine "undocumented immigrant." Except in a few
instances where these terms appear in quotations or titles, this book does
not use either. Instead, people who are potentially removable from the
United States are described as such: as potentially removable or simply as
removable. This has the benefit of avoiding political catchphrases while
simultaneously increasing legal accuracy.

I take a similar position regarding the term used to describe people
generally who are not United States citizens. The INA uses "alien," a term
that is patently offensive because it conjures images of invasion, danger,
and otherworldness from which only military might and the occasional
superhero can protect us. The term "immigrant" lacks the offensiveness of

---

46. For more on appeals to the BIA, see 8 C.F.R. §1003.3 and IMMIGRATION COURT
PRACTICE MANUAL §§ 6.1-6.2 (last revised June 10, 2013).
47. INA § 242(h)(2).

"alien," but it is also not suitable for general use in a legal text because it has a very specific legal meaning.[48] It is, as lawyers like to put it, a "term of art" that essentially means a person not a United States citizen or national authorized to live and work in the United States indefinitely. Where it appears in this book, therefore, immigrant is used interchangeably with "lawful permanent resident" or "permanent resident."

To refer to people who were not United States citizens when they came to the United States, this book uses the term "migrant." A migrant can become a United States citizen through naturalization, but even then they never lose that essential characteristic of having traveled to the United States from another country. In addition, using "migrant" allows me to distinguish between "immigrants" and people who lack authorization to be in the United States without entangling myself in the dead-end political rhetoric of "illegal alien" versus "undocumented immigrant."

Chapter Outline

To properly understand crimmigration law's three parts, it is necessary to discuss each in detail. The rest of the book takes on this task.

In three chapters, Part 1 will address the most significant substantive and procedural effects that attach to a criminal record in immigration court. Chapter 2 begins this discussion by identifying the principal methods through which the Immigration and Nationality Act authorizes removal of individuals who have committed a crime. This will entail discussions of the aggravated felony, controlled substance offense, and crimes involving moral turpitude grounds of removal, as well as immigration law's peculiar definition of "conviction." Chapter 3 follows by discussing various options that exist for noncitizens to remain in the United States despite having been convicted of a crime. In particular, this chapter addresses cancellation of removal for lawful permanent residents and nonlawful permanent residents, protection under the Convention Against Torture, readjustment of status, waivers available under INA § 212(h), and options for relief under now-repealed (but still relevant) INA § 212(c). After two chapters about substantive immigration law's

---

48. INA § 101(a)(15).

emphasis on criminal activity, chapter 4 turns to procedural issues that arise in immigration law proceedings involving crime. In particular, chapter 4 addresses the contentious issue of obligatory detention of many noncitizens who have been convicted of a crime. It first explains the legislative origins of INA § 236(c), the statute's so-called mandatory detention provision; then it recounts the Supreme Court's decision to uphold this power. This chapter also includes a discussion of avenues for avoiding a finding that the mandatory detention provision applies and closes with a discussion of recent federal cases limiting the scope of § 236(c) detention.

After Part 1's examination of the immigration court system, Part 2 turns to the criminal justice system's treatment of people thought not to be United States citizens. Chapter 5 begins this discussion by addressing the highly important and ground-shifting developments in Sixth Amendment right to counsel doctrine affecting criminal defense attorneys who represent noncitizen clients. The Supreme Court's decision in *Padilla v. Kentucky* takes center stage in this chapter. First, it explains the *Padilla* Court's reasoning and the line of cases that has developed since then, including the Court's 2013 decision in *Chaidez v. United States*[49] holding that *Padilla* does not apply retroactively. The chapter then explores the criminal defense attorney's obligations under *Padilla*. Chapter 6 follows by turning to immigration activity that constitutes a federal crime. In particular, this chapter takes a close look at illegal entry and illegal reentry, the two most commonly prosecuted immigration crimes. In addition to explaining the conduct that these offenses sanction, this chapter addresses prosecutorial trends and common defense strategies. Lastly, this chapter includes a discussion of key policy initiatives that have facilitated federal prosecutions of immigration crimes, notably Operation Streamline and fast-track plea agreements. The book's focus on the criminal justice system ends in chapter 7 with an examination of the criminal law methods used by states to regulate immigration. In particular, this chapter discusses state crimes specifically targeting noncitizens and state law limitations on bail for some noncitizens. This chapter also discusses types of laws that have been deemed beyond the scope of states' powers,

---

49. 133 S. Ct. 1103 (2013).

notably provisions of Arizona's well-known Senate Bill 1070, which the Supreme Court held unconstitutional.

Lastly, Part 3 moves beyond the substantive and procedural legal developments addressed in the first two parts and instead hones in on the tools that state and federal law enforcement officials have used to enforce crimmigration law. Chapter 8 begins Part 3 by highlighting the area of the country that is most often associated with immigration law enforcement—the nation's border. Here the book discusses unique legal features of border policing, with a special emphasis on the Mexican border region. In particular, it addresses the permissibility of suspicionless searches at ports of entry, the allowable use of race-based criteria to enforce immigration law along the border, and overlapping authorization granted to law enforcement agencies regarding drug and immigration laws. The next chapter, chapter 9, returns to detention, but with a focus on the development of the immigration detention system and consequences of detaining individuals pending removal, including the recent drastic expansion in the use of detention to enforce federal immigration laws. In an effort to give readers a sense of what detainees experience, this chapter discusses conditions within immigration detention centers. It also addresses alternatives to detention. Chapter 10 follows by chronicling the pivotal role that states and localities have filled in enforcing crimmigration law in recent years. Particular attention is given to the Secure Communities program, 287(g) program, and the use of ICE detainers to identify and apprehend potentially removable individuals. The chapter also discusses the creation of "sanctuary city" policies throughout the country.

Further Reading

César Cuauhtémoc García Hernández, *Creating Crimmigration*, 2013 BYU L. Rev. 1457.

Juliet Stumpf, *The Crimmigration Crisis*, 56 Am. U. L. Rev. 367 (2006).

Yolanda Vazquez, *Advising Noncitizen Defendants on the Immigration Consequences of Criminal Convictions*, 20 Berkeley La Raza L. J. 31 (2010).

CRIMINALS IN THE IMMIGRATION LAW SYSTEM

As the Introduction explained, immigration law has long been the vehicle through which people considered to have something valuable to contribute to the United States have been welcomed into the country while also giving government officials the means by which to exclude people deemed undesirable. What has changed over the decades has simply been the criteria by which the federal government has sifted through the masses of people who seek admission every year. For many years, exclusion and deportation turned on race or national origin. First the Chinese, then Asians generally, and later southern and eastern Europeans were explicitly barred entry or their numbers were limited severely by statutes that did little if anything to conceal their racist intentions. In the early twentieth century, leftist radicals—anarchists, socialists, communists, and others—were given much the same unwelcome treatment. Many were kept out of the country and countless others were rounded up and deported.

Today the preferred measure of undesirability is crime. Beginning in the 1980s and continuing in every major immigration law amendment since then, Congress has steadily raised the immigration law stakes for people who have been convicted of—and, in some instances, merely committed—a crime. In recent years these statutory provisions have taken center stage in immigration courts around the country. Almost half of people removed from the United States between 2010 and 2012, for example, had been convicted of a crime. Overall, more than half a million people with a criminal record were removed during that three-year stretch.[1] Though not all of these were removed on the basis of that conviction, DHS did seek to remove over 250,000 people between 2007 and 2012 because of a conviction.[2] The discrepancy lies in the fact that some people convicted of a crime lack authorization to be present in the United States. As a result, DHS frequently takes the path of least resistance by pursuing removal on that basis rather than go through the complicated analysis that is required to determine whether a particular conviction leads to removal.

Part 1 addresses that complexity. The following three chapters detail the current state of the statutes and case law that place so much emphasis on criminal activity within the immigration court system.

———————

  1. U.S. DEP'T OF HOMELAND SECURITY, IMMIGRATION ENFORCEMENT ACTIONS: 2012 ANNUAL REPORT 6 tbl.7 (2013).
  2. Transactional Records Access Clearinghouse, *Nature of Charge in New Filings Seeking Removal Orders Through December 2013*, http://trac.syr.edu/phptools/immigration/charges/apprep_newfiling_charge.php.

CHAPTER 2

Crime-Based Removal

The Immigration and Nationality Act (INA) lists numerous crimes that potentially lead to removal. Depending on how one counts, INA § 212(a)(2) alone includes roughly a dozen subsections authorizing exclusion based on criminal activity. Its deportation counterpart, INA § 237(a)(2), includes another fifteen. One of these, the provision authorizing deportation upon conviction of an aggravated felony, in turn consists of twenty-one subsections, some of which have their own subparts.

Rather than attempt a comprehensive analysis of each of these provisions, this book discusses doctrinal requirements that arise in crime-based removal regardless of which provision is involved before turning to in-depth discussions of the three most frequently used provisions: aggravated felonies, crimes involving moral turpitude, and controlled substance offenses.[1]

---

1. Transactional Records Access Clearinghouse, *Charges Asserted in Deportation Proceedings in the Immigration Courts: FY 2002-FY 2011 (Through July 26, 2011)*, http://trac.syr.edu/immigration/reports/260/include/detailchg.html.

Conviction and Commission

A conviction is required before most crime-based consequences apply, but there are important exceptions that practitioners need to consider. The main section of the INA in which crime-based deportation (not inadmissibility) grounds are listed, § 237(a)(2), explicitly requires a conviction before authorizing deportation for most grounds. The provision targeting people who have engaged in a crime involving moral turpitude states, for example, that it applies only to a migrant who "is convicted" of such an offense.[2] Section 237(a)(2)'s other subsections use similar language.

One exception applies to the general rule that deportation for criminal activity requires a conviction. INA § 237(a)(1)(A) allows for deportation of "[a]ny alien who at the time of entry or adjustment of status was . . . inadmissible." That is, any migrant who should have been excluded from the United States but was not can be expelled at a later date. The deportable-if-initially-inadmissible power circumvents the typical conviction requirement because the section of the INA that lists most of the criminal bases for excluding migrants from the United States, § 212(a)(2), does not require a conviction. Unlike § 237(a)(2)'s consistent references to a conviction, § 212(a)(2) uses varying language to describe its broader reach. One of the most important inadmissibility provisions—the section that applies to people who have engaged in a crime involving moral turpitude or controlled substance offense—refers to "any alien convicted of, or who admits having committed, or who admits committing acts which constitute the essential elements of" a crime involving moral turpitude or controlled substance offense.[3] A conviction, therefore, is equivalent to an admission of having committed a particular crime or, short of that, an admission to having engaged in conduct that satisfies the elements of a particular crime.

In a series of cases across many years, the Board of Immigration Appeals (BIA) has identified four requirements for an admission of having committed a particular crime or the elements of a crime. The migrant must have admitted to having engaged in conduct that is unquestionably a

---

2. INA § 237(a)(2)(A)(i)(I).
3. INA § 212(a)(2)(A)(i).

specific crime in the jurisdiction in which it was committed;[4] the conduct must necessarily involve moral turpitude or a controlled substance (in the United States or where it was committed);[5] any admission made to a United States government official must have been preceded by an "understandable" and "substantially similar" explanation of the relevant crime;[6] and the admission must be made freely and voluntarily.[7] An "element" of an offense had been thought to be simply any mental state or conduct that the prosecution must prove beyond a reasonable doubt that a criminal defendant committed for a conviction to occur.[8] Recent developments, including at the BIA, suggest that elements are also only those facts that the jury unanimously agreed the defendant committed.[9]

Though this four-part requirement might appear burdensome for the government to meet, it is sufficiently malleable to include responses that migrants give to questions from immigration officials. Many migrants, after all, approach immigration proceedings with a desire to be forthright. While that is commendable, it can also lead to immigration law problems. Attorneys, therefore, must be cognizant that admitting to having committed a crime is treated equivalently to a conviction and strategize accordingly.

While migrants do occasionally admit to having committed crimes, convictions remain the standard-bearer means through which immigration consequences arise from criminal activity. After decades of defining "conviction" through BIA case law, Congress entered the fray in 1996 with a statutory definition that remains unchanged. INA § 101(a)(48)

---

4. Matter of J---, 2 I&N Dec. 285, 287 (BIA 1945); see Matter of E-N--, 7 I&N Dec. 153, 154-55 (BIA 1956) (no admission where migrant admitted having engaged in statutory rape, but it was not clear from admission whether this was a felony that rendered the migrant inadmissible or a misdemeanor that rendered him admissible).

5. See Matter of S---, 8 I&N Dec. 409, 415 (BIA 1959) (discussing admission to crime involving moral turpitude).

6. See Matter of P---, 4 I&N Dec. 252, 254 (BIA 1951) ("the definition need only be substantially similar to the particular statutory definition of the offense . . . but need not be identical to the law of the jurisdiction in which the crime was committed"); Matter of J---, 2 I&N Dec. at 287 (explaining that the crime must be defined "in understandable terms").

7. Matter of G---, 1 I&N Dec. 225, 227 (BIA 1942).

8. See Pazcoguin v. Radcliffe, 292 F.3d 1209, 1215 (9th Cir. 2002).

9. Matter of Chairez, 26 I&N Dec. 349, 354 (BIA 2014); see Rendon v. Holder, 764 F.3d 1077, 1086 (9th Cir. 2014).

provides multiple alternative definitions of a conviction. Importantly, this definition applies retroactively.[10] Under the most straightforward option, a conviction occurs if a court enters a "formal judgment of guilt" against a defendant. In the federal criminal system this would involve a formal announcement in writing of any plea or verdict accepted by the court plus the sentence imposed.[11]

The second statutory route leading to a conviction addresses situations in which the criminal court has withheld adjudication—that is, it has stopped the judicial process of determining whether criminal liability exists. BIA case law that governed immigration law's understanding of the term "conviction" prior to 1996 held that deferred adjudication processes did not end in a conviction.[12] Many states have such procedures. Though their requirements vary, they have in common a desire to mitigate some of the consequences of a conviction in exchange for requiring the defendant to meet certain conditions. Importantly for immigration law, they accomplish this mitigation by instructing the court to accept a plea but not enter a judgment of guilt. Deferred adjudication essentially stops the criminal proceeding in its tracks while the defendant has an opportunity to meet the conditions imposed. If the defendant satisfies those conditions, the criminal charge is dropped. If the defendant does not satisfy the conditions, the court enters a finding of guilt and imposes a sentence.

State courts routinely use deferred adjudication procedures, but in the 1990s Congress was not pleased with the immigration law results. Indeed, it noted that "aliens who have clearly been guilty of criminal behavior and whom Congress intended to be considered 'convicted' have escaped the immigration consequences normally attendant upon a conviction."[13] As part of its massive overhaul of immigration law in 1996, Congress rectified what it saw as a problem by supplanting the BIA's position. Now a conviction can occur even if the criminal court deferred adjudication. In INA § 101(a)(48)(A)(i) and (ii), Congress provided that, in these situations,

---

10. Garnica-Vasquez v. Reno, 210 F.3d 558, 560 (5th Cir. 2000).
11. *See* Fed. R. Crim. P. 32(k)(1).
12. *See* Matter of Ozkok, 19 I&N Dec. 546 (BIA 1988).
13. H.R. Conf. Rep. No. 828 (1996), *reprinted in* 104th CONG., 2d SESS., CONG. REC. H10899, at 224 (Sept. 24, 1996).

a conviction occurs if there is a finding of guilt, the migrant pleaded guilty or nolo contendere, or "admitted sufficient facts to warrant a finding of guilt" and "the judge ordered some form of punishment, penalty, or restraint on the alien's liberty." Courts interpret the final component of this definition—imposition of a punishment, penalty, or restraint on liberty—rather broadly to include any punitive sanction. Incarceration obviously meets this threshold. So too does a court-imposed requirement that a criminal defendant pay court costs.[14] The end result is that an outcome that is not considered a conviction for criminal law purposes may be considered a conviction for immigration law purposes. As such, criminal defense attorneys and prosecutors must be especially cognizant of potential immigration consequences when crafting a plea bargain that appears to involve a favorable criminal law outcome.

Despite the breadth of the conviction definition, it is not limitless. For one, a conviction for immigration law purposes cannot result from anything that is not a criminal proceeding. Importantly, this means that an adjudication of guilt will not be considered a conviction unless the defendant was provided the constitutional protections "normally attendant upon a criminal adjudication." Failure to provide a defendant with access to appointed counsel, the right to a jury trial, or require the prosecution to meet its case beyond a reasonable doubt would not satisfy the conviction requirement.[15] Neither would a juvenile delinquency determination that reflects the standards Congress adopted in the Federal Juvenile Delinquency Act (FJDA).[16] The FJDA provides a special mechanism by which some individuals who are less than twenty-one years old and committed a crime prior to their eighteenth birthday can avoid a criminal sanction.[17]

14. Matter of Cabrera, 24 I&N Dec. 459, 462 (BIA 2008); *but see* Retuta v. Holder, 591 F.3d 1181, 1189 (9th Cir. 2010) (concluding that a suspended fine does not satisfy the punishment, penalty, or restraint requirement).
15. Matter of Eslamizar, 23 I&N Dec. 684, 687 (BIA 2004); *see* Castillo v. Atty. Gen., 729 F.3d 296 (3d Cir. 2013).
16. Matter of Devison, 22 I&N Dec. 1362, 1365–66 (BIA 2001) (discussing the Federal Juvenile Delinquency Act, 18 U.S.C. § 5031-5042); *but see* Matter of V-X-, 26 I&N Dec. 147 (BIA 2013) (Michigan juvenile offender adjudication is not analogous to the FJDA, thus it is a conviction).
17. 18 U.S.C. § 5031.

Second, it has long been thought that for a conviction to result in adverse immigration consequences, it must have become final.[18] A conviction becomes final when all direct appeals have been waived or concluded. In most state court systems, this means a decision by the state's highest court on the merits of a claim or an order denying discretionary review. The BIA cast some doubt on that position and some circuits have followed its lead at least toward deferred adjudication.[19] In the main, though, attorneys should remember that it remains true that a conviction must be final for immigration consequences to attach.

Categorical Approach

After concluding that a particular person has in fact been convicted for immigration law purposes, the next step in the analysis is to determine whether that conviction constitutes a removable offense. This step appears complicated because the analytical method prescribed by the Supreme Court—the categorical approach—is not intuitive. Fortunately, the actual analysis required is not beyond reach.

Since the late nineteenth century when Congress first linked immigration status to criminality, courts have needed a method of determining whether a migrant will suffer immigration consequences based on a conviction. Since that time they have used a categorical analysis, meaning that the immigration judge or reviewing court only analyzes the statutory definition of the crime.[20] The court does not explore the facts underlying the conviction.

Though courts have long used the categorical approach in immigration law, today courts usually credit a pair of Supreme Court decisions about criminal sentencing law with providing its modern foundation. The first

18. *See* Pino v. Landon, 349 U.S. 901 (1955); *Matter of Montiel*, 26 I&N Dec. 555 (BIA 2015) (finding that removal proceedings may be delayed through administrative closure pending criminal proceedings).

19. Matter of Punu, 22 I&N Dec. 224, 230–34 (BIA 1998) (Grant, concurring); *see* Orabi v. Atty. Gen., 738 F.3d 535, 541–42 (3d Cir. 2014) (discussing deferred adjudication); Griffiths v. INS, 243 F.3d 45, 54 (1st Cir. 2001) (same); Moosa v. INS, 171 F.3d 994, 1009 (5th Cir. 1999) (not limiting its analysis to deferred adjudication).

20. *See* Alina Das, *The Immigration Penalties of Criminal Convictions: Resurrecting Categorical Analysis in Immigration Law*, 86 N.Y.U. L. Rev. 1669, 1688 (2011); *see also id.* at 1749–60 (collecting federal court, Attorney General, and BIA opinions beginning in 1913).

of these two cases, *Taylor v. United States*,[21] explained how the categorical approach operates, but in a case concerning a sentencing enhancement under the Anti-Drug Abuse Act of 1986.[22] According to the *Taylor* Court, the categorical approach "generally requires the trial court to look only to the fact of conviction and the statutory definition of the prior offense" to determine if a defendant is subject to a sentencing enhancement.[23] The second case, *Shepard v. United States*, added that when the statute of conviction can be divided into discrete prongs, some of which would result in a sentencing enhancement while others would not, courts may also examine the "charging document, written plea agreement, transcript of plea colloquy, and any explicit factual finding by the trial judge to which the defendant assented."[24] *Shepard*'s expansion is referred to as the "modified categorical approach."

In effect, this means that attorneys and courts must perform a three-step analysis. First, it is necessary to identify the federal immigration category or categories relevant to a migrant's situation. This requires perusing the INA for potentially applicable bases of removal. In a case involving a Georgia conviction for possession of marijuana with intent to distribute, for example, DHS contended that the migrant was removable for having been convicted of "illicit trafficking in a controlled substance," a type of aggravated felony.[25] Now comes the most important part of the first step—determining what Congress meant by "illicit trafficking in a controlled substance." To do this, courts examine the definition of the removable offense category in the abstract, what is called the "generic" definition of that crime category.[26] In *Taylor*, the sentencing case that launched the modern categorical approach framework, the Court grappled with what Congress meant when it used the word "burglary" in a sentencing enhancement statute. Because Congress did not specify how it construed "burglary," the Court concluded "that Congress meant by 'burglary' the

---

21. 495 U.S. 575 (1990).
22. Pub. L. No. 99-570, 100 Stat. 3207 (1986).
23. *Taylor*, 495 U.S. at 602.
24. 544 U.S. 13, 16 (2005).
25. *See* Moncrieffe v. Holder, 133 S. Ct. 1678 (2013).
26. *See* Descamps v. United States, 133 S. Ct. 2276, 2283 (2013); *Moncrieffe*, 133 S. Ct. at 1684.

generic sense in which the term is now used in the criminal codes of most
States." As used in most state penal codes, the Court added, "burglary"
consists of the following elements: unlawful or unprivileged entry into,
or remaining in, a building or structure, with intent to commit a crime.
Interpreting "burglary" for federal law purposes to have a certain set of
elements gives it a "uniform definition independent of the labels employed
by the various States' criminal codes."[27] In other words, the generic definition means that a defendant will be considered to have been convicted of
a "burglary" and receive the sentencing enhancement required by federal
law if the state offense of conviction contains the elements the Court identified and only that. The same holds true of terms used in the INA.

The categorical approach's second step entails examining the least culpable conduct[28] that is necessarily required for a conviction to occur under the statute of conviction. To do this, courts identify the elements of
an offense by turning to the text of the statute that the migrant was convicted of violating, as well as binding case law interpreting that statute.
In particular, when dealing with a state law offense immigration courts
look to see how the courts of the state in which the migrant was convicted
interpret the offense. Immigration courts rely on state legislatures and
state courts because the states, and not Congress or the federal courts,
are authorized to enact and interpret state criminal laws. Indeed, federal
tribunals, including federal administrative bodies such as the immigration courts, have no authority to contradict state courts' interpretation
of state criminal law.[29] State courts, therefore, are the final authority on
the meaning of state law. As an illustration of the states' primacy in interpreting their own state law, even the U.S. Supreme Court turned to the
Florida penal code and Florida Supreme Court when trying to identify
the elements of Florida's statute criminalizing driving under the influence
of alcohol. The statute, the Court explained, provided basic information
about the crime's elements, while the state supreme court added key information about the lack of mental state required for a conviction.[30] Oddly,

---

27. *Taylor*, 495 U.S. at 592, 598–99.
28. *See* Mellouli v. Lynch, No. 13-1034, 2015 WL 2464047, slip op. at 6 (June 1, 2015)
(quoting Moncrieffe v. Holder, 133 S. Ct. 1678, 1684-85 (2013)).
29. *See* City of Chicago v. Morales, 119 S. Ct. 1849, 1861 (1999).
30. Leocal v. Ashcroft, 543 U.S. 1, 6 (2004).

the Supreme Court recently reserved the question of whether it is actually appropriate for courts to consider state judicial opinions interpreting a state statute's text, but it's hard to see what alternative exists.[31]

Equipped with an understanding of what Congress meant when it included a particular term in its list of crimes that can result in removal (step 1) and an understanding of what the legislature and courts of the jurisdiction in which a migrant was convicted required for a conviction (step 2), courts can move to the third step of the categorical approach: identifying whether a match exists between the federal immigration category and the statute of conviction. This is the most important and complicated step in the categorical analysis. A court must decide whether all conduct punishable under a given state statute (the outcome of step 2) meets the generic definition of the federal immigration category (the outcome of step 1). If there is a "realistic probability, not a theoretical possibility, that the State would apply its statute to conduct that falls outside the generic definition of a crime" as used for immigration law purposes, then it is not possible to conclude that the migrant has been convicted of that removable offense.[32]

The Supreme Court illustrated this mismatch between state criminal law and federal immigration law, as well as its effect, in *Descamps v. United States*, a decision about whether "burglary" under California law constitutes "burglary" under the Armed Career Criminal Act, a sentencing enhancement statute.[33] The Court held that it did not because the state statute, as interpreted by California courts, "'defines burglary more broadly' than the generic offense" used for federal immigration law purposes.[34] Specifically, California's burglary offense punishes entry into specified locations with the intent to commit larceny or any felony. Importantly, the state crime includes punishment of lawful entries done with this intent, for example, entering a store during business hours with the intent to shoplift. In contrast, the generic definition of "burglary"

---

31. Descamps v. United States, 133 S. Ct. 2276, 2291 (2013) (reserving the question of whether courts should consider state judicial interpretations of a state statute).

32. Gonzales v. Duenas-Alvarez, 549 U.S. 183, 193 (2007); *see, e.g.,* United States v. Teran-Salinas, 767 F.3d 453, 460–62 (5th Cir. 2014) (adopting reasonable probability requirement); Ramos v. U.S. Atty. Gen., 709 F.3d 1066, 1071–72 (11th Cir. 2013) (same); Familia Rosario v. Holder, 655 F.3d 739, 749 (7th Cir. 2011) (same).

33. 133 S. Ct. 2276, 2281–82 (2013).

34. *Id.* at 2285 (quoting *Taylor v. United States*, 495 U.S. 575, 599 (1990)).

used for immigration law purposes requires an unlawful entry. Because the state punishes conduct that is not a removable offense, there is no match between the state crime and the federal immigration category.[35] A California conviction for burglary, therefore, is not equivalent to "burglary" as used for immigration law purposes, meaning this conviction cannot result in removal under the burglary basis.

California's burglary statute exemplifies an important complication that attorneys frequently encounter: many statutes list multiple alternative facts that can support a conviction. California's burglary statute, for example, requires the "intent to commit grand or petit larceny or any felony."[36] Similarly, some Utah crimes require that the defendant have acted with "intent, knowledge, or recklessness."[37] California courts do not require that the prosecution prove and the jury agree that the defendant acted with the intent to commit any particular offense. They simply require that the jury agree that the defendant had the intent to commit one of the listed crimes: larceny or any felony.[38] For their part, the Utah courts do not require that the jurors agree on which of the three mental states the defendant acted with. The jury only has to agree that the defendant acted with one of the three mental states listed in the statute: intent, knowledge, or recklessness.[39] In cases involving disjunctive statutes like California's burglary statute or Utah's mental state provision, courts must determine whether these alternative facts are elements of the offense or merely alternative means of committing a crime. This is a critical distinction because the modified categorical approach can be used to identify which crime the defendant was convicted of violating if the statute includes alternative elements and is thus divisible, but it cannot be used when a statute simply includes alternative means of commission. To determine whether a disjunctive statute lists alternative means or alternative elements requires understanding what constitutes an "element" of an offense. Though courts and lawyers toss this word around with

35. *See Descamps*, 133 S. Ct. at 2285–86.
36. CAL. PENAL CODE § 459.
37. UTAH CODE ANN. § 76-2-102.
38. Rendon v. Holder, 764 F.3d 1077, 1084 (9th Cir. 2014).
39. Matter of Chairez, 26 I&N Dec. 349, 355 (BIA 2014) (discussing State v. Russell, 733 P.2d 162, 164–68 (Utah 1987)).

remarkable frequency, there is surprisingly little case law explaining its meaning. Is the mental state requirement of a crime that requires acting with "intent, knowledge, or recklessness" an element? Addressing a Utah statute in *Matter of Chairez*, the BIA held that an offense's elements "are those facts about the crime which '[t]he Sixth Amendment contemplates that a jury—not a sentencing court—will find . . . unanimously and beyond a reasonable doubt.'"[40] In a follow-up decision, the BIA recognized that the federal circuits are currently hashing out how to best interpret the categorical approach and not all have issued a precedential decision about whether to follow the BIA's view.[41]

When a statute is divisible, an immigration judge must therefore determine under which alternative set of elements the migrant was convicted to decide whether a conviction constitutes a removable offense.[42] This analysis is called the "modified categorical approach" and "serves a limited function: It helps effectuate the categorical analysis when a divisible statute, listing potential offense elements in the alternative, renders opaque which element played a part in the defendant's conviction."[43] The modified categorical approach allows courts to "examine a limited class of documents to determine which of a statute's alternative elements formed the basis of the defendant's prior conviction."[44] Though it has never provided an exhaustive list, the Supreme Court has explained that courts can examine "the statutory definition, charging document, written plea agreement, transcript of plea colloquy, and any explicit factual finding by the trial judge to which the defendant assented."[45] They cannot, however, consider police reports or complaints.[46] In effect, courts can consider documents produced by or under the direction of the criminal court that presided over the conviction. They cannot consider documents that may have spurred a criminal investigation or prosecution. This is a reasonable

---

40. 26 I&N Dec. 349, 353 (BIA 2014) (quoting *Descamps*, 133 S. Ct. at 2288); *see* Rendon v. Holder, 764 F.3d 1077, 1087–88 (9th Cir. 2014) (following Matter of Chairez).
41. Matter of Chairez, 26 I&N Dec. 478, 481–82 (BIA 2015).
42. *See Descamps*, 133 S. Ct. at 2281; Nijhawan v. Holder, 557 U.S. 29, 35 (2009).
43. *Descamps*, 133 S. Ct. at 2283.
44. *Id.* at 2284.
45. Shepard v. United States, 544 U.S. 13, 16 (2005).
46. Matter of Teixeira, 21 I&N Dec. 316, 319–20 (BIA 1996).

Practice Pointer

Determining whether a statute is divisible determines whether the modified categorical approach is permissible. When a statute is disjunctive, attorneys and courts must therefore focus on whether the statute lists alternative elements or alternative means of commission. Statutes listing alternative elements are divisible, thus the modified categorical approach is permitted. If the statute merely lists alternative means of committing the crime, then it is indivisible and only the categorical approach is allowed.

limitation because, in an era when defendants frequently plead guilty or nolo contendere, charging documents do not necessarily reflect the crime that a defendant was convicted of violating.

Two unique departures from the categorical and modified categorical approaches exist, which merit special attention. First, the Supreme Court has adopted a "circumstance-specific" analysis when examining the fraud or deceit type of aggravated felony. This provision encompasses an offense that "involves fraud or deceit in which the loss to the victim or victims exceeds $10,000."[47] If courts were to apply the usual categorical or modified categorical approach described above, the fraud or deceit category would have "little, if any, meaningful application" because, at the time that Congress enacted this financial threshold, only eight states had fraud or deceit offenses that include as an element of the crime a financial loss in the vicinity of $10,000, as the Court recognized in *Nijhawan v. Holder*.[48] Congress, the Court concluded, would not have meant for this basis of removal to apply in "so limited and so haphazard a manner."[49] Instead, the Court continued under the assumption that Congress must have intended for courts to examine "the specific way in which an offender committed the crime on a specific occasion."[50] Granting immigration courts the power to "look to the facts and circumstances underlying an offender's conviction" represents a dramatic and important move away from courts' traditionally steadfast reliance on the categorical approach.[51] To date, however, courts have

---

47. INA § 101(a)(43)(M)(i).
48. 557 U.S. 29, 39–40 (2009).
49. Nijhawan v. Holder, 557 U.S. 29, 40 (2009).
50. *Id.* at 33.
51. *Id.* at 34.

largely refrained from applying the circumstance-specific approach to other grounds of removal, as the Supreme Court suggested in a recent decision.[52] (For one application of the circumstance-specific approach to an exemption from removal, see the Controlled Substance Offense section below.)

The second peculiar departure from the categorical approach concerns a rescinded but still relevant analytical method that allowed courts to consider the facts underlying a conviction. In *Matter of Silva-Trevino*, Attorney General Michael Mukasey, having directed the BIA to refer the case to him,[53] announced a new method of determining whether a conviction constitutes a crime involving moral turpitude. In addition to using the categorical and modified categorical approach, the attorney general instructed immigration judges to "consider any additional evidence the adjudicator determines is necessary or appropriate to resolve accurately the moral turpitude question."[54] This additional step in the analysis represented a significant deviation from the categorical approach's focus on the statute of conviction and the modified categorical approach's recognition that a small set of documents created by or at the direction of the criminal court may shed light on the particular elements of a crime that the migrant was convicted of. It was not, however, without limit. In a subsequent case, the BIA explained that *Silva-Trevino* did not permit an immigration judge to "leapfrog" over the modified categorical approach "to rely on sources outside the record of conviction, even though the record of conviction evidence fully resolves the issue."[55] Instead, *Silva-Trevino*'s "additional evidence" prong was available only "[w]hen the record of conviction is inconclusive."[56]

For all the dramatic change that *Silva-Trevino* promised to bring to the traditional analytical approach used in immigration courts, the federal courts significantly muted its impact. Several circuits refused to adopt Attorney General Mukasey's approach, including, notably, the Fifth Circuit

52. Mellouli v. Lynch, No. 13-1034, 2015 WL 2464047, slip op. at 5 n.3 (June 1, 2015). *But see, e.g.,* United States v. Mendoza, 2015 WL 1591244, at *3 (5th Cir. April 9, 2015) (regarding money laundering); Bianco v. Holder, 624 F.3d 265, 272–73 (5th Cir. 2010) (regarding domestic violence).
53. *See* 8 C.F.R. § 1003.1(h)(1)(i).
54. Matter of Silva-Trevino, 24 I&N Dec. 687, 704 (A.G. 2008).
55. Matter of Ahortalejo-Guzman, 25 I&N Dec. 465, 468 (BIA 2011).
56. Matter of Silva-Trevino, 24 I&N Dec. at 690.

in Silva-Trevino's own appeal.[57] In its decision, the Fifth Circuit explained
that it would not follow the Attorney General's framework because there
was nothing ambiguous about the INA's requirement that removability
turn on whether a migrant was "convicted of" a crime involving moral
turpitude. Congress, after all, defined the term "conviction" in the INA.
Moreover, courts long used the categorical approach to glean what a person was convicted of and, as a general matter of statutory interpretation,
Congress is presumed to know how the courts have interpreted a term.[58]
Congress can surely allow immigration judges to go beyond the categorical
and modified categorical approaches by considering evidence outside the
record of conviction by simply amending the INA, but it has not done so.
Instead, at every turn it has either reiterated its reliance on convictions or,
as it did in 1996 when it adopted the statutory definition of "conviction,"
actually further cemented its support for a formal adjudication of guilt
rather than allowing immigration judges to conduct fact-finding inquiries as the attorney general's decision instructed. Meanwhile, only a small
number of circuits have adopted the *Silva-Trevino* analysis as a reasonable
interpretation of a statute within the agency's expertise.[59] Responding to
the circuit split that *Silva-Trevino* caused and the way in which it departed
from the Supreme Court's repeated emphasis on the categorical approach,
Attorney General Eric Holder vacated Mukasey's opinion in April 2015.[60]
Holder's opinion, however, left intact for now BIA decisions relying on
Silva-Trevino, thus Mukasey's reasoning remains relevant to a limited
extent.[61]

The categorical approach's "focus on the elements, rather than the facts,
of a crime," as the Supreme Court explained the categorical approach in

---

57. *See* Silva-Trevino v. Holder, 742 F.3d 197 (5th Cir. 2014); Olivas-Motta v. Holder,
716 F.3d 1199 (9th Cir. 2013); Prudencio v. Holder, 669 F.3d 472 (4th Cir. 2012); Fajardo
v. U.S. Attorney General, 659 F.3d 1303 (11th Cir. 2011); Jean-Louis v. Attorney General
of U.S., 582 F.3d 462 (3d Cir. 2009).

58. *Silva-Trevino*, 742 F.3d at 202–03.

59. *See* Bobadilla v. Holder, 679 F.3d 1052 (8th Cir. 2012); Ali v. Mukasey, 521 F.3d
737 (7th Cir. 2008).

60. Matter of Silva-Trevino, 26 I&N Dec. 550, 550 (A.G. 2015).

61. *Id.*

Descamps, strikes many attorneys as odd.[62] Shouldn't a migrant face immigration consequences if she did something Congress deems worthy of removal rather than subject a migrant to these consequences only if attorneys and courts can hash out the meaning of a statute and limited set of documents obtained from the criminal court? The Court's answer is a resounding "no," and it has provided three reasons in support. First, the categorical and modified categorical approach emphasizes Congress's decision to trigger removal upon a "conviction" for a removable offense. Congress has the ability to tie removal to commission of certain conduct or an exploration of the facts surrounding a conviction—and indeed has done so in some situations[63]—but when it uses the word "conviction," courts must give meaning to that term. Doing this ensures that everyone convicted of the same removable offense is treated identically instead of removal turning on what someone did and could have been convicted of.[64]

Second, using the categorical and modified categorical analysis prevents sentencing courts and immigration courts from treading on findings of fact that the Sixth Amendment reserves to juries and, if the defendant waives the jury trial right, judges in criminal proceedings. For a criminal penalty to attach to any conduct, the Sixth Amendment requires that a jury or judge determine beyond a reasonable doubt that the defendant actually engaged in that conduct, and then repeat this finding for conduct that satisfies every element of a crime. Except for finding that a defendant was previously convicted of a crime, a finding by a lower standard of proof or by another party would not meet constitutional muster.[65] That constitutional problem, the Court explained, "counsel[s] against allowing a sentencing court to 'make a disputed' determination 'about what

---

62. Descamps v. United States, 133 S. Ct. 2276, 2285 (2013).

63. *See, e.g.*, INA § 212(a)(2)(A)(i) (providing that a migrant who is "convicted of, or who admits having *committed*, or who admits *committing* acts which constitute the essential elements of" a crime involving moral turpitude or controlled substance offense is inadmissible); Nijhawan v. Holder, 557 U.S. 29, 36 (2009) (adopting the "circumstance-specific" approach for the fraud or deceit type of aggravated felony).

64. *Descamps*, 133 S. Ct. at 2287–88.

65. Apprendi v. New Jersey, 530 U.S. 466, 477 (2000).

the defendant and state judge must have understood as the factual basis of the prior plea,' or what the jury in a prior trial must have accepted as the theory of the crime."[66] In overturning a Ninth Circuit decision allowing sentencing courts to look beyond the conviction statute and records, the Court added, "The Sixth Amendment contemplates that a jury—not a sentencing court—will find such facts, unanimously and beyond a reasonable doubt. And the only facts the court can be sure the jury so found are those constituting elements of the offense—as distinct from amplifying but legally extraneous circumstances."[67] The same reasoning applies to the immigration context.

Third, allowing immigration courts to venture beyond the categorical and modified categorical approach would require them to conduct mini-trials that they are not equipped to do. It would be possible to allow immigration judges to ask respondents in removal proceedings about what happened that led to their criminal law problems. Immigration judges could ask the same thing of complainants, witnesses, and arresting police officers. In effect, immigration judges could take all manner of evidence about the facts underlying a conviction. But doing this would simply reproduce the criminal court's work. Furthermore, criminal courts are designed to hear testimony, make credibility determinations, and weigh evidence relevant to criminal activity. Immigration courts, in contrast, are poorly equipped to do this. They lack the detailed procedures that criminal courts rely on to increase the reliability of their adjudications and decrease the likelihood that a criminal proceeding will be driven by little more than intuition. There is nothing about immigration courts that inherently prevents them from becoming indistinguishable from criminal courts. But neither Congress nor the Justice Department in which the immigration courts sit has equipped them to do this, and the Supreme Court has shown no interest in forcing immigration courts to engage in high-stakes analyses that they are not prepared to do.

---

66. *Descamps*, 133 S. Ct. at 2289 (quoting Shepard v. United States, 544 U.S. 13, 25 (2005) (plurality opinion)).
67. *Descamps*, 133 S. Ct. at 2288.

Problem 2.1

Sam pleaded guilty to aggravated criminal sexual abuse in Illinois. At the time of his conviction, the state statute provides: "A person commits aggravated criminal sexual abuse if that person commits an act of sexual penetration or sexual conduct with a victim who is at least 13 years of age but under 17 years of age and the person is at least 5 years older than the victim." After some legal research, you learn that, for purposes of federal law, a minor is commonly defined as someone less than sixteen years old. To prepare your legal strategy you need to determine whether this is an indivisible statute requiring use of the categorical approach only or a divisible statute allowing use of the modified categorical approach as well.

This is almost certainly an indivisible statute, thus only the categorical approach is permissible to analyze whether it will result in removability. The Illinois statute clearly states that the offense punishes certain sexual acts against a person in the thirteen- to seventeen-year-old age range. The prosecution is not required to show and the jury (or judge) is not required to decide that the victim was of any specific age, so long as the victim was somewhere in the thirteen to seventeen range. According to the Ninth Circuit, this age range includes people who are not similarly protected by federal law. United States v. Acosta-Chavez, 727 F.3d 903, 908–09 (9th Cir. 2013). Though it is possible that the victim of Sam's actions was less than sixteen years old, as the state statute is written there is no way to disaggregate the victim's age from the statutory age range without exploring the underlying facts. Those facts might reveal more about the victim's age, but they would not tell an immigration court whether the state judge who accepted Sam's guilty plea necessarily pinned down the victim's age. The Illinois legislature could have written the statute as a series of alternatives—for example, by defining a minor as a person who is thirteen, fourteen, fifteen, or sixteen—but it did not. Instead, it defined a minor as someone within a multi-year age range, some of which come within the federal definition of minor and others who do not. Thus the immigration judge cannot determine whether Sam was convicted of engaging in this conduct against a person defined as a minor for purposes of federal law or whether he was convicted of engaging in this conduct against a person who Illinois defines as a minor but federal law does not. As such, this is an indivisible statute.

Aggravated Felonies

The stakes are seldom higher than when a migrant faces a criminal prosecution for or has been convicted of a crime that might constitute an "aggravated felony."[68] Migrants convicted of an aggravated felony are barred from receiving the most charitable form of relief available under the current version of the INA, cancellation of removal, as well as voluntary departure at the conclusion of removal proceedings.[69] They must be held in immigration detention without bond while removal proceedings are ongoing and, if ordered removed, until removal actually occurs.[70] After being removed, they are permanently barred from obtaining authorization to reenter the United States.[71] If they do enter without authorization they are subject to as much as a twenty-year prison term, though most are sentenced to much less.[72] They are also indirectly barred from becoming a United States citizen through the naturalization process because an aggravated felony conviction means they lack the good moral character that is required.[73] Added to that, the INA also limits judicial review of removal decisions based on aggravated felony convictions.[74]

Despite its name, the aggravated felony basis of removal is not limited to egregious crimes. In fact, the definition is sufficiently broad to include many misdemeanors. It also includes crimes that would not strike many people as especially aggravated—small-dollar theft offenses, for example. None of that matters because the "aggravated felony" phrase is a term of art that Congress can define however it likes. It has done just that in impressive detail at INA § 101(a)(43). This section, in the words of the U.S. Court of Appeals for the Seventh Circuit, "functions like a dictionary, in that it provides us with Congress' definition of the term 'aggravated felony.'"[75] Some parts of this definition refer to crimes with great specificity while other parts describe "broad categor[ies] of

---

68. INA § 237(a)(2)(A)(iii); *see* INA § 101(a)(43).
69. INA § 240A(a)(3) (cancellation of removal for LPRs); INA § 240A(b)(1)(C) (cancellation of removal for non-LPRs); INA § 240B(a)(1) (voluntary departure).
70. INA § 236(c); *see* Demore v. Kim, 538 U.S. 510, 517 (2003) (recognizing possibility of habeas challenge to detention decision pursuant to § 236(c)).
71. INA § 212(a)(2)(A)(9)(A)(i).
72. INA § 276(b)(2).
73. INA § 316(a); § 101(f)(8).
74. INA § 242(a)(2)(C).
75. Guerrero-Perez v. INS, 242 F.3d 727, 736–37 (7th Cir. 2001).

crimes."[76] Likewise, some of the crimes listed seem at home under the "aggravated felony" umbrella—murder and rape, for example[77]—while finding others on the list is bound to furrow more eyebrows—altering a passport or perjury.[78]

There is a special concern that arises for migrants who are not lawful permanent residents who have been convicted of an offense that an ICE officer thinks constitutes an aggravated felony. INA § 238(b) allows ICE to issue an administrative order of removal for a nonpermanent resident who has been convicted of an aggravated felony. The person in removal proceedings then has fourteen days to seek judicial review in a U.S. Court of Appeals.[79] The reality, though, is that most people do not seek judicial review. The practical effect, therefore, is that nonpermanent residents can be deemed aggravated felons and removed without an immigration judge ever deciding whether the ICE officer's assessment was correct. At least in circuits that have concluded that the Fifth Amendment Due Process Clause requires informing migrants of the possibility of relief, individuals removed pursuant to § 238's summary removal provisions may be able to collaterally attack the removal order in a subsequent illegal reentry prosecution (see chapter 6).

Though it has such a significant impact on immigration law, the aggravated felony is a relative newcomer to the immigration law lexicon. It made its debut in 1988 as part of the Anti-Drug Abuse Act (ADAA of 1988).[80] At that time, the term "aggravated felony" included only three crimes—murder, drug trafficking, and illicit trafficking in firearms.[81] After a series of expansions, today there are twenty-one categories of aggravated felonies enumerated at INA § 101(a)(43), and several of those categories include subsections.

---

76. Padilla v. Kentucky, 559 U.S. 356, 378 (2010) (Alito, J., concurring) (quoting Michael John Garcia & Larry M. Eig, Cong. Res. Serv. Report for Congress, *Immigration Consequences of Criminal Activity* n.p. (Oct. 23, 2006), *available at* http://trac.syr.edu/immigration/library/P1338.pdf).

77. INA § 101(a)(43)(A).

78. INA §§ 101(a)(43)(P)(i), (S).

79. INA § 238(b)(3) (granting fourteen days for judicial review); § 242(a)(5) (explaining judicial review to courts of appeal).

80. Anti-Drug Abuse Act of 1988, Pub. L. 100–690, 102 Stat. 4181, § 7341-50 (1988).

81. *Id.* at § 7342.

Importantly, according to the BIA, the aggravated felony deportation basis applies no matter how long ago the conviction occurred. Indeed, the statute explicitly states that a conviction for an aggravated felony "at any time after admission" renders a person deportable.[82] This means that many old convictions can become problematic for migrants who think they have put that trouble behind them. At least two circuits, the Seventh and Ninth, disagree with the BIA, though, and instead conclude that the aggravated felony deportation provision does not apply to convictions that occurred prior to November 18, 1988, the date the ADAA of 1988 became effective.[83]

In addition, the aggravated felony definition that currently exists applies even to a crime that would not have been considered an aggravated felony at the time it was committed or the migrant was convicted. Take, for example, a 1995 conviction for a fraud offense in which the victim lost $25,000. At the time, the relevant provision required a loss of at least $200,000. Congress reduced the loss amount to $10,000 in 1996.[84] Had this migrant consulted an immigration attorney about the potential immigration consequences of a conviction while the criminal prosecution was pending, the conscientious attorney, after researching the relevant INA provision, would have learned that this crime would not be considered an aggravated felony. That would have been correct at the time of conviction, but what matters for removal purposes is whether it is correct at the time of removal proceedings. Clearly it is not. This individual has been convicted of a fraud type of aggravated felony as the term is currently defined and it does not matter how it was defined at the time of conviction.[85]

---

82. INA § 237(a)(2)(A)(iii).

83. Ledezma-Galicia v. Holder, 636 F.3d 1059, 1079-80 (9th Cir. 2010); see Zivkovic v. Holder, 724 F.3d 894, 911 (7th Cir. 2013). Other circuits concluded that the aggravated felony definition does not apply to deportation or exclusion actions initiated prior to September 30, 1996. See, e.g., Saqr v. Holder, 580 F.3d 414, 421 (6th Cir. 2009).

84. Illegal Immigration Reform and Immigrant Responsibility Act, 110 Stat. 3009-628, § 321.

85. See Matter of Truoung, 22 I&N Dec. 1090, 1096 (BIA 1999).

Practice Pointer

Changes to civil immigration law can apply retroactively. Congress, for example, can add a basis of removal to the INA today and have it apply to people who engaged in that conduct yesterday. Because no one can predict what Congress will do, attorneys would be wise to advise migrant clients that the only sure way to avoid removal is to become a United States citizen through the naturalization process. Attorneys need to remember, however, that applying for naturalization involves investigation of the applicant's background and can result in initiation of removal proceedings if the government believes that the applicant is potentially removable.

A. Illicit Trafficking

Among the most contested aggravated felony categories is the illicit drug trafficking provision. Located at INA § 101(a)(43)(B), the provision provides in whole that "illicit trafficking in a controlled substance (as defined in section 802 of title 21), including a drug trafficking crime (as defined in section 924(c) of title 18)" is an aggravated felony. On its face this text reveals little more than that Congress thought "drug trafficking" crimes to be a subset of "illicit trafficking" offenses. To fully unravel this provision, though, the Supreme Court parsed the definitional phrases in parenthesis. The first parenthetical simply points to a section of the federal Controlled Substances Act (CSA), 21 U.S.C. § 802, that defines the phrase "controlled substance" for federal law purposes as one of a long list of drugs enumerated in one of five schedules—all the usual suspects plus plenty of less familiar substances.[86] Because § 802 does not actually define "illicit trafficking," the Court in *Lopez v. Gonzales* gave the terms their "everyday understanding" and concluded that "ordinarily 'trafficking' means some sort of commercial dealing."[87] In contrast, the second parenthetical points to a section of the federal penal code, 18 U.S.C. § 924(c)(2), that defines "drug trafficking" as "any felony punishable under the Controlled Substances Act (21 U.S.C. § 802)."

To determine whether a particular state offense is an illicit trafficking aggravated felony, therefore, courts explore two routes. One option

---

86. *See* 21 U.S.C. § 802. The five schedules are actually located at 21 U.S.C. § 812.
87. 549 U.S. 47, 53 (2006).

consists of asking whether the crime necessarily involves commercial dealing. If it does, then the offense falls within the first parenthetical's definition. The second possibility asks whether the offense is punishable as a
felony under the CSA. If so, the offense falls within the second parenthetical's definition. In *Lopez*, the Court applied this analysis to aiding and
abetting another person's possession of cocaine, which state law equated
to simple possession of cocaine. Most state simple possession crimes, the
Court explained, do not involve commerce so it fails the first parenthetical definition.[88] Second, simple possession is punished as a misdemeanor
under federal law, so it also fails the second parenthetical definition.[89] As
such, the Court concluded that simple possession offenses usually do not
constitute illicit trafficking aggravated felonies.

While *Lopez* clearly signaled that a crime that neither involves commercial dealing nor is punishable as a federal felony falls within the illicit
trafficking category, what happens if a state could have prosecuted certain criminal conduct in a way that would have been a federal felony?
The Supreme Court confronted this issue four years after *Lopez* in
Carachuri-Rosendo v. Holder.[90] Mr. Carachuri-Rosendo, a long-time lawful permanent resident, had been convicted in Texas of two misdemeanor
simple possession offenses: one involving less than two ounces of marijuana
and the other a single tablet of the common antianxiety medication Xanax.
Because both convictions fell squarely into the *Lopez* Court's holding that
simple possession ordinarily lacks the commercial dealing required of illicit
trafficking, the Court turned to whether Carachuri-Rosendo's convictions
were punishable as a felony under the CSA.[91]

The key twist in this case was that federal law allows for second and
subsequent simple possession offenses to be punished as recidivist felony
offenses.[92] Felony implications, however, do not arise automatically by
virtue of the fact that a defendant has previously been convicted of simple
possession. Instead, the prosecutor is required to follow a detailed pro-

---

88. *See id.* at 54.
89. *Id.* at 52 (discussing 21 U.S.C. § 844(a)).
90. 560 U.S. 563 (2010).
91. *Id.* at 574.
92. 21 U.S.C. § 844(a).

cedure: charge the existence of the prior offense before trial or entry of a guilty plea, notify the defendant of the government's intent to pursue a recidivist offender enhancement, and give the defendant the opportunity to challenge the validity of the prior conviction (e.g., on the basis that the prior conviction is not a simple possession offense or that the prosecutor has identified the wrong person).[93] Like many states, Texas requires a similar process before enhanced punishment can be meted out on recidivist offenders.[94] The prosecutor in Mr. Carachuri-Rosendo's case, however, failed to follow the required process. In fact, "the prosecutor specifically elected to '[a]bandon' a recidivist enhancement under state law," according to the Court.[95] The "mere possibility" that Mr. Carachuri-Rosendo could have been prosecuted and convicted as a recidivist offender in such a way that would have been analogous to a felony under the CSA does not mean that he was *actually convicted* of a crime that is itself punishable as a felony under federal law."[96] Given the INA's requirement that a migrant be convicted of an aggravated felony to be deportable, this distinction makes all the difference. For a second or subsequent simple possession conviction to be deemed an illicit trafficking type of aggravated felony, the state must have relied on procedures comparable to the recidivist offender procedure required under the CSA. Anything short of this will not be deemed illicit trafficking.

Problem 2.2

Omar, a lawful permanent resident studying at a university in South Dakota, was caught smoking marijuana in his dorm room. He was convicted of possession of between two ounces and one-half pound of marijuana, a felony under S.D. Codified Laws § 22-42-6. Does Omar's conviction constitute illicit trafficking?

Probably not. Applying the two-part analysis announced in Lopez v. Gonzales *ask first whether South Dakota's possession offense necessarily involves commercial*

(continued)

---

93. *See* 21 U.S.C. § 851(a)-(c).
94. Tex. Penal Code § 12.43; *see* Tex. Penal Code § 12.42 (analogous provision applicable to felonies).
95. *Carachuri-Rosendo*, 560 U.S. at 579.
96. *Id.* at 581–82.

> *dealing. The South Dakota Supreme Court defines "possession" as used in § 22-42-6 as "signif[ying] dominion or right of control over a controlled substance or marijuana with knowledge of its presence and character." State v. Goodroad, 442 N.W.2d 246, 251 (S.D. 1989). Commerce is not a part of this definition, thus there is a very strong argument to be made that commerce is not a required component of the state's possession offense.*
>
> *Continuing with the Lopez analysis, next consider whether Omar's state conviction is punishable as a felony under the CSA. This is also straightforward. Federal law punishes simple possession as a misdemeanor. Unless DHS shows that this was a second or subsequent conviction and that the state prosecutor followed a recidivist offender process similar to what is required under the CSA, see 21 U.S.C. § 851(a)-(c), Omar's conviction is not punishable as a felony under the CSA.*
>
> *Consequently, Omar's conviction is unlikely to be considered an illicit trafficking aggravated felony.*

B. Crime of Violence

A second type of aggravated felony that presents a host of thorny issues is the "crime of violence" provision. INA § 101(a)(43)(F) provides that "a crime of violence (as defined in section 16 of title 18, but not including a purely political offense) for which the term of imprisonment [is] at least one year" is an aggravated felony. Aside from the one-year prison term requirement, the major component of the crime of violence definition turns on the two-pronged definition referenced in the parenthetical phrase: 18 U.S.C. § 16(a) defines a crime of violence as "an offense that has as an element the use, attempted use, or threatened use of physical force against the person or property of another," while § 16(b) targets "any other offense that is a felony and that, by its nature, involves a substantial risk that physical force against the person or property of another may be used in the course of committing the offense." Because these are alternative definitions, each prong has to be analyzed separately.

The first of the two subsections focuses on whether a conviction necessarily requires that physical force be used, attempted, or threatened. This definition consists of two parts—one defines the phrase "physical force," and another asks what Congress meant when it included the word "use." Both are guided by the Supreme Court's admonition that, even though a legislature can define words in a statute however it likes, the crime-of-violence type of aggravated felony envisions "a category of violent, active crimes."[97] Turning first to the "physical force" requirement, the BIA "conclude[d] that the 'physical force' necessary to establish that an offense is a 'crime of violence' for purposes of the Act must be 'violent' force, that is, force capable of causing physical pain or injury to another person."[98] The word "use," meanwhile, "requires active employment."[99] As the Court explained this interpretation in *Leocal v. Ashcroft,*

> While one may, in theory, actively employ *something* in an accidental manner, it is much less natural to say that a person actively employs physical force against another person by accident. Thus, a person would 'use . . . physical force against' another when pushing him; however, we would not ordinarily say a person 'use[s] . . . physical force against' another by stumbling and falling into him.[100]

The practical consequence of the Court's interpretation of "use" is that the crime of violence aggravated felony excludes strict liability crimes—that is, offenses that do not include a mens rea requirement—as well as offenses that require a mental state of "negligent or merely accidental conduct."[101] Combined, the interpretations of § 16(a)'s two parts means that an offense constitutes a crime of violence under § 16(a) only if it has as an element the actual, attempted, or threatened active employment of violent force capable of causing pain or injury to another's person or property.[102]

The second crime of violence definition applies somewhat more broadly. Rather than hone in on an element of a crime, § 16(b) "simply covers offenses that naturally involve a person acting in disregard of the risk that physical force might be used against another in committing an

---

97. Leocal v. Ashcroft, 543 U.S. 1, 11 (2004).

98. Matter of Velasquez, 25 I&N Dec. 278, 283 (BIA 2010) (applying Johnson v. United States, 559 U.S. 133 (2010)).

99. *Leocal*, 543 U.S. at 9.

100. *Id.*

101. *See id.* at 9–10.

102. *See* Matter of Velasquez, 25 I&N Dec. 278, 283 (BIA 2010).

offense."[103] Importantly, the severity of the injury that results from the crime is irrelevant. What matters is whether the crime inherently involves a substantial risk that physical force will be used, with those terms being defined just as they are for § 16(a).[104] Strict liability offenses do not meet this requirement because they can be committed without the defendant being cognizant of the risks; a person who is unaware of a risk certainly cannot disregard that risk. The same goes for offenses that require a mens rea of negligent or accidental conduct.[105] As the Court explained in *Leocal*, a case involving a conviction under Florida's driving under the influence of alcohol offense, "In no 'ordinary or natural' sense can it be said that a person risks having to 'use' physical force against another person in the course of operating a vehicle while intoxicated and causing injury."[106]

New York's first- and second-degree manslaughter offenses are a good illustration of § 16(b)'s substantial risk factor. The state's first-degree manslaughter statute punishes a person who "[w]ith intent to cause serious physical injury to another person . . . causes the death of such person or of a third person" or "[w]ith intent to cause the death of another person, he causes the death of such person . . . under circumstances which do not constitute murder."[107] In contrast, the second-degree manslaughter statute punishes a person who "recklessly causes the death of another person."[108] According to the Second Circuit, first-degree manslaughter is a crime of violence under § 16(b), because to be convicted "the accused must cause a human death while acting with the specific intent to do so or, at least, with the specific intent to cause serious physical injury." Therefore, "inherent in the nature of that offense is a substantial risk that the perpetrator may intentionally use physical force in committing the crime."[109] Second-degree manslaughter, however, does not satisfy § 16(b)'s definition because "[t]he offense encompasses many situations in which the defendant applies no physical force to the victim, and more importantly, situations that do not

---

103. *Leocal*, 543 U.S. at 10.
104. *See id.* at 10 n.7.
105. *See id.* at 11.
106. *Id.*
107. N.Y. PENAL § 125.20(1).
108. *Id.* at § 125.15(1).
109. Vargas-Sarmiento v. Dep't of Justice, 448 F.3d 159, 172 (2nd Cir. 2006).

involve any risk that the defendant will apply force to the victim."[110] If the crime can be committed without using force, then clearly a conviction can result without showing that the defendant disregarded a substantial risk that force would be used. First-degree manslaughter, therefore, is a crime of violence under § 16(b), while second-degree murder is not.

Given the crime of violence category's complexity, it is no surprise that the courts continue to address unresolved nuances. For one, since *Leocal* was issued, several courts of appeals have concluded that, under *Leocal*'s reasoning, conduct committed recklessly does not satisfy the crime of violence definition, a question that the *Leocal* Court explicitly did not answer.[111] The Second Circuit, for example, explained that "'§ 16(b) contemplates only *intentional* conduct and refers only to those offenses in which there is a substantial likelihood that the perpetrator will *intentionally* employ physical force, . . . not [to] an accidental, unintended event.'"[112] Second, there remains some uncertainty about whether the reference to a felony in § 16(b) means a felony under state law or federal law.[113] Because Congress tends to prefer a uniform application of INA provisions no matter where in the country the conviction occurs, there is a strong argument to be made that federal law should govern—that is, in order to satisfy § 16(b), the offense must be one that is punishable as a felony under the federal penal code. Militating in the opposite direction, however, is the fact that courts frequently note that the crime was punished as a felony under the relevant state law, thereby satisfying § 16(b)'s felony

---

110. Jobson v. Ashcroft, 326 F.3d 367, 373 (2nd Cir. 2003).

111. *Leocal*, 543 U.S. at 13.

112. *Vargas-Sarmiento*, 448 F.3d at 170 (quoting Dalton v. Ashcroft, 257 F.3d 200, 208 (2nd Cir. 2001)); *see* United States v. Zuniga-Soto, 527 F.3d 1110, 1124 (10th Cir. 2008 (holding that "a *mens rea* of recklessness does not satisfy use of physical force requirement" under the crime of violence definition used by the U.S. Sentencing Guidelines, which, in relevant part, is identical to 18 U.S.C. § 16(a)); United States v. Torres-Villalobos, 487 F.3d 607, 615–17 (8th Cir. 2007) ("[T]he Court's reasoning suggests that crimes requiring only reckless disregard for the risk of physical injury to another are not crimes of violent"); Garcia v. Gonzales, 455 F.3d 465, 469 (4th Cir. 2006) ("recklessness, like negligence, is not enough to support a determination that a crime is a 'crime of violence.'"); United States v. Vargas-Duran, 356 F.3d 598, 599 (5th Cir. 2004) (interpreting a sentencing enhancement provision of the U.S. Sentencing Guidelines that is identical to 18 U.S.C. § 16(a) and "hold[ing] that the 'use' of force requires that a defendant intentionally avail himself of that force").

113. *See* Covarrubias Teposte v. Holder, 632 F.3d 1049, 1052 (9th Cir. 2010).

requirement.[114] It is likely to be some time before this issue is cleared up. Third, the BIA muddled § 16(b) analyses by holding that immigration judges must consider the "ordinary case" that results in conviction under a particular statute rather than the least culpable conduct that could be punished as is traditionally examined under the categorical approach.[115]

Controlled Substance Offenses

While the immigration consequences of an aggravated felony conviction are more severe than any other category of crime, immigration officials also have at their disposal a sweeping provision that ensnares most drug offenses. Going back at least to 1922, immigration law has penalized distribution of a small number of narcotics.[116] But beginning in 1986, the INA has included sweeping language intended to put almost every migrant involved in drug activity in jeopardy of removal.[117]

The controlled substance offense provision, as it is frequently referred to, appears as a basis of deportation and inadmissibility in slightly different form. The deportation ground, located at INA § 237(a)(2)(B)(i), provides that "[a]ny alien who at any time after admission has been convicted of a violation of (or a conspiracy or attempt to violate) any law or regulation of a State, the United States, or a foreign country relating to a controlled substance (as defined in section 802 of title 21), other than a single offense involving possession for one's own use of 30 grams or less of marijuana, is deportable." Its inadmissibility counterpart, INA § 212(a)(2)(A)(i)(II), provides that "any alien convicted of, or who admits having committed, or who admits committing acts which constitute the essential elements of . . . a violation of (or a conspiracy or attempt to violate) any law or regulation of a State, the United States, or a foreign country relating to a controlled substance (as defined in section 802 of title 21), is inadmissible."

Both forms of the controlled substance offense provision require careful navigation of state drug laws and the federal CSA, especially when

---

114. *See* Ortega-Mendez v. Gonzales, 450 F.3d 1010, 1015–16 (5th Cir. 2006).
115. Matter of Francisco-Alonzo, 26 I&N Dec. 594, 600 (BIA 2015).
116. Act of May 26, 1922, ch. 202, Pub. L. No. 227, 42 Stat. 596 , §§ 2(c), 2(e) (authorizing deportation for being involved in the importation of opium, coca leaves, or cocaine).
117. Anti-Drug Abuse Act of 1986, Pub. L. No. 99-570, § 1751(a)-(b), 100 Stat. 3207 (amending INA § 212(a)(23), 8 U.S.C. § 1182(a)(23) (2012), and INA § 241(a)(11), 8 U.S.C. § 1251(a)(11)).

dealing with an offense involving possession of a particular drug. Since 1965, while interpreting a now-repealed statutory provision, the BIA has steadfastly maintained that a state drug possession crime can result in deportation or exclusion only if the government shows that the conviction necessarily involved a substance punished by federal drug laws.[118] More recently it explained that this applies to "crimes involving the possession or distribution of a *particular* drug."[119] The two provisions now in the INA explicitly require that the phrase "controlled substance" be interpreted as defined in 21 U.S.C. § 802, the definitional section of the federal CSA. The CSA, including Code of Federal Regulations sections where updates are added, provides an extensive list of illicit substances that includes all the usual suspects in five parts called "schedules," with Schedule I containing the substances deemed most pernicious and Schedule V the least threatening.[120] Marijuana and heroin, for example, are listed in Schedule I,[121] cocaine in Schedule II,[122] and anabolic steroids in Schedule III.[123] Much less common substances such as the highly addictive opiod called "properidine" and the sedative "mecloqualone" are also included.[124]

Though it is tempting to assume that every substance regulated by state drug laws appears in one of the five CSA schedules, that is not correct. New York, for example, lists chorionic gonadotropin, a hormone sometimes abused as a means to lose weight, as a controlled substance, but the CSA does not.[125] Likewise, many states prohibit possession of khat, a leaf

---

118. *See* Matter of Paulus, 11 I&N Dec. 274, 276 (BIA 1965); *but see* Matter of Espinoza, 25 I&N Dec. 118, 121 (BIA 2009) (noting that the BIA has refused to extend Matter of Paulus to crimes other than possession).

119. Matter of Espinoza, 25 I&N Dec. at 121.

120. *See* 21 U.S.C. §§ 812(b), (c); 8 C.F.R. § 1308.11–1308.15 (providing updated versions of Schedule I through V).

121. 21 U.S.C. § 812, Schedule I, §§ (b)(10), (c)(10).

122. 21 U.S.C. § 812, Schedule II, § (a)(4).

123. 21 U.S.C. § 812, Schedule III, § (e).

124. 21 U.S.C. § 812, Schedule I, § (a)(40) (properidine); 8 C.F.R. § 1308.11(e)(2) (mecloqualone).

125. NEW YORK PUBLIC HEALTH LAW § 3306, Schedule III, § (g). For a discussion of an immigration court's application of the CSA to New York's listing of chorionic gonadotropin, see crImmigration.com, *IJ: Not All Drug Convictions Are Controlled Substance Offenses* (Nov. 5, 2013), http://crimmigration.com/2013/11/05/ij-not-all-drug-convictions-are-controlled-substance-offenses.aspx.

long used as a stimulant in East Africa, but the CSA does not.[126] To borrow
a hypothetical scenario that the Third Circuit proposed, "Suppose, then,
that Pennsylvania—which has its own controlled-substances schedules to
which it is free to add substances not in the federal lists—chose to include
tobacco in its schedules, and that [a migrant] was convicted of possessing tobacco paraphernalia. Given the express exclusion of tobacco from
the federal list of controlled substances, it would be a complete anomaly
to then place [a migrant] in removal proceedings for possessing tobacco
paraphernalia."[127] Ensuring that this does not happen, however, requires
an attorney's vigilance.

In addition, the statute includes a simple "relating to" requirement
that courts have interpreted quite broadly: the state, federal, or foreign
country offense must relate to a controlled substance. As the BIA explained, "the 'relating to' concept has a broad ordinary meaning, namely,
'to stand in some relation; to have bearing or concern; to pertain; refer;
to bring into association with or connection with.'"[128] Unlike language
that might restrict the clause's reach, the "relating to" language that actually appears in the statute is thought to involve "conduct associated
with the drug trade in general."[129] Indeed, the BIA has deemed "preparatory crimes" such as attempt, conspiracy, facilitation, and solicitation to
relate to a controlled substance "when the underlying substantive crime
involves a drug offense," because the preparatory offense is so closely
tied to the underlying substantive crime that the former "'takes its character and its quality from the nature of the law toward whose violation
it is . . . directed.'"[130] Applying this interpretation, the Board concluded
that a law prohibiting "possession of an item intentionally used for

---

126. *See* Argaw v. Ashcroft, 395 F.3d 521, 524–26 (4th Cir. 2005); 1 UELMEN &
HADDOX, DRUG ABUSE AND LAW SOURCEBOOK § 3:35.
127. Rojas v. Attorney General, 728 F.3d 203, 209 (3d Cir. 2013).
128. Matter of Espinoza, 25 I&N Dec. 118, 120 (BIA 2009).
129. *Id.* at 121.
130. Matter of Beltran, 20 I&N Dec. 521, 525–26 (BIA 1992) (quoting Matter of
Bronsztejn, 15 I&N Dec. 281, 282 (BIA 1974); *see* Matter of Zorilla-Vidal, 24 I&N Dec.
768, 770 (BIA 2009); *but see* Coronado-Durazo v. INS, 123 F.3d 1322, 1324–25 (9th Cir.
1997).

manufacturing, using, testing, or enhancing the effect of a controlled substance"—in this instance, a marijuana pipe—necessarily relates to a controlled substance.[131]

Though "relating to" is read expansively, it is not without limits. A crime's coincidental association with a controlled substance is insufficient—for example, a conviction for unlicensed distribution of prescription drugs "that also happen to contain 'controlled substances'" because the relationship between the distribution offense and the illegal drug trade is too attenuated and because treating all unlicensed distribution convictions as controlled substance offenses would capture a lot of conduct not regulated by the federal CSA.[132] Additionally, a crime that is linked to an underlying offense but is "separate and apart from the underlying crime"—such as "accessory after the fact, [that] by its nature, takes place after the completion of the principal crime, [and] therefore does not require any planning and involvement in the principal drug-trafficking crime"—does not take its "character and quality" from the underlying drug crime.[133] For its part, the Ninth Circuit made much of the fact that the statutory provision explicitly references "a conspiracy or attempt to violate" a law relating to a controlled substance. To give meaning to this language, the court explained, requires excluding other preparatory offenses such as solicitation.[134] More importantly, in the eyes of the Supreme Court, the BIA has stretched the "relating to" phrase "to the breaking point." In *Mellouli v. Lynch*, the Court held that a person is subject to removal under the controlled substance offense provision only if the government "connect[s] an element of the alien's conviction to a drug" listed in the federal CSA.[135]

Though the deportation and inadmissibility controlled substance offense provisions share many similarities, they differ in two important ways. First, the deportation provision sanctions convictions only, while the

---

131. Matter of Espinoza, 25 I&N Dec. at 120.
132. Borrome v. Attorney General, 687 F.3d 150, 161–62 (3d Cir. 2012).
133. Matter of Batista-Hernandez, 21 I&N Dec. 955, 960 (BIA 1997).
134. Coronado-Durazo v. INS, 123 F.3d 1322, 1324–25 (9th Cir. 1997) (rejecting Matter of Beltran, 20 I&N Dec. 521, 525–26 (BIA 1992).
135. Mellouli v. Lynch, No. 13-1034, 2015 WL 2464047, slip op. at 13-14 (June 1, 2015).

inadmissibility provision also affects people who admit to having committed a controlled substance offense or who admit to having committed the
elements of a controlled substance offense. While this seems like a quibble, it
can pose a major problem for people who admit to having engaged in minor
illegal drug use without having been caught or prosecuted. A young man
seeking admission into the United States, for example, was deemed inadmissible because he told a psychiatrist who screened him as part of the visa application process that he had occasionally smoked marijuana in the past.[136]

Problem 2.3

Audrey is a twenty-three-year-old British citizen who lives and works in Denver on
a nonimmigrant visa. After marijuana was legalized in Colorado in January 2014,
Audrey began to buy marijuana from a licensed vendor once or twice a month. In
June 2014, she spent a week abroad visiting family. On her return the Customs and
Border Protection agent who questioned her at the airport asked whether she had
ever used marijuana. Well aware that she had done so in compliance with state law,
Audrey responded that she had. Is Audrey subject to the inadmissibility version of
the controlled substance offense, INA § 212(a)(2)(A)(i)(II)?

*If the CBP agent informed Audrey that using marijuana is a crime (see Convic-
tion and Commission section above for "admission" requirements), then Audrey
is likely inadmissible under INA § 212(a)(2)(A)(i)(II). Though Audrey engaged
in conduct that is legal in Colorado, marijuana remains a "controlled substance"
under the federal CSA and possessing it remains a federal crime.*

Second, the deportation basis includes an important exception for a
minor marijuana possession conviction—involving 30 grams or less for
one's own use—that does not appear in the inadmissibility provision. This
is a rather narrow exception, but one that offers a crucial second chance
for many migrants convicted of a common low-level drug crime. The statutory text clearly restricts the exception to simple possession convictions and
even then only to such convictions involving 30 grams or less of marijuana.
Convictions involving more than 30 grams of marijuana or involving other
controlled substances fall outside the exception. The trickiest part of the
exception undoubtedly goes to the phrase "single offense." Does this refer

---

136. *See* Pazcoguin v. Radcliffe, 292 F.3d 1209, 1217–18 (9th Cir. 2002), *as amended
on denial of reh'g and reh'g en banc*, 308 F.3d 934 (9th Cir. 2002).

to the number of crimes that a migrant was convicted of or does it ask about the underlying conduct that gave rise to a conviction or convictions? According to the BIA, "single offense" refers to "a specific number of occasions" no matter how many discrete crimes were involved so long as "they were constituent parts of a single act of simple marijuana possession."[137] Determining whether a crime fits this description, the Board added, requires a "'circumstance-specific' inquiry, that is, an inquiry into the nature of the alien's conduct. It does not suggest a focus on the formal elements of generic offenses."[138] Applying this framework, the Board concluded that a migrant convicted of simple possession of less than 10 grams of marijuana and possession of drug paraphernalia—namely the plastic bag in which the marijuana was contained—met the statutory exception.[139]

Problem 2.4

Travis, a lawful permanent resident, was pulled over in Illinois by a police officer who noticed that his rear taillight was not working. While speaking to Travis, the police officer saw what appeared to be Oxycontin pills on the car floor. Knowing that these pills were frequently sold and used illegally, the officer asked Travis if that was indeed Oxycontin, and Travis said it was. He was subsequently convicted of simple possession of a controlled substance. The judge sentenced him to one year in jail and a $500 fine, but the jail time was suspended. Is Travis subject to the controlled substance offense deportation basis, INA § 237(a)(2)(B)(i)?

Travis is likely deportable under INA § 237(a)(2)(B)(i) because Illinois, 720 Illinois Comp. Stat. 570/206(xiv), and federal drug laws, 21 C.F.R. § 1308.12(b)(1)(xiii), both regulate the possession of the principal ingredient in Oxycontin, the opioid oxycodone. Since Travis's conviction did not involve marijuana, he is not eligible for the exception that applies to a single conviction for possession of 30 grams or less of marijuana for personal use.

Crimes Involving Moral Turpitude

Aggravated felonies and controlled substance offenses may get more limelight, but another category, crimes involving moral turpitude, undoubtedly

---

137. Matter of Davey, 26 I&N Dec. 37, 39 (BIA 2012).
138. *Id.* at 39 (citing *Nijhawan v. Holder*, 557 U.S. 29, 34 (2009)); *see* Matter of Dominguez-Rodriguez, 26 I&N Dec. 408, 411 (BIA 2014) (reaffirming Matter of Davey).
139. Matter of Davey, 26 I&N Dec. at 41.

wins the prize for causing the most headaches among crimmigration practitioners. Despite having been part of immigration law statutes since 1891,[140] no one, it seems, can figure out what the phrase means. Congress has never bothered to define it. Instead, the BIA's standard definition revolves around ever-shifting views of morality. "Moral turpitude," the Board explained in a frequently quoted passage, "refers generally to conduct that shocks the public conscience as being inherently base, vile, or depraved, contrary to the rules of morality and the duties owed between man and man, either one's fellow man or society in general."[141]

Part of the confusion surrounding the crime involving moral turpitude category is that the phrase's "inherently base, vile, or depraved" definition is itself not particularly illuminating. The BIA and courts often seem unsure whether this includes an intent requirement or whether strict liability offenses can come within its reach. At times the BIA and courts have suggested that this category of removable offenses "necessarily involves an evil intent or maliciousness in carrying out a reprehensible act."[142] At other times, however, the Board has explained that "[t]he presence or absence of a corrupt or vicious mind is not controlling."[143] Likewise, though there is general agreement that the category encompasses only crimes that are inherently wrong rather than those that are wrong only because they have been prohibited by statute, the Board and courts do not always agree about how to categorize a particular offense. The crime of failure to register as a sex offender offers an interesting example. In a case concerning California's failure to register offense, the BIA concluded that it was a crime involving moral turpitude largely by relying on the fact that "[a] principal purpose of the statute is to safeguard children and other citizens from exposure to danger from convicted sex offenders," an obligation that is "simply too important not to heed."[144] Whether or not the underlying sex offense is base, vile, or depraved—due the peculiarities of the categorical

---

140. Immigration Act of March 3, 1891, § 1, ch. 551, 26 Stat. 1084.
141. Matter of Short, 20 I&N Dec. 136, 139 (BIA 1989).
142. Efagene v. Holder, 642 F.3d 918, 921–22 (10th Cir. 2011) (citing Matter of Flores, 17 I&N Dec. 225, 227 (BIA 1980)); see Matter of P-, 3 I&N Dec. 56, 59 (BIA 1948).
143. Matter of Medina, 15 I&N Dec. 611, 614 (BIA 1976).
144. Matter of Tobar-Lobo, 24 I&N Dec. 143, 146 (BIA 2007).

approach—the failure to register crime is not, the Tenth Circuit explained in a case involving Colorado's analogous crime, because it targets conduct that is wrong only because the legislature relatively recently enacted a statute prohibiting specified conduct. For instance, a person can be convicted for registering six business days after changing residences instead of five. In the Tenth Circuit's view, this and similar requirements indicate that the offense is "regulatory in nature"—that is, it is "designed to aid in law enforcement" rather than punish.[145] Or, as the Ninth Circuit put it in a case involving California's offense, "Registration statutes can serve important purposes by helping to prevent future sex crimes, and assisting law enforcement in apprehending recidivist offenders. But registration is not itself a socially desirable good."[146] The Ninth and Tenth Circuits' decisions in effect represent judicial push back by the courts of appeals of the BIA's wide view of the crime involving moral turpitude provisions.[147] If they were to agree that any conduct that stems from a heinous crime is a crime involving moral turpitude simply because a legislature has prohibited it, then almost anything could fall into this category.

Courts, lawmakers, and commentators have harshly criticized this definition for most of the time that it has been part of immigration law. Just a quarter century after its introduction to immigration law, a member of Congress complained, "No one can really say what is meant by saying a crime involving moral turpitude."[148] In a dissenting opinion, Justice Robert Jackson asked, "How should we ascertain the moral sentiments of masses of persons on any better basis than a guess?"[149] Even the BIA has described it as a "nebulous concept."[150] Among the most strident modern examples deriding its imprecision is a 2010 decision in which the Ninth Circuit devoted several pages to doing nothing more than criticizing the concept. The phrase "moral

145. See *Efagene*, 642 F.3d at 924.
146. Plasencia-Ayala v. Mukasey, 516 F.3d 738, 748 (9th Cir. 2008), *overruled on other grounds by* Marmolejo-Campos v. Holder, 558 F.3d 903, 911 (9th Cir. 2009). The Ninth Circuit subsequently reaffirmed its *Plasencia-Ayala* analysis of the merits of the California sex offender registration offense. Pannu v. Holder, 639 F.3d 1225, 1228 (9th Cir. 2011).
147. See also Mohamed v. Holder. 769F. 3d 885, 889–90 (4th Cir. 2014).
148. Jordan v. DeGeorge, 341 U.S. 223, 233–34 (1951) (Jackson, J., dissenting).
149. *Id.* at 238.
150. Matter of Flores, 17 I&N Dec. 225, 227 (BIA 1980).

turpitude," the court lamented, contains "inherent ambiguity," and the only thing consistent about it is "the consistent failure of either the BIA or our own court to establish any coherent criteria for determining which crimes fall within that classification and which crimes do not."[151] Recognizing the difficulty of pinpointing what satisfies this ambiguous definition, the court added that because there are no "consistent or logical rules to follow as we determine whether a crime (other than one involving fraud) involves moral turpitude, our most useful guidance often comes from comparing the crime with others that we have previously deemed morally turpitudinous."[152]

While this is a practical remedy for a thorny problem, its lack of principled core means determinations of what constitutes a crime involving moral turpitude sometimes lead to surprising, even seemingly conflicting, results. Rape and voluntary manslaughter have been held to be crimes involving moral turpitude, but statutory rape and manslaughter in the second degree not so.[153] Such disagreements appear even within a single court in relatively short order. The Ninth Circuit, for example, concluded in 1958 that knowingly and willfully making a false statement with the intent to obtain a passport involves moral turpitude, but four years later decided that making a false statement to a government agency does not.[154]

Wavering opinions about what constitutes a crime involving moral turpitude has not kept the provision from surviving a constitutional challenge that it is "void for vagueness." This doctrine, intended to ensure that individuals are informed that certain conduct has been prohibited, finds its roots in the Due Process Clause's requirement that people receive notice of what they ought to avoid doing—or at the very least, what they may do at the risk of reprisal.[155] As the Supreme Court explained, a law is void for

---

151. Nuñez v. Holder, 594 F.3d 1124, 1130 (9th Cir. 2010).

152. *Id.* at 1131.

153. *See* Ng Sui Wing v. United States, 46 F.2d 755, 756 (7th Cir. 1931) (rape involves moral turpitude); Matter of Franklin, 20 I. & N. Dec. 867, 870 (BIA 1994) (voluntary manslaughter is not a crime involving moral turpitude); Matter of Guevara Alfaro, 25 I. & N. Dec. 417, 424 (B.I.A. 2011) (statutory rape does not categorically involve moral turpitude); Mongiovi v. Karnuth, 30 F.2d 825, 826 (W.D.N.Y. 1929) (manslaughter in the second degree does not involve moral turpitude).

154. *See* Hirsch v. INS, 308 F.2d 562, 567 (9th Cir. 1962); Bisaillon v. Hogan, 257 F.2d 435, 437–38 (9th Cir. 1958).

155. *See* United States v. Williams, 553 U.S. 285, 304 (2008).

vagueness "if it is so vague and standardless that it leaves the public uncertain as to the conduct it prohibits or leaves judges and jurors free to decide, without any legally fixed standards, what is prohibited and what is not in each particular case."[156] In a key 1951 decision, *Jordan v. DeGeorge*, the Court held that, for all its imperfections, the crime involving moral turpitude provision does not suffer this fatal flaw.[157] Importantly, that case involved a fraud offense and the Court made much of this fact. Whatever it might mean "in less obvious cases does not render that standard unconstitutional for vagueness" in all instances, including, importantly, those before the Court.[158] A judge on the Eighth Circuit would later refer to the *Jordan* Court's explanation as "an intellectual sleight of hand"—the provision survived because the particular type of crimes at issue in *Jordan*, fraud offenses, had long been deemed morally turpitudinous.[159] Despite the Supreme Court's narrow reasoning, it has become almost an article of faith that, short of congressional repeal, the crime of moral turpitude provision is with us to stay.

As it currently reads, the INA includes three crime involving moral turpitude provisions. One authorizes exclusion from the United States, while the other two allow for deportation.[160] Like the two controlled substance offense provisions, the crime involving moral turpitude basis of inadmissibility can be triggered by a conviction, an admission to having committed a crime involving moral turpitude, or an admission to having committed the essential elements of a crime involving moral turpitude.[161] The two deportation bases, however, require a conviction.[162]

Additionally, the three crime involving moral turpitude provisions differ in scope. The inadmissibility provision contains two important exceptions. One excepts crimes committed before the migrant reached eighteen years of age and more than five years before applying for admission into

---

156. Giaccio v. State of Penn., 382 U.S. 399, 402–03 (1966).
157. *See* 341 U.S. 223, 232 (1951).
158. *Id.*
159. Franklin v. INS, 72 F.3d 571, 594 (8th Cir. 1995) (Bennett, J., dissenting).
160. INA §§ 212(a)(2)(A)(i)(I) (inadmissibility), 237(a)(2)(A)(i)(I) (deportation), § 237(a)(2)(A)(ii) (deportation for multiple crime involving moral turpitude convictions).
161. INA § 212(a)(2)(A)(i)(I).
162. *See* 237(a)(2)(A)(i)(I), § 237(a)(2)(A)(ii).

the United States.[163] The second exception, frequently referred to as the "petty offense exception," provides a pass for crimes punishable by no more than one year imprisonment and, if the migrant was convicted, the sentence did not exceed six months imprisonment.[164]

The two deportation provisions build on each other. One provision authorizes deportation of a migrant convicted of a crime involving moral turpitude punishable by a sentence of at least one year (regardless of the sentence actually imposed) so long as the crime was committed within five years of admission.[165] The five years since commission is extended to ten years for a subset of people admitted into the United States as a result of having cooperated with a criminal investigation.[166] Perhaps because this provision includes a minimum possible sentence requirement and a clause that operates akin to a statute of limitations, the second provision drops these requirements while increasing the number of convictions. It authorizes deportation of a migrant "who at any time after admission is convicted of two or more crimes involving moral turpitude, not arising out of a single scheme of criminal misconduct, regardless of whether confined therefor and regardless of whether the convictions were in a single trial."[167] Under this provision the sentence possible and actually imposed is irrelevant. What does matter, however, is whether the convictions arose from a "single scheme of criminal misconduct." That ambiguous phrase, the BIA explained in a 1992 case that it reaffirmed in 2011, refers to "acts, which although separate crimes in and of themselves, were performed in furtherance of a single criminal episode, such as where one crime constitutes a lesser offense of another or where two crimes flow from and are the natural consequence of a single act of criminal misconduct."[168] For example, a person who breaks into a store with intent to commit larceny and, while engaged in that conduct, assaults someone with a deadly

---

163. INA § 212(a)(2)(A)(ii)(I).
164. INA § 212(a)(2)(A)(ii)(II).
165. INA § 237(a)(2)(A)(i).
166. See INA § 237(a)(2)(A)(i) (referencing admissions under INA § 245(j), which in turn references INA § 101(a)(15)(S)).
167. INA § 237(a)(2)(A)(ii).
168. Matter of Adetiba, 20 I&N Dec. 506, 511 (BIA 1992); see Matter of Islam, 25 I&N Dec. 637, 641 (BIA 2011).

weapon would fall within the single scheme requirement.[169] A person who used two stolen credit cards at four locations in adjoining counties to make five purchases in a matter of hours, however, would not.[170]

The most pressing issue to have affected the crime involving moral turpitude bases of inadmissibility and deportation in recent years has centered on the proper analytical method to use to determine whether a crime falls into this category. In a 2008 decision, Attorney General Michael Mukasey exercised his power as the head of the Justice Department to decide any case pending before the BIA. In *Matter of Silva-Trevino*, he announced that the traditional categorical and modified categorical approaches used to analyze immigration law statutory text would be supplemented by a broad and unprecedented additional step. If the categorical and modified categorical approaches did not clear up whether a crime involves moral turpitude, immigration judges could "consider any additional evidence the adjudicator determines is necessary or appropriate to resolve accurately the moral turpitude question."[171] This step vastly expands the range of information immigration officials can consider. Immigration judges and the BIA, for example, have turned to police reports and testimony by the migrant—previously off limits—to glean whether the migrant's conduct involved moral turpitude.[172] Among the reasons that Attorney General Mukasey offered for adding this step was his perception that the circuits disagreed on the proper analytical method to use and that the statutory language is ambiguous, thus, under ordinary principles of administrative law, authorizing the agency to carve out some semblance of clarity from Congress's unclear language.[173]

---

169. Matter of Adetiba, 20 I&N Dec. at 509.

170. *See* Matter of Islam, 25 I&N Dec. at 638.

171. Matter of Silva-Trevino, 24 I&N Dec. 687, 704 (A.G. 2008)

172. *See, e.g.,* Matter of Guevara Alfaro, 25 I&N Dec. 417, 724 (BIA 2011) (considering respondent's testimony); Matter of Christian Alejandro Bayardi, 2010 WL 4822986, *2 (BIA Nov. 9, 2010) (unpublished) (considering police report); Matter of Shohaib Alam Qazi, 2009 WL 3818032, *3 (BIA Oct. 30, 2009) (unpublished) (same). For cases stating that immigration judges could not examine police reports, see Shepard v. United States, 544 U.S. 13, 16 (2005); *see* Matter of Teixeira, 21 I&N Dec. 316, 319–20 (BIA 1996). In *Descamps v. United States*, the Court rejected an approach that allowed immigration judges to consider facts not in the record of conviction. *See* 133 S. Ct. 2276, 2287–88 (2013).

173. *See* Matter of Silva-Trevino, 24 I&N Dec. at 693, 695.

The courts of appeals have largely disagreed with his assessment. Significantly, the Fifth Circuit rejected Attorney General Mukasey's framework in Mr. Silva-Trevino's own case. Like the Third, Fourth, Ninth, and Eleventh Circuits, the Fifth Circuit concluded that there is nothing ambiguous about the conviction requirement.[174] There may be sufficient ambiguity in the phrase "moral turpitude" to justify courts' deferring to the BIA or AG, but when it comes to whether or not a conviction exists, Congress, the court explained, has spoken quite clearly. Indeed, INA § 101(a)(48)(A) provides a detailed definition of "conviction" that unmistakably spells out just what Congress thinks the term means.[175] Another section, INA § 240(c)(3)(B), even includes a list of documents that "shall constitute proof of a conviction," and nothing in the statute indicates that Congress intended for an immigration judge to rely on other evidence as proof of a conviction.[176] Nor do words such as "committing" or "involving" render ambiguous the conviction requirement.[177] In addition, courts have long used the uniform analysis known as the categorical approach, augmented by the modified categorical approach (see Categorical Approach section above), to determine whether a conviction qualifies as a certain type of crime subject to removal (e.g., whether an assault conviction qualifies as a crime involving moral turpitude).[178] Using the categorical and modified categorical approaches, courts "look to the elements of the statutory offense to ascertain the least culpable conduct hypothetically necessary to sustain a conviction under the statute."[179] If it is possible that the migrant was convicted for having engaged in nonturpitudinous conduct, eligibility for removal has not been established. Further, Congress

---

174. Silva-Trevino v. Holder, 742 F.3d 197, 200–01 (5th Cir. 2014); *see* Olivas-Motta v. Holder, 746 F.3d 907, 911 (9th Cir. 2013); Prudencio v. Holder, 669 F.3d 472, 482 (4th Cir. 2012); Fajardo v. U.S. Atty. Gen., 659 F.3d 1303, 1310 (11th Cir. 2011); Guardado-Garcia v. Holder, 615 F.3d 900, 902 (8th Cir. 2010); Jean-Louis v. Attorney General, 582 F.3d 462, 470 (3d Cir. 2009).

175. *See Jean-Louis*, 582 F.3d at 474.

176. *See Silva-Trevino*, 742 F.3d at 200–01 (citing 8 U.S.C. § 1229a(c)(3)(B)).

177. *See Prudencio*, 669 F.3d at 482.

178. *See Silva-Trevino*, 742 F.3d at 200–01.

179. *Jean-Louis*, 582 F.3d at 471.

is presumed to be aware of judicial interpretations of statutory language. When it does not act to alter how courts interpret a statute or, as with the crime involving moral turpitude provisions, Congress amends the statute repeatedly without indicating any disagreement with the universal judicial interpretation, courts conclude that Congress means for courts to continue doing as they have been. Given varying combinations of these reasons, these circuits have concluded that there is no reason to defer to Attorney General Mukasey's sudden departure from the categorical and modified categorical approaches. In April 2015, Attorney General Eric Holder vacated Mukasey's decision.[180]

Civil Immigration Enforcement Priorities

Despite a sizeable budget, DHS cannot identify and remove everyone in the United States in violation of immigration law. Enforcement priorities can and do shift.[181] To its credit, under the Obama Administration DHS has explicitly articulated its civil immigration enforcement priorities in a series of memoranda. Secretary of Homeland Security Jeh Johnson announced the department's current priorities in a November 2014 memorandum that lays out a three-tiered priority system identifying which migrants ICE, CBP, and CIS officials ought to target for detention and removal.[182] The type of crime-related conduct that fits into each priority

---

180. *Matter of Silva-Trevino*, 26 I&N Dec. 550, 550 (A.G. 2015).

181. *See*, e.g., John Morton, Director, Immigr. & Customs Enforcement, to All Field Office Directors et al., *Exercising Prosecutorial Discretion Consistent with the Civil Immigration Enforcement Priorities of the Agency for the Apprehension, Detention, and Removal of Aliens* (June 17, 2011), available at http://www.ice.gov/doclib/secure-communities/pdf/prosecutorial-discretion-memo.pdf; John Morton, Director, Immigr. & Customs Enforcement, to All ICE Employees, *Civil Immigration Enforcement: Priorities for the Apprehension, Detention, and Removal of Aliens* (March 2, 2011), available at http://www.ice.gov/doclib/news/releases/2011/110302washingtondc.pdf; John Morton, Assistant Secretary, Immigr. & Customs Enforcement, to All ICE Employees: *Civil Immigration Enforcement: Priorities for the Apprehension, Detention, and Removal of Aliens* (June 30, 2010), http://www.ice.gov/doclib/news/releases/2010/civil-enforcement-priorities.pdf.

182. Jeh Charles Johnson, Secretary, U.S. Dep't of Homeland Security, to Thomas S. Winkowski, Acting Director, Immigr. & Customs Enforcement et al., *Policies for the Apprehension, Detention and Removal of Undocumented Immigrants* (Nov. 20, 2014), available at http://crimmigration.com/wp-content/uploads/2015/03/PD-11202014.pdf.

level is summarized in the box below. Each priority category also includes conduct that is not related to criminal activity; that conduct is not listed below.

Practice Pointer

This is only a summary of DHS's civil immigration enforcement priorities. For a complete list, see http://crimmigration.com/wp-content/uploads/2015/03/PD-11202014.pdf. Migrants who fit the Priority 1 criteria are to receive the greatest attention.

- *Priority 1:* Migrants who pose a national security, border security, or public safety threat. This includes migrants apprehended at the border trying to enter the country unlawfully; those with gang ties; migrants "convicted of an offense classified as a felony in the convicting jurisdiction, other than a state or local offense for which an essential element was the alien's immigration status;" and those convicted of an aggravated felony.
- *Priority 2:* Migrants with three or more misdemeanor convictions "other than minor traffic offenses or state or local offenses for which an essential element was the alien's immigration status;" migrants convicted of a "significant misdemeanor," defined as "an offense of domestic violence; sexual abuse or exploitation, burglary; unlawful possession or use of a firearm; or . . . [offenses] for which the individual was sentenced to time in custody of 90 days or more (the sentence must involve time to be served in custody, and does not include a suspended sentence)."
- *Priority 3:* Migrants with a final order of removal issued on or after January 31, 2014.

Further Reading

Categorical and Modified Categorical Approach
Alina Das, *The Immigration Penalties of Criminal Convictions: Resurrecting Categorical Analysis in Immigration Law*, 86 N.Y.U. L. Rev. 1669 (2011).

Aggravated Felonies
Rosemary Cakmis, *Construing "Crimes of Violence" After Johnson v. United States*, 15 Bender's Immigr. Bull. 795 (June 1, 2010).

Crimes Involving Moral Turpitude
Mary Holper, *Deportation for a Sin: Why Moral Turpitude is Void for Vagueness*, 90 Neb. L. Rev. 647 (2012).

CHAPTER 3

Relief from Crime-Based Removal

There is no doubting that removal frequently results from involvement in all manner of criminal activity. But all hope is not lost. Migrants can and do obtain relief from removal even when they have a criminal record. Multiple forms of relief are available, each with its own eligibility criteria. This chapter addresses the principal avenues of relief available: cancellation of removal, waivers under INA § 212(h), readjustment of status, relief under the long-repealed former § 212(c), and withholding of removal.

Cancellation of Removal

The most significant form of relief available under the current version of the INA is cancellation of removal. Enacted in 1996, cancellation allows an immigration judge to balance a migrant's past troubles against the equities in her favor. If the scale weighs more heavily toward the equities, then the immigration judge is authorized to halt removal and let the applicant stay in the United States as a lawful permanent resident. There is no overstating the significance of cancellation. Quite simply, it lets a migrant start life in the United States anew with her criminal record firmly left in the past and a blank slate on which to craft a future.

There are two types of cancellation—one is limited to migrants who are already lawful permanent residents, while the other applies to any migrant including those who lack authorization to be in the United States. Each type involves its own eligibility criteria. Perhaps because cancellation represents such a powerful second chance, eligibility for both is rather constrained.

A. Cancellation of Removal for Lawful Permanent Residents

Section 240A(a) allows immigration judges to "cancel removal of, and adjust to the status of an alien lawfully admitted for permanent residence" a migrant who is removable. Because the statute references migrants who have been admitted to permanent residence, this type of cancellation is frequently described as "cancellation of removal for lawful permanent residents" or, more succinctly, "cancellation for LPRs." In a reference to the application form on which such cancellation requests must be made, Form EOIR 42A, practitioners and judges often shorthand even more by describing it simply as "42A cancellation." Moreover, its focus on LPRs means that individuals who have been granted permission to visit, live in, or work in the United States but who have not been granted permanent resident status are not eligible for this type of cancellation.

In addition to being a lawful permanent resident, the statute lists three required criteria. First, an applicant must have been a lawful permanent resident for at least five years.[1] For most migrants who have been granted permanent residence, this tends to be a straightforward question of counting days. Complications arise, however, when the cancellation applicant obtained LPR status by fraud—for example, when a migrant is granted permanent residence on the basis of a bigamous marriage that he did not disclose. In those instances, the Board has held that the migrant has not been "lawfully admitted for permanent residence" as the statute requires.[2] It also presents difficult evidentiary issues when an applicant is unsure about her immigration status history. Many migrants are understandably unclear about what specific legal status allows them to live in the United States and when exactly they obtained it. Attorneys, therefore, should never rely on a

---

1. INA § 240A(a)(1).
2. Matter of Koloamatangi, 23 I&N Dec. 548, 549 (BIA 2003).

client's recollection alone; always obtain verifiable documentation of a client's immigration status either directly from the client, from DHS through a Freedom of Information Act request, or at least in the Ninth Circuit, through a request pursuant to *Dent v. Holder* which requires the government to turn over records in their possession in the migrant's "A file" without a FOIA request.[3]

Second, the applicant must have continuously resided in the United States for at least seven years "after having been admitted in any status."[4] As a preliminary matter, this requires that the applicant entered the United States after presenting herself to an immigration officer and being allowed to proceed into the country, the statutory definition of "admission."[5] The definition of "admission" includes an important exception for people who were granted parole (and are therefore lawfully in the United States) that preclude them from satisfying the "admission" requirement.[6] Furthermore, the second eligibility criterion means that a cancellation applicant must have continuously resided in the United States after admission as a lawful permanent resident or a "nonimmigrant" visitor for these seven years even if she has failed to abide by the terms of admission (e.g., by remaining in the United States after the duration allowed by a nonimmigrant visa expired).[7] A nonimmigrant is anyone who was admitted into the United States on a temporary visa pursuant to INA § 101(a)(15). These include ordinary short-term visas to visit the United States for pleasure as well as visas that allow migrants to visit for much longer and work here. Lastly, though the INA does not define "continuous residence," it does define "residence" as "the place of general abode," which in turn "means his principal, actual dwelling place in fact, without regard to intent."[8] In effect, then, "continuous residence" means that the migrant has generally made her home in the United States. Presumably leaving for short stints would not break the "continuous" nature of this residence.[9] Only members of the military are allowed to leave for longer periods without consequence.[10]

---

3. Dent v. Holder, 627 F.3d 365, 374 -75 (9th Cir. 2010).
4. INA § 240A(a)(2).
5. INA § 101(a)(13)(A).
6. INA § 101(a)(13)(B).
7. Matter of Blancas-Lara, 23 I&N Dec. 458, 460–61 (BIA 2002).
8. INA § 101(a)(33).
9. *See, e.g.*, De Rodriguez v. Holder, 724 F.3d 1147, 1151–52 (9th Cir. 2013) (thirteen-day trip abroad does not break continuous residence).
10. INA § 240A(d)(3).

Third, migrants are ineligible for cancelation for LPRs if they have been convicted of an aggravated felony. This limitation is both broad and narrow. It is a wide-reaching exclusion because the INA's aggravated felony definition consists of twenty-one parts. Perhaps surprisingly, this bar due to criminal convictions is narrow because it does not capture any other criminal basis for removal. LPRs convicted of a controlled substance offense or a crime involving moral turpitude are eligible for LPR cancellation so long as the crime is not also an aggravated felony. Many common crimes meet these constraints. Simple drug possession offenses, for example, are controlled substance offenses, but not illicit trafficking.[11]

B. Cancellation of Removal for Nonpermanent Residents

Section 240A(b) allows immigration judges to cancel the removal of removable migrants regardless of the migrant's immigration status. Even unauthorized migrants are eligible for this type of cancellation, frequently described as "cancellation of removal for nonpermanent residents" or just "42B cancellation" because of the official form that must accompany all such requests Form EOIR-42B. Despite its name, lawful permanent residents may also seek relief under this provision.[12] As with cancellation for LPRs, the INA imposes several specific eligibility criteria.

First, to ensure that only people with a significant connection to the United States are granted cancellation, Congress limited eligibility to individuals who have met a minimal presence requirement in the United States. With the exception of members of the military, an applicant for cancellation of removal for non-LPRs must have been "physically present in the United States for a continuous period of not less than 10 years immediately preceding the date of such application."[13] Time in any immigration status counts toward the ten-year requirement, even time spent in the United States without authorization. The "continuous period," however,

---

11. *See* Lopez v. Gonzales, 549 U.S. 47, 59 (2006) (simple possession is not illicit trafficking); Alsol v. Mukasey, 548 F.3d 207, 208 (2d Cir. 2008) (conceding that simple possession is a controlled substance offense).

12. Matter of A-M-, 25 I&N Dec. 66, 75 (BIA 2009).

13. INA § 240A(b)(1)(A) (providing continuous presence requirement); INA § 240A(d) (3) (exempting military members).

ends if the migrant leaves the United States for a single ninety-day period or multiple trips abroad totaling more than 180 days.[14]

Second, applicants must show that they have had good moral character during the ten years preceding application.[15] Though the INA leaves some room for immigration judges to make individualized determinations of whether an applicant has met the good moral character requirement, it does list several actions that prevent a finding of good moral character.[16] Most of these are in some way related to criminal activity. One provision prohibits immigration judges from concluding that someone who has ever been imprisoned for at least 180 days is a person of good moral character.[17] Another section provides that migrants convicted of or who committed most of the crime-based grounds of inadmissibility have failed to show good moral character, but only if this crime was committed during the ten-year period.[18] A third provision precludes anyone convicted of an aggravated felony.[19] Though this section suggests that it applies to all aggravated felony convictions, Congress was clear that it applies only to convictions occurring on or after November 29, 1990.[20]

Third, the statute precludes eligibility to people who have been convicted of almost all the crime-based grounds of removal.[21] Anyone convicted of a crime that results in inadmissibility under INA § 212(a)(2) or deportability under INA § 237(a)(2) or 237(a)(3) cannot receive cancellation for non-LPRs. This is a far-reaching exclusion since these provisions, combined, cover all crimes involving moral turpitude, controlled substance offenses, and aggravated felonies. A migrant convicted of any removable offense, therefore, is unlikely to qualify for non-LPR cancellation.

Fourth, the applicant is required to prove that her removal would result in "exceptional and extremely unusual hardship" to a United States citizen or lawful permanent resident spouse, parent, or child.[22] Hardship to other

14. INA § 240A(d)(2).
15. INA § 240A(b)(1)(B).
16. INA § 101(f).
17. INA § 101(f)(7).
18. INA § 101(f)(3).
19. INA § 101(f)(8).
20. Immigration Act of 1990, P.L. 101-649, 104 Stat. 4978, § 509.
21. INA § 240A(b)(1)(C).
22. INA § 240A(b)(1)(D).

family members or to the applicant herself is irrelevant. In practice, this often proves to be the most difficult eligibility criterion to satisfy. The BIA has made no qualms about the fact that Congress meant for this to be a tough hurdle that only the truly extraordinary cases will overcome. When Congress added the cancellation of removal section to the INA, including its "exceptional and extremely unusual hardship" standard, it simultaneously repealed an "extreme hardship" requirement. This change, the BIA explained, was Congress's attempt to raise the hardship standard so as to narrow the number of migrants who could obtain relief.[23] Indeed, Congress itself explained that the legislators who moved the proposal through the House of Representatives "deliberately changed the required showing of hardship from 'extreme hardship' to 'exceptional and extremely unusual hardship' to emphasize that the alien must provide evidence of harm to his spouse, parent, or child substantially beyond that which ordinarily would be expected to result from the alien's deportation."[24] The trauma that might be expected to ordinarily accompany separation, therefore, is simply not sufficient to meet this elevated hardship requirement.

Difficult though it is to show exceptional and extremely unusual hardship, it is possible. Courts tend to focus on "the ages, health, and circumstances of qualifying lawful permanent resident and United States citizen relatives."[25] No one factor is dispositive; rather, an immigration judge must assess hardship factors in their totality.[26] Analyzing those factors, the BIA concluded that a single mother met the hardship standard when she showed that, if removed to México, she would be devoid of the robust family support she had in the United States, all of whom were either United States citizens or lawful permanent residents and all of whom played an active role in the lives of her four United States citizen children.[27] Importantly, the children did not speak Spanish well and were unfamiliar with México, thus, they could be expected to have a difficult time adjusting to life there.[28] Moreover, the applicant's ex-husband—the children's father—was

---

23. *See* Matter of Monreal, 23 I&N Dec. 56, 58–59 (BIA 2001).
24. H.R. Rep. No. 104-828, at 213 (1996).
25. Matter of Monreal, 23 I&N Dec. at 63.
26. Matter of Gonzalez-Recinas, 23 I&N Dec. 467, 472 (BIA 2002).
27. *Id.* at 471.
28. *Id.*

not part of their lives, and, in fact, was himself in removal proceedings, thus the children could not be expected to stay in the United States with him.[29] Interestingly, the Board noted that it is permissible to consider the impact on the applicant to the extent that affects the qualifying relatives.[30] In this way, the Board weighed the fact that the economic hardship that the applicant was likely to feel if removed would necessarily transfer onto her children since they were entirely dependent on her for financial support.[31] Illustrating that "[t]he BIA will sometimes reach opposite conclusions in cases that have many factual similarities,"[32] the Board was not convinced by a single mother of two United States citizen children given that the children's father provided economic support and was part of their lives, the applicant's siblings in the United States were unauthorized, the applicant had not shown that her children would be deprived of education if they relocated with their mother, and the applicant had accumulated assets in the United States that "would surely help her in establishing a new life in Mexico."[33] In the end, only "compelling" cases meet the exceptional and extremely unusual hardship requirement.[34]

C. Stop-Time Rule

One perpetually befuddling component of both types of cancellation is the so-called stop-time rule.[35] At its simplest, the stop-time rule identifies the moment at which the continuous residence required to receive cancellation for LPRs and the continuous physical presence required to obtain cancellation for non-LPRs ends. Somewhat surprisingly, the requirement imposed on LPR cancellation applicants that they have been an LPR for at least five years is not subject to the stop-time rule. The BIA takes the position that the stop-time rule applies to all convictions, even those that occurred before the rule was added to the INA in 1996.[36] At least two

---

29. *Id.* at 469.
30. *Id.* at 471.
31. *Id.*
32. Ettiene v. Holder, 659 F.3d 513, 518 (6th Cir. 2011).
33. Matter of Andazola, 23 I&N Dec. 319, 323–24 (BIA 2002).
34. Matter of Monreal, 23 I&N Dec. 56, 59 (BIA 2001).
35. INA § 240A(d)(1).
36. *See* Matter of Robles-Urrea, 24 I&N Dec. 22, 27–28 (BIA 2006); Matter of Perez, 22 I&N Dec. 689, 691 (BIA 1999).

circuits, however, have rejected this view, instead holding that the stop-time rule is not retroactive; it applies only to offenses committed on or after April 1, 1997, the date the stop-time rule's statutory text took effect.[37]

From this relatively straightforward starting place, things get complicated. To begin with, the stop-time rule kicks in to end accrual of continuous residence or continuous physical presence when one of two events occurs. The first option is that time ceases to accrue when DHS serves the respondent with a Notice to Appear (NTA) indicating that removal proceedings have formally begun.[38] In the BIA's view, this is true even if the NTA does not state the time and date of the removal hearing as INA § 239(a)(1)(G)(i) seems to require.[39]

The second situation that stops accrual of time is more convoluted. In whole, it provides that the stop-time rule is triggered "when the alien has committed an offense referred to in section 212(a)(2) that renders the alien inadmissible to the United States under section 212(a)(2) or removable from the United States under section 237(a)(2) or 237(a)(4)."[40] This clause consists of two subparts. Subpart one consists of the phrase "when the alien has committed an offense referred to in section 212(a)(2)." This language indicates that the migrant must have committed a crime listed in INA § 212(a)(2). Use of the word "committed" is key because most of § 212(a)(2) requires a conviction before a migrant is deemed inadmissible. Despite referencing § 212(a)(2), the stop-time rule does not require a conviction.[41] Instead, subpart one looks first for the date the crime was committed and only then asks whether that crime could result in inadmissibility under § 212(a)(2). Subpart two consists of everything beginning with the word "renders." This language requires that the offense that the migrant committed must also result in inadmissibility under § 212(a)(2) or deportabililty under §§ 237(a)(2) or (a)(4).[42] For example, the BIA concluded that the stop-time rule applied to a migrant who was convicted

---

37. *See* Jeudy v. Holder, 768 F.3d 595, 605 (7th Cir. 2014); Sinotes-Cruz v. Gonzales, 468 F.3d 1190, 1202–03 (9th Cir. 2006).

38. INA § 240A(d)(1)(A).

39. *See* Matter of Camarillo, 25 I&N Dec. 644, 652 (BIA 2011).

40. INA § 240A(d)(1)(B).

41. *See* Matter of Perez, 22 I&N Dec. 689, 693 (BIA 1999).

42. *See id.*

of possession of cocaine because he committed an offense referred to in INA § 212(a)(2)(A)(i)(II), the crime involving moral turpitude basis of inadmissibility, and his conviction rendered him deportable under INA § 237(a)(2)(B)(i), the controlled substance offense basis of removal. The migrant's continuous presence therefore ceased accruing the day he committed the possession offense.[43] In contrast, a migrant convicted of a firearms offense that rendered him deportable under INA § 237(a)(2)(C) did not trigger the stop-time rule because § 212(a)(2) does not refer to firearms offenses.[44] Likewise, conviction for a crime involving moral turpitude within five years of admission rendered a migrant deportable under INA § 237(a)(2)(A)(i), but it did not trigger the stop-time rule because it fell within the petty offense exception to the crime involving moral turpitude basis of inadmissibility, thus it could not be deemed "an offense referred to in section 212(a)(2)."[45]

D. Burden

Whose obligation is it to show that an applicant for cancellation meets the statutory eligibility requirements? The INA leaves no room to doubt that the burden rests on the migrant's shoulders.[46] A regulation adds that if the available evidence indicates that a basis for mandatory denial of relief "may apply," the migrant must show by a preponderance of the evidence that it does not.[47] This means, for example, that a migrant seeking cancellation of removal for LPRs must provide enough evidence to convince an immigration judge that she has not been convicted of an aggravated felony.[48] Similarly, an applicant for cancellation for non-LPRs must show that she has not been convicted of a controlled substance offense since that is an offense listed in INA § 212(a)(2).[49] To do this, the applicant must be

---

43. *See id.*

44. *See* Matter of Campos-Torres, 22 I&N Dec. 1289, 1292 (BIA 2000).

45. *See* Matter of Garcia, 25 I&N Dec. 332, 334–35 (BIA 2010).

46. INA § 240(c)(4)(A); *see* Matter of Almanza-Arenas, 24 I&N Dec. 771, 774 (BIA 2009) (concluding that the burden is on the applicant for all applications for relief filed on or after May 11, 2005), *rev'd by* Almanza-Arenas v. Holder, 771 F.3d 1184, 1194 (9th Cir. 2014).

47. 8 C.F.R. § 1240.8(d).

48. *See* INA § 240A(a)(3).

49. *See* INA § 240A(b)(1)(C).

sure to meet any corroboration requirements that the immigration judge
imposes or demonstrate that she does not have access to the necessary
evidence and cannot reasonably obtain it.[50]

Carrying the burden always makes obtaining relief more difficult for
migrants. It gets truly complicated, however, when a migrant is unable to
gather enough evidence to convince an immigration judge that the preponderance of the evidence indicates she is not ineligible for relief. The
Board takes the position that an inconclusive record is insufficient to meet
the applicant's burden.[51] A number of federal courts agree.[52] This is true
even if the applicant submits every criminal history document kept by the
court in which she was convicted, thus there can be no claim that she was
to blame for not finding additional evidence. At least two courts, however,
takes the opposite position: an inconclusive record of conviction is sufficient to meet the applicant's burden.[53] Perhaps the Supreme Court will
clarify which is the proper path to take, but until that happens, attorneys
need to be aware of the circuit case law that applies in their jurisdiction.
Meanwhile, it is worth noting that the BIA's position leaves some ambiguity. In *Matter of Almanza-Arenas*, the Board explained, "the respondent
did not submit the requested documentation at the resumed hearing and
gave no reason for failing to do so."[54] The Board does not hint at what
kind of explanation would have been sufficient, but its language suggests
that part of the fatal flaw in *Almanza-Arenas* was the migrant's failure to
provide any explanation. The practical effect of the BIA's position and this
circuit split is that immigration defense attorneys should be quite careful about counseling clients to concede removal when a sound argument
otherwise is available. No matter how strong the migrant's argument for

---

50. INA § 240(c)(4)(B); *see* Matter of Almanza-Arenas, 24 I&N Dec. 771, 774–75
(BIA 2009), *rev'd by Almanza-Arenas*, 771 F.3d at 1194.

51. *See* Matter of Almanza-Arenas, 24 I&N Dec. at 774–75 (BIA 2009), *rev'd by
Almanza-Arenas*, 771 F.3d at 1194 (where the record of conviction is inconclusive, the
court must presume the least culpable means of conviction).

52. *See* Young v. Holder, 697 F.3d 976, 990 (9th Cir. 2012) (en banc), *abrogation recognized in Almanza-Arenas*, 771 F.3d at 1193–94; Salem v. Holder, 647 F.3d 111, 116 (4th
Cir. 2011); Garcia v. Holder, 584 F.3d 1288, 1289–90 (10th Cir. 2009).

53. *See Almanza-Arenas*, 771 F.3d at 1194; Martinez v. Mukasey, 551 F.3d 113, 121
(2nd Cir. 2008).

54. 24 I&N Dec. at 775, *rev'd by Almanza-Arenas*, 771 F.3d at 1194.

cancellation of removal may be, conceding removal has the possibility of entangling her when the burden shifts to her to show she is eligible for relief and the conviction records available are inconclusive.

Practice Pointer

Conceding removability is often tempting. It is almost always an uphill battle to successfully challenge the government's claim that a migrant with a criminal history is removable. Plus, migrants are often detained while removal proceedings are pending, giving them an incentive to move the process along as quickly as possible (for a detailed discussion of immigration detention, see chapters 4 and 9). Attorneys, however, need to be sure to properly gauge the risk of obtaining relief from removal and counsel migrants accordingly. Part of that advice needs to include clear warnings of the consequences of returning to the United States without authorization (for a discussion of the federal crime of illegal reentry, see chapter 6).

E. Discretion

The final consideration for migrants applying for either type of cancellation concerns the exercise of discretion. Both cancellation provisions specify that the Attorney General "may" cancel the removal of migrants who meet the statutory eligibility requirements discussed above.[55] This small word matters a lot. After all is said and done with the eligibility requirements that the INA clearly lays out, the migrant must still convince an immigration judge (who acts as the Attorney General's surrogate) that she merits a favorable exercise of discretion.[56]

Discretionary decisionmaking is inherently flexible. As the Board put it, "there is no inflexible standard for determining who should be granted discretionary relief, and each case must be judged on its own merits."[57] In evaluating each case, immigration judges "must balance the adverse factors evidencing the alien's undesirability as a permanent resident with the social and humane considerations presented in his (or her) behalf to determine whether the granting of . . . relief appears in the best interest of

---

55. Matter of A-M-, 25 I&N Dec. 66, 76 (BIA 2009).
56. 8 C.F.R. § 1240.8(d).
57. Matter of C-V-T, 22 I&N Dec. 7, 11 (BIA 1998).

this country."[58] Adverse factors include the existence of a criminal record and "its nature, recency, and seriousness," as well as other indications of "bad character or undesirability as a permanent resident of this country" that may not have turned into a criminal offense.[59] Favorable factors include the applicant's family ties in the United States, how long she has lived here, military service, work history, property or business ties, and involvement in the community.[60] Immigration judges will also consider evidence of rehabilitation "and other evidence attesting to a respondent's good character," factors that are especially relevant for individuals who have been involved in criminal activity.[61]

212(h) Waiver

Another means of obtaining relief from removal is the waiver of inadmissibility provided by INA § 212(h). This waiver applies only to specified grounds of inadmissibility: a crime involving moral turpitude, two or more convictions, prostitution, certain serious criminal offenses, and a controlled substance offense. It cannot be used to waive any basis for deportation. Moreover, it is available only to individuals who can show that a United States citizen or lawful permanent resident spouse, parent, son, or daughter would suffer "extreme hardship" if the applicant were removed. Though the § 212(h) provision's language is fairly straightforward, four important nuances exist. The first twist concerns controlled substance offenses, the second relates to a bar for people convicted of an aggravated felony, the third addresses the hardship requirement, and the fourth is about the possibility that an otherwise ineligible applicant has rehabilitated.

Section 212(h) does not apply to all controlled substance offenses. Rather, it can waive "a single offense of simple possession of 30 grams or less of marijuana" and no other crimes that might render the applicant removable under INA § 212(a)(2)(A)(i)(II). A single simple possession conviction involving 31 grams of marijuana, a conviction for possession of

58. *Id.* (quoting Matter of Marin, 16 I&N Dec. 581, 584–85 (BIA 1978)).
59. Matter of C-V-T, 22 I&N Dec. at 11.
60. *Id.*
61. *Id.*

any other controlled substance, or two marijuana possession convictions regardless of quantity, for example, could not be waived. As with all relief applications, it is up to the applicant to show that a conviction falls within § 212(h)'s strict parameters.[62] The Board is clear that the applicant must do so by a preponderance of the evidence.[63] Beyond that, the statutory text requires unpacking. Since the waiver applies only to "a single offense," the Board had to determine what Congress meant by the term "offense." In *Matter of Martinez*, the Board concluded that "offense" "refer[s] to the specific unlawful acts that made the alien inadmissible, rather than to any generic crime."[64] In other words, what matters is not how many crimes the applicant was convicted of violating or admitted to committing. Instead, immigration courts are to look to see whether the activity that results in inadmissibility under INA § 212(a)(2)(A)(i)(II) consists of "a specific type of conduct (simple possession) committed on a specific number of occasions (a 'single' offense) and involv[ed] a specific quantity (30 grams or less) of a specific substance (marijuana)," or whether the inadmissible conduct "relates to" such an offense.[65] This is a crucial interpretation of § 212(h) because many people are charged with simple possession of drug paraphernalia instead of simple possession of marijuana itself. In other instances, defendants are charged with simple possession of marijuana and simple possession of drug paraphernalia. The BIA's interpretation of § 212(h) means that such individuals remain eligible for a § 212(h) waiver if they can show that the unlawful activity was all related to a single incident of simple possession of 30 grams or less of marijuana. If they can't, then they are not eligible for a §212(h) waiver.

The second key nuance about § 212(h) to consider is the statute's unfavorable view of people convicted of an aggravated felony. The statute provides that a migrant "who has previously been admitted to the United States as an alien lawfully admitted for permanent residence" is ineligible

---

62. INA § 240(c)(4)(A); *see* Matter of Martinez, 25 I&N Dec. 118, 123 (BIA 2009).
63. Matter of Martinez, 25 I&N Dec. at 125.
64. *Id.* at 124.
65. *Id.*

for a waiver if "since the date of such admission the alien has been convicted of an aggravated felony." Does this mean that all LPRs convicted of
an aggravated felony are ineligible? The BIA certainly takes that position.
It claims that an LPR with an aggravated felony conviction is ineligible
if she entered the United States as an LPR or became an LPR while in
the United States through adjustment of status (discussed below).[66] One
circuit agrees.[67] Every other circuit to decide the issue, however, takes a
contrasting position, holding that migrants who entered the United States
as LPRs are subject to § 212(h)'s aggravated felony bar, but those who
became LPRs while in the United States through the adjustment of status
process are not because they were not "admitted" into the United States
as LPRs.[68] Illustrating this reasoning, the Fifth Circuit explained, "for the
§ 212(h) bar to apply: when the alien is granted permission, after inspection, to enter the United States, he must then be admitted as an LPR."
But, the court added, "for aliens who adjust post-entry to LPR status,
§ 212(h)'s plain language demonstrates unambiguously Congress' intent
not to bar them from *seeking* a waiver of inadmissibility."[69] In this vein,
the Sixth Circuit explained that had Congress wanted to bar everyone
who becomes an LPR from obtaining a 212(h) waiver, that "result could
quite easily have been obtained by saying something much simpler, such
as: No waiver shall be granted under this subsection in the case of a lawful permanent resident if . . . since the date of obtaining such status the
alien has been convicted of an aggravated felony."[70] Congress, of course,

---

66. *See* Medina-Rosales v. Holder, 778 F.3d 1140, 1145 (10th Cir. 2015); Matter of
Rodriguez, 25 I&N Dec. 784, 789 (BIA 2012); *see also* Matter of Koljenovic, 25 I&N
Dec. 219, 225 (BIA 2010) (adopting similar conclusion regarding seven-year continuous
residence requirement); Matter of Paek, 26 I&N Dec. 403, 407 (BIA 2014) (same regarding
admission as a "conditional permanent resident" under INA § 216(a)).
67. *See* Roberts v. Holder, 745 F.3d 928, 932 (8th Cir. 2014).
68. *See* Medina-Rosales v. Holder, 778 F.3d 1140, 1145 (10th Cir. 2015); Husic v.
Holder, 776 F.3d 59, 66 (2d Cir. 2015); Stanovsek v. Holder, 768 F.3d 515, 517–18 (6th
Cir. 2014); Negrete-Ramirez v. Holder, 741 F.3d 1047, 1054 (9th Cir. 2014); Papazoglou
v. Holder, 725 F.3d 790, 794 (7th Cir. 2013); Leiba v. Holder, 699 F.3d 346, 356 (4th Cir.
2012); Lanier v. U.S. Atty. Gen., 631 F.3d 1363, 1366–67 (11th Cir. 2011); Martinez v.
Mukasey, 519 F.3d 532, 546 (5th Cir. 2008); *see also* Hanif v. Attorney General of the
U.S., 694 F.3d 479, 484 (3d Cir. 2012) (reaching identical holding regarding seven-year
continuous residence requirement).
69. Martinez, 519 F.3d at 544, 546.
70. Stanovsek, 768 F.3d at 517.

did not include such a statement. (A separate and little used exception applies for applicants who have continuously resided as an LPR for at least seven years prior to the initiation of removal proceedings.[71])

The third nuance to consider in § 212(h) analysis hones in on the waiver's hardship requirement. In most situations the § 212(h) waiver requires that an applicant show by a preponderance of the evidence that a United States citizen or lawful permanent resident spouse, parent, son, or daughter would suffer "extreme hardship" if the applicant were removed.[72] Though this hardship standard is less onerous than the "exceptional and extremely unusual hardship" requirement for cancellation of removal for nonlawful permanent residents,[73] it is nonetheless satisfied "only in cases of great actual or prospective injury" to a qualifying relative.[74] To determine whether extreme hardship exists, the Board considers a wide range of factors, including "the presence of lawful permanent resident or United States citizen family ties to this country; the qualifying relative's family ties outside the United States; the conditions in the country or countries to which the qualifying relative would relocate and the extent of the qualifying relative's ties to such countries; the financial impact of departure from this country; and, finally, significant conditions of health, particularly when tied to an unavailability of suitable medical care in the country to which the qualifying relative would relocate."[75]

Since the extreme hardship requirement presents an "onerous" obstacle to migrants, courts and attorneys contemplating the applicability of § 212(h) need to be aware that the hardship requirement is sometimes irrelevant. Individuals inadmissible only on the basis of prostitution activity can avoid the hardship requirement by showing that their admission would not adversely impact "national welfare, safety, or security," or, alternatively, that they have been rehabilitated.[76] Similarly, migrants inadmissible for any other reason covered by § 212(h) can avoid the hardship

---

71. INA § 212(h).

72. INA § 212(h)(1)(B).

73. INA § 240A(b)(1)(D).

74. Matter of Ngai, 19 I&N Dec. 245, 246 (BIA 1984).

75. Matter of Cervantes-Gonzalez, 22 I&N Dec. 560, 565–66 (BIA 1999) (discussing the "extreme hardship" requirement under INA § 212(i)).

76. INA § 212(h)(1)(A)(i)–(iii).

requirement by showing that the activity that makes them inadmissible occurred more than fifteen years ago and they have rehabilitated or, alternatively, their admission would not negatively affect "national welfare, safety, or security."[77]

After all is said and done, the § 212(h) waiver is granted only at the Attorney General's discretion.[78] Acting on the AG's behalf, immigration judges balance an applicant's adverse factors, including criminal history, against her life's equities. This is not so for individuals inadmissible as a result of being involved in "violent or dangerous crimes." In those instances, 8 C.F.R. § 1212.7(d) presumes that immigration judges "will not favorably exercise discretion." This presumption will be overcome only in "extraordinary circumstances," including where an applicant shows that removal "would result in exceptional and extremely unusual hardship."[79] Though this standard departs quite drastically from INA § 212(h)'s reliance on "extreme hardship," several federal courts of appeals have upheld the regulation, reasoning that the regulation addresses the AG's exercise of discretion, which is a different requirement than the extreme hardship mandated by the statute.[80] Importantly, neither the statute nor regulations define "violent or dangerous crimes." The decision that adopted the heightened discretionary standard that was subsequently codified into § 1212.7(d) suggests that only the most heinous crimes should fall into this category. That case involved a woman who admitted to hitting and shaking a nineteen-month-old child in her care, then failing to seek medical attention for the child. The child ultimately died.[81] In adopting the presumption against granting an extreme hardship waiver, Attorney General John Ashcroft described the crime as "depraved" and the injuries to the child as "extraordinary."[82] The obviously heinous nature of these actions suggests that "violent or dangerous crimes" should be construed narrowly.

---

77. INA § 212(h)(1)(A)(i)–(iii).
78. INA § 212(h)(2).
79. 8 C.F.R. § 1212.7(d).
80. *See* Samuels v. Chertoff, 550 F.3d 252, 257 (2nd Cir. 2008); Pimental v. Mukasey, 530 F.3d 321, 325 (5th Cir. 2008); Mejia v. Gonzales, 499 F.3d 991, 995–96 (9th Cir. 2007).
81. *See* Matter of Jean, 23 I&N Dec. 373, 374 (A.G. 2002).
82. *Id.* at 383.

Adjustment of Status

Migrants can obtain lawful permanent resident status through one of two ways: by applying at the United States embassy or consulate in their country of citizenship (known as consular processing) or by asking the United States government to adjust their status from within the United States. The second route, known as adjustment of status, allows a migrant to request recognition as a lawful permanent resident without going through the time-consuming and expensive process of returning to one's country of citizenship. It has the important added benefit of allowing migrants to avoid bars to admission that apply to individuals who were in the United States without authorization then left.[83] More than half of people who have become lawful permanent residents in recent years have done so through adjustment of status—roughly 550,000 people in fiscal year 2012 alone.[84]

Two forms of adjustment of status exist. The first and most common is available to migrants who were admitted or paroled into the United States and are in the country at the time of applying.[85] The second type—known as "245(i) adjustment" due to the section of the INA in which it is located—applies to individuals who entered without inspection and for whom an immigration petition was filed on or before April 30, 2001.[86] The 2001 deadline means that the number of people eligible for 245(i) adjustment is rapidly dwindling.

Adjustment of status is only available to individuals who are eligible for admission into the United States on the date of application. As a result, the only migrants who can adjust their status are "immediate relatives" of United States citizens or migrants who are currently eligible for admission through a family or employment-based route.[87] Migrants who are not immediate relatives must be sure that an immigrant visa is currently available for them. The INA provides a complicated formula by which to

83. INA § 212(a)(9)(B).
84. RANDALL MONGER & JAMES YANKAY, U.S. LEGAL PERMANENT RESIDENTS: 2012 ANNUAL FLOW REPORT 2 tbl.1 (2013).
85. INA § 245(a).
86. INA § 245(i).
87. INA § 201(b)(2)(A)(i) (defining "immediate relative"); § 203(a) (listing family-based immigration routes); § 203(b) (providing employment-based immigration options).

measure this, but the Department of State provides a much more user-friendly gauge in the monthly Visa Bulletins it posts online.[88] Importantly, most migrants who are not immediate relatives are ineligible to adjust their status if they worked without authorization or were present in the United States without authorization.[89] An exception to this bar exists for technical violations of lawful status.[90]

Because adjustment applicants must be admissible at the time of applying, adjustment is particularly attractive to migrants who would be inadmissible if they left the United States after having been here without authorization for at least six months. Individuals who have been unlawfully present in the United States for more than 180 days but less than one year are inadmissible for three years.[91] Those who have been unlawfully present for at least one year are inadmissible for ten years.[92] Both provisions are triggered the moment a person leaves the United States. Staying in the United States and seeking adjustment of status, therefore, allows these individuals to avoid having to spend many years away from the life they have created here.

All of the criminal bases of inadmissibility in INA § 212(a) apply to adjustment applications. For individuals with a criminal history, the value of adjustment lies in the discrepancy that exists between bases of deportation listed in INA § 237(a) and the inadmissibility grounds of § 212(a). In some instances, it is possible to rely on a § 212(h) waiver to avoid a finding of inadmissibility even when a migrant is deportable. For example, migrants who are convicted of an aggravated felony are deportable, but they are not inadmissible if the offense is neither a crime involving moral turpitude, controlled substance offense, nor falls into any other inadmissibility category.

Perhaps counterintuitively, adjustment of status pursuant to INA § 245(a) is available to people who are already lawful permanent residents.

88. Visa Bulletins are posted on the Department of State's Bureau of Consular Affairs web site at http://travel.state.gov/content/visas/english/law-and-policy/bulletin.html.

89. INA 245(c)(2), (c)(8). An exception to this bar exists for technical violations of lawful status. Technical violations defined at 8 C.F.R. § 245.1(d)(2)(ii)–(iv).

90. See 8 C.F.R. § 245.1(d)(1) (defining "lawful immigration status"); 8 C.F.R. § 245.1(d)(2) (defining fault and technical violations).

91. INA § 212(a)(9)(B)(i)(I).

92. INA § 212(a)(9)(B)(i)(I)(II).

That is, it is possible to "readjust" one's status from lawful permanent resident to lawful permanent resident. The statute, after all, merely requires that an adjustment applicant have been "admitted or paroled" into the United States. All LPRs have successfully undergone this process. Of course, the same criteria apply on readjustment as apply to migrants seeking adjustment for the first time—candidates for readjustment of status must be admissible into the United States at the time of applying.

Problem 3.1

Sidney, a Haitian citizen, entered the United States clandestinely in 1986. Nine years later, in 1995, when Sidney was sixteen, the former Immigration and Naturalization Service approved an immigrant visa petition filed on his behalf by Sidney's United States citizen father. Two years later Sidney was convicted of burglary and sentenced to two years imprisonment. After his release, Sidney married a United States citizen. Sidney was recently placed in removal proceedings during which an immigration judge concluded that his conviction is both an aggravated felony and crime involving moral turpitude. Is Sidney eligible for adjustment of status?

Sidney is likely eligible for adjustment of status. Despite the fact that he entered without inspection, he is the immediate relative of a United States citizen (his spouse), INA § 201(b)(2)(A)(i), and his father submitted a petition on Sidney's behalf well before the April 30, 2001, deadline required for adjustment of status pursuant to INA § 245(i). The difficult question that remains is whether his conviction disqualifies him from eligibility by making him inadmissible. It does not. The fact that burglary is an aggravated felony, INA § 101(a)(43)(G), doesn't disqualify him because an aggravated felony is not a basis of inadmissibility. In the decision from which this example is drawn, the BIA explained that burglary is also a crime involving moral turpitude. Matter of Michel, 21 I&N Dec. 1101, 1103 (BIA 1998). A CIMT conviction is a basis of inadmissibility, thus Sidney is inadmissible. INA § 212(a)(2)(A)(i)(I). He can get around that inadmissibility, however, by obtaining a waiver under INA § 212(h). That waiver is unavailable to individuals who have previously been admitted as LPRs and convicted of an aggravated felony. Sidney seems to fit this description except that the Board held that the aggravated felony bar in § 212(h) does not apply to migrants who have not been granted LPR status. Matter of Michel, 21 I&N Dec. at 1104. Sidney, therefore, is not precluded from applying for a § 212(h) waiver. If he can show that a qualifying relative will suffer the required "extreme hardship," he might obtain a waiver of inadmissibility thus allowing him to adjust his status.

Section 212(c) Relief

Each type of relief from removal discussed above remains ensconced in the current INA. Another form of relief that continues to resonate with attorneys is actually found in a provision that Congress repealed in 1996 when it enacted cancellation of removal. Former § 212(c) existed in one form or another for roughly eight decades and, at its most charitable, granted the Attorney General the power to waive virtually any criminal basis of inadmissibility (admittedly, at the time this consisted almost entirely of crimes involving moral turpitude).[93] Despite the statute's apparent applicability to grounds of inadmissibility only, several courts of appeals and the BIA concluded that it had to apply to bases of deportation as well to avoid due process and equal protection problems.[94] The statute remained in this form until 1990 when Congress amended § 212(c) to bar anyone convicted of an aggravated felony and who had served a term of imprisonment of at least five years.[95] Six years later, in April 1996, Congress further limited § 212(c)'s reach by barring people convicted of an aggravated felony, drug offenses, certain weapons offenses or national security violations, and multiple crimes involving moral turpitude.[96] Later that year, in September 1996, Congress entirely repealed § 212(c) relief.[97]

This, however, is not the end of the story. Congress was not clear about whether it intended § 212(c)'s repeal to apply retroactively, and the federal circuits took differing positions. Eventually the Supreme Court had to resolve this disagreement. In *INS v. St. Cyr*, the Court held that § 212(c) continues to be available to individuals who met the eligibility criteria when they were convicted.[98] Naturally, as time passes this is an ever-smaller pool of people. Nonetheless, § 212(c) availability is sufficiently important that it returned to the Supreme Court in 2011. In *Judulang v. Holder*,

---

93. *See* INS v. St. Cyr, 533 U.S. 289, 294 (2001) (discussing Immigration Act of 1917, § 3, 39 Stat. 875, 878).

94. *See* Francis v. INS, 532 F.2d 268, 273 (2nd Cir 1976); Matter of Silva, 16 I&N Dec. 26, 30 (BIA 1976).

95. Immigration Act of 1990, § 511, P.L. 101-649, 104 Stat. 4978, 5052.

96. Anti-Terrorism and Effective Death Penalty Act of 1996, Pub. L. 104-132, § 440, 110 Stat. 1214 (1996).

97. Illegal Immigration Reform and Immigrant Responsibility Act of 1996, Pub. L. No. 104-208, § 304, 110 Stat. 3009 (1996).

98. 533 U.S. 289, 326 (2001).

the Court rejected the "comparable grounds" or "statutory counterpart" approach that the BIA had long used to determine which grounds of deportation could be waived under § 212(c).[99] That approach, the Court announced, is "unmoored from the purpose and concerns of the immigration laws," thus it is "arbitrary and capricious."[100]

Having been sent back to the drawing board, the BIA announced a multi-part eligibility framework that relies quite heavily on the amendments Congress adopted in 1996. According to the Board, lawful permanent residents with at least seven consecutive years of lawful unrelinquished domicile remain eligible for § 212(c) relief if they meet other criteria.[101] They cannot have engaged in terrorism, espionage, sabotage, or other threats to national security.[102] Individuals convicted between November 29, 1990, and April 24, 1996, are barred if convicted of one or more aggravated felonies for which they served an aggregate term of imprisonment of at least five years.[103] Anyone convicted between April 24, 1996, and April 1, 1997, is ineligible if removal or deportation proceedings began on or after April 24, 1996, and is deportable for having committed an aggravated felony, controlled substance offense, certain firearms offenses under INA § 237(a)(2)(C), any offense listed in INA § 237(a)(2)(D) (relating to espionage or sabotage), or multiple crimes involving moral turpitude, or has been convicted of at least one aggravated felony that resulted in at least five years imprisonment.[104] No one convicted of any crime on or after April 1, 1997, is eligible.[105] Any migrant who meets these requirements is eligible to seek § 212(c) relief *"unless* the applicant is subject to the grounds of inadmissibility under sections 212(a)(3)(A), (B), (C), or (E), or (10)(C) of the Act," none of which address ordinary criminal activity.[106] Clearly determining whether a given individual remains eligible for § 212(c) relief requires very careful review. If eligible, an applicant may

---

99. 132 S. Ct. 476, 490 (2011).

100. *Id.*

101. Matter of Abdelghany, 26 I&N Dec. 254, 259 (BIA 2014).

102. *Id.* at 259–60.

103. *Id.* at 272.

104. *Id.*

105. *Id.* at 260.

106. *Id.* at 266.

then seek the immigration judge's favorable exercise of discretion.[107] As with other discretionary determinations, an immigration judge must weigh all factors, including rehabilitation, on a case-by-case basis.[108]

Withholding of Removal and Deferral of Removal

The INA and the Convention Against Torture provide an additional form of relief from removal, withholding of removal. The Torture Convention, meanwhile, provides for yet another form of relief, deferral of removal. Though these are distinct bases of relief, they are sufficiently similar that they are frequently adjudicated simultaneously.

Importantly, withholding and deferral are different from the forms of relief discussed above in three significant ways. First, withholding and deferral do not provide any particular type of legal status for a successful applicant. Instead, they merely prevent the government from removing a migrant to the country where persecution or torture is likely to result.[109] Second, every type of relief from removal discussed above is discretionary. That is, it is ultimately up to the Attorney General—in practice, represented by an immigration judge—whether a migrant who meets the statutory eligibility criteria is allowed to remain in the United States. Withholding of removal is different. It is a mandatory form of relief. This means that, except principally for individuals convicted of a "particularly serious crime," a person who meets the statutory eligibility criteria provided in INA § 241(b)(3) cannot be removed. Likewise, the only individuals who meet the Torture Convention's eligibility requirements who can be removed are those convicted of a particularly serious crime. Even those individuals, however, remain eligible for deferral of removal. There is no hardship inquiry or balancing of equities. For this reason, deferral of removal represents a powerful form of relief. Third, withholding and deferral stem from international law. In § 241(b)(3), Congress codified the international law principle of nonrefoulement, a French term that simply means that states cannot return a person to a location where she will be persecuted. The 1951 Convention Relating to the Status of Refugees and the 1984

---

107. *See* Matter of Marin, 16 I&N Dec. 581, 585–87 (BIA 1978).
108. *See* Matter of Edwards, 20 I&N Dec. 191, 196 (BIA 1990).
109. Matter of I-S- & C-S-, 24 I&N Dec. 432, 434 (BIA 2008) (discussing 8 C.F.R. § 208.16(f)).

Convention Against Torture cemented the principle of nonrefoulement into international law.[110] This norm, in turn, arises from the Universal Declaration of Human Rights' assurance that "[e]veryone has the right to seek and to enjoy in other countries asylum from persecution."[111]

A. Withholding of Removal Under INA § 241(b)(3)

Obtaining withholding is difficult. A migrant is eligible for withholding pursuant to the INA only if her "life or freedom would be threatened . . . because of the alien's race, religion, nationality, membership in a particular social group, or political opinion."[112] Though the statute uses the term "threatened," a regulation actually requires a showing of past persecution or that future persecution is more likely than not due to one of the five protected grounds.[113] A substantial eligibility bar applies to individuals who have been convicted of a "particularly serious crime."[114] Though the INA does not define the phrase "particularly serious crime," it does state that a conviction for one or more aggravated felonies for which the migrant served an aggregate term of imprisonment of at least five years shall be considered a particularly serious crime.[115] Many crimes fit within this exception.

Aside from the wide reach of the particularly serious crime exception, withholding under the INA is best described as a near absolute bar on removal rather than an absolute bar for another reason. Individuals who receive withholding under § 241(b)(3) are ordered removed and can actually be removed to a safe third country at any time.[116] Admittedly, this is not common.

---

110. *Convention and Protocol Relating to the Status of Refugees art. I(a)(2)*, http://www.unhcr.org/3b66c2aa10.html; *Convention Against Torture and Other Cruel, Inhuman, or Degrading Treatment or Punishment art. 3*, http://www.ohchr.org/EN/ProfessionalInterest/Pages/CAT.aspx.

111. *Universal Declaration of Human Rights art. 14*, http://www.un.org/en/documents/udhr/index.shtml#a14.

112. INA § 241(b)(3)(A).

113. 8 C.F.R. § 208.16(b)(1), (2); *see* Ivanisvili v. U.S. Dep't of Justice, 433 F.3d 332, 339 (2nd Cir. 2006) (applying the regulatory requirement of "persecution"); Hadjimehdigholi v. INS, 49 F.3d 642, 647 (10th Cir. 1995) (same).

114. INA § 241(b)(3)(B)(ii).

115. INA § 241(b)(3).

116. Matter of I-S- & C-S-, 24 I&N Dec. 432, 434 (BIA 2008) (discussing 8 C.F.R. § 208.16(f)).

B. Withholding of Removal under the Convention Against Torture

To obtain withholding of removal under the Convention Against Torture, a migrant must show "that it is more likely than not that he or she would be tortured if removed."[117] There is no requirement that the torture be on the basis of a protected ground as with withholding under INA § 241(b)(3).[118] Torture consists of nothing less than extremely cruel and inhuman treatment.[119] The few individuals who meet this high threshold may nonetheless be removed if convicted of a particularly serious crime.[120]

C. Deferral of Removal under the Convention Against Torture

Unlike the two versions of withholding of removal, deferral of removal operates as an absolute bar to removal. Indeed, deferral is explicitly available only to individuals who would have received withholding under the Convention Against Torture but for a conviction for a particularly serious crime.[121] An individual granted deferral is ordered removed, only actual removal is postponed while the risk of torture continues.[122]

Problem 3.2

Clark, a Mexican citizen, entered the United States sixteen years ago using a border crossing card. At the time Clark was seventeen years old. Rather than return to México, Clark moved to Phoenix to live with his parents and siblings. After many years of living and working in the Phoenix area, Clark was recently convicted of possessing roughly 15 grams of marijuana after which he was placed in removal proceedings. Four months ago Clark married a United States citizen. Is Clark eligible for relief?

The border crossing card authorizes a person to visit the United States for up to thirty days and travel within twenty-five miles of the border. Clearly Clark has exceeded those limitations, thus he is removable. Since Clark is not a lawful permanent resident there is no doubt that he is not eligible for cancellation of removal for lawful permanent residents. INA § 240A(a).

(continued)

---

117. 8 C.F.R. § 208.16(c)(2).
118. Aliyev v. Mukasey, 549 F.3d 111, 116 n.5 (2nd Cir. 2008).
119. 8 C.F.R. § 208.18(a)(2).
120. 8 C.F.R. § 208.16(d)(2).
121. 8 C.F.R. § 208.17(a).
122. 8 C.F.R. § 208.17(a), (b)(iv).

He may, however, be eligible for cancellation of removal for nonlawful permanent residents. INA § 240A(b). One problem that Clark faces, though, is that his drug possession conviction is a controlled substance offense under INA § 212(a)(2)(A)(i)(II), thus he has been convicted of an offense under § 212(a)(2). This renders him ineligible for cancellation for non-LPRs. INA § 240A(b)(1)(C). As an aside, his conviction also presents a problem meeting non-LPR cancellation's good moral character requirement and nothing indicates that his United States citizen wife or any other qualifying relative would suffer "exceptional and extremely unusual hardship" if Clark were removed. See INA § 240A(b)(1)(B), (D).

Clark's hopes of remaining in the United States are not yet dashed. He might be able to adjust his status to that of a lawful permanent resident. INA § 245(a). He was clearly inspected and admitted into the country when he arrived using his border crossing card. As the spouse of a United States citizen, he is an immediate relative, INA § 201(b)(2)(A)(i), thus there is a visa available for him immediately as required by INA § 245(a)(3). The only question left to resolve is whether Clark's conviction makes him inadmissible. Because his conviction is unquestionably a controlled substance offense under INA § 212(a)(2)(A)(i)(II), at first blush, it appears that he is inadmissible. He might, however, qualify for a waiver of inadmissibility under INA § 212(h). That provision grants immigration judges the power to waive INA § 212(a)(2)(A)(i)(II) so long as the conviction involved "a single offense of simple possession of 30 grams or less of marijuana." If Clark can carry the burden of showing that his conviction involved 15 grams of marijuana, he still has a chance of adjusting his status. The fatal problem for Clark appears when we reach the hardship requirement. Unless Clark can show that his removal would result in "extreme hardship" to his wife or another qualifying relative, he does not meet the eligibility requirements for adjustment of status. Clark, therefore, is likely out of luck.

Nothing indicates that Clark might be eligible for withholding of removal or deferral of removal.

Further Reading

Laura Murray-Tjan, *Waivers of Inadmissibility Under Sections 212(h) and 209(c) of the Immigration and Nationality Act: Strategies for Success When the Government Alleges a "Violent or Dangerous" Crime*, 11-07 IMMIGR. BRIEFINGS 1 (July 2011).

CHAPTER 4

Immigration Detention

This chapter addresses what is likely the most poignant feature of removal proceedings short of removal itself: civil immigration detention. It begins by delving into the legislative origins of detention, a task that requires a quick visit to the late nineteenth century when federal immigration law was coming into its own. The chapter then turns to the authority that immigration officials currently possess to detain migrants. It closes with a detailed examination of the INA's current mandatory detention provisions.

Importantly, this chapter does not address law enforcement initiatives related to detention such as the use of immigration detainers and the reliance on private prisons. Those topics are taken up in chapters 9 and 10.

Historical Origins

The practice of regularly detaining newcomers stretches back to the late nineteenth century. Beginning in 1875, Congress enacted a series of laws that increasingly excluded greater numbers of migrants, with a special emphasis on arriving Chinese. Government officials charged with identifying excludable individuals naturally needed time to do so, and migrants had to go somewhere while officials sorted through the new arrivals—keeping migrants on the ships they came on became infeasible rather quickly. In response, Congress enacted the first statute explicitly authorizing immigration detention in 1891.[1] Two years later Congress returned to immigration detention when it enacted the first mandatory detention statute.[2]

For its part, the Supreme Court has never questioned detention's integral role in immigration law enforcement. In one of the earliest cases involving immigration detention to reach the Court, it explained, "We think it clear that detention or temporary confinement, as part of the means necessary to give effect to the provisions for the exclusion or expulsion of aliens, would be valid."[3] More recently, the Court has relied on this statement to reaffirm its view that "detention during deportation proceedings [i]s a constitutionally valid aspect of the deportation process."[4]

Just as consistently, the Court has described the detention that accompanies immigration proceedings as civil rather than criminal.[5] This is an important distinction. Confinement that arises from criminal proceedings is subject to a host a constitutional and statutory limitations that do not apply to civil detention. The Fourth Amendment's exclusionary rule, for example, a device intended to incentivize police compliance with constitutional safeguards, is unavailable in removal proceedings except for egregious or widespread constitutional violations, thus raising the likelihood that someone will be penalized through use of evidence obtained in violation of the Fourth Amendment.[6] Likewise, the Fifth Amendment's Double Jeopardy Clause prohibits multiple punishments for the same offense, but because immigration detention is not deemed punitive the Clause is irrelevant. The Sixth Amendment's right to counsel also does not apply to individuals facing the possibility of losing their liberty at the hands of immigration officials.

---

1. *See* Act of Mar. 3, 1891, ch. 551, § 8, 26 Stat. 1084, 1085.
2. Act of March 3, 1893, ch. 206, § 5, 27 Stat. 569, 570.
3. Wong Wing v. United States, 163 U.S. 228, 235 (1896).
4. Demore v. Kim, 538 U.S. 510, 523 (2003).
5. Zadvydas v. Davis, 533 U.S. 678, 690 (2001).
6. *See* Puc-Ruiz v. Holder, 629 F.3d 771, 777, 778 (8th Cir. 2010); *see also* INS v. Lopez-Mendoza, 468 U.S. 1032, 1050–51 (1984).

Interestingly enough, the Court has never actually explained why immigration detention is civil. Instead, it merely repeats its assumption that immigration detention is civil because the immigration proceedings of which detention is part are civil.[7] There is plenty of reason to doubt that the Court's civil characterization is defensible. Pointing to the heavy intertwinement of criminal and immigration law that fills this book's pages, academics and advocates have begun to attack the Court's frail assumption that immigration detention is civil. Thus far, however, courts have failed to heed their calls.

Modern Immigration Detention Authorizations

As in the late nineteenth century, today two types of immigration detention authorizations exist. The first allows immigration law enforcement officers and immigration judges to detain if they believe it is merited in a particular situation. The second type of detention requires that they do so when a migrant meets particular criteria enumerated by Congress. The following sections address each in turn.

Discretionary Detention

Immigration law enforcement officers have broad authority to detain migrants suspected of violating immigration law. By regulation, most frontline officers working for CBP or ICE can question or arrest.[8] As an initial matter, they are allowed "to interrogate any alien or person believed to be an alien as to his right to be or to remain in the United States."[9] A number of courts have interpreted this provision as authorizing an investigatory stop (i.e., a *Terry* stop). As such, immigration officials may temporarily seize a person to investigate their compliance with immigration law if they have reasonable suspicion that the individual is engaged in wrongdoing, including potentially violating immigration law.[10] Secondarily, certain immigration officials may issue an administrative arrest warrant along

---

7. *See Zadvydas*, 533 U.S. at 690 ; Carlson v. Landon, 342 U.S. 524, 537–38 (1952).
8. 8 C.F.R. § 287.5(a)(1), (c).
9. INA § 287(a)(1).
10. Au Yi Lau v. INS, 445 F.2d 217, 223 (D.C. Cir. 1971); *see* Ojeda-Vinales v. INS, 523 F.2d 286, 287 (2nd Cir. 1975); 8 C.F.R. § 287.8(b)(1).

with a notice to appear in immigration court for removal proceedings.[11] If an immigration official has "reason to believe" a migrant has violated immigration law "and is likely to escape before a warrant can be obtained for his arrest," the statute permits the migrant's arrest.[12] Courts have interpreted this "reason to believe" requirement as equivalent to the probable cause necessary for an arrest under Fourth Amendment jurisprudence.[13] Because the Fourth Amendment prohibits an arrest for the mere purpose of investigating whether criminal activity occurred,[14] courts have no choice but to interpret the INA's "reason to believe" language in this way. Despite this reference to the traditional level of suspicion required under the Fourth Amendment, it is unclear whether probable cause means the same thing in the administrative immigration arrest context as it does in the traditional criminal law enforcement context. At least one court—the District of Columbia Circuit—explicitly requires a lower threshold. According to that court in *Blackie's House of Beef, Inc. v. Castillo,* searches conducted by immigration officials of commercial premises must be supported by "sufficient specificity and reliability to prevent the exercise of unbridled discretion by law enforcement officials" but do not require individualized suspicion as is traditionally required by the Fourth Amendment.[15] Other courts disagree. One federal district court referred to *Blackie's* as "a radical departure from established fourth amendment doctrine."[16] Another has read the D.C. Circuit's interpretation to apply, at most, only to searches but not seizures.[17]

---

11. INA § 236(a); *see* 8 C.F.R. § 287.5(e)(2) (listing officials authorized to issue arrest warrants); *see* 8 C.F.R. § 236.1(b) (providing that an arrest warrant may be issued along with an NTA or any time prior to completion of removal proceedings).

12. INA § 287(a)(2); *see* 8 C.F.R. § 287.8(c)(2).

13. *See* United States v. Quintana, 623 F.3d 1237, 1239 (8th Cir. 2010); United States v. Varkonyi, 645 F.2d 453, 458 (5th Cir. 1981); Tejeda-Mata v. INS, 626 F.2d 721, 725 (9th Cir. 1980); Ojeda-Vinales v. INS, 523 F.2d 286, 288 (2nd Cir. 1975); United States v. Cantu, 519 F.2d 494, 496 (7th Cir. 1975) (interpreting the "reason to believe" requirement of INA § 287(a)(4)); Au Yi Lau v. INS, 445 F.2d 217, 222 (D.C. Cir. 1971).

14. Brown v. Illinois, 422 U.S. 590, 605 (1975).

15. 659 F.2d 1211, 1224–25 (D.C. Cir. 1981).

16. Intl. Molders' & Allied Workers' Local Union No. 164 v. Nelson, 643 F. Supp. 884, 891 (N.D. Cal. 1986).

17. Illinois Migrant Council v. Pilliod, 531 F. Supp. 1011, 1020 (N.D. Ill. 1982).

An arrested migrant must be taken "without unnecessary delay" before a different immigration officer (unless no other officer is available and finding one requires unnecessary delay) "having authority to examine aliens as to their right to enter or remain in the United States."[18] A regulation requires that this normally happen within 48 hours of arrest.[19] If immigration officials decide that there is prima facie evidence that an arrested person is potentially removable and not subject to expedited removal (applicable to certain arriving migrants[20]) or reinstatement of removal,[21] they must refer the migrant to an immigration judge by filing a notice to appear.[22] At any time, though, immigration officials authorized to issue arrest warrants may release a migrant not subject to mandatory detention so long as the official believes the migrant does not pose a risk to people or property and is likely to appear for removal proceedings.[23] ICE may impose a bond amount or release the migrant on her own recognizance.[24]

No matter what ICE elects to do about granting bond or setting a bond amount, immigration judges have independent authority to decide whether continued detention is appropriate or required, and, if not, setting a bond amount.[25] In determining whether to release a detained migrant, immigration judges consider the migrant's dangerousness and flight risk.[26] Among the factors they consider in assessing dangerousness and flight risk are:

(1) whether the alien has a fixed address in the United States; (2) the alien's length of residence in the United States; (3) the alien's family ties in the United States, and whether they may entitle the alien to

---

18. INA § 287(a)(2); 8 C.F.R. § 287.3(a).

19. 8 C.F.R. § 287.3(d).

20. *See* INA § 235(b)(1).

21. INA § 241(a)(5).

22. 8 C.F.R. § 287.3(b).

23. 8 C.F.R. § 236.1(c)(8).

24. 8 C.F.R. § 287.3(d); *see* Memorandum from Johnny Williams, *Exec. Assoc. Comm., ICE Office of Field Operations, Guidance Regarding the Release of an Alien on an Order of Release on Recognizance, Detention and Deportation Field Officer's Manual (DDFM)* (Jan. 26, 2003), http://www.ice.gov/doclib/foia/dro_policy_memos/guidanceregardingreleaseofalienonorderofreleaseonrecognizance01262003.pdf.

25. 8 CF.R. § 236.1(d)(1); 8 C.F.R. § 1003.19; *see* 8 C.F.R. § 1003.14(a) (explaining that immigration judges can consider bond requests even if no NTA has been filed).

26. Matter of Saelee, 22 I&N Dec. 1258, 1261 (BIA 2000).

reside permanently in the United States in the future; (4) the alien's employment history; (5) the alien's record of appearance in court; (6) the alien's criminal record, including the extensiveness of criminal activity, the recency of such activity, and the seriousness of the offenses; (7) the alien's history of immigration violations; (8) any attempts by the alien to flee prosecution or otherwise escape from authorities; and (9) the alien's manner of entry to the United States.[27]

This is not an exhaustive list, and no one factor is dispositive. While criminal history is important, "criminal history alone will not always be sufficient to justify denial of bond on the basis of dangerousness. Rather, the recency and severity of the offenses must be considered."[28] Moreover, an immigration judge has "broad discretion" to weigh these and other factors as she believes appropriate.[29] An immigration judge may order the release of migrants who merit a favorable exercise of discretion and are not subject to mandatory detention. Immigration judges may release migrants on their own recognizance or on a bond of at least $1,500.[30]

While flight risk and dangerousness remain the two criteria immigration judges typically consider in making detention decisions, in certain extraordinary circumstances they appear to be able to deviate from this framework. In 2003, Attorney General John Ashcroft announced in *Matter of D-J-* that immigration judges may take into account national security interests implicated by "mass migrations" of unauthorized migrants.[31] To release a Haitian migrant who entered the United States without authorization along with 215 others threatened the nation's security "by diverting valuable Coast Guard and [Defense Department] resources from counterterrorism and homeland security interests," Ashcroft concluded, and "would give rise to adverse consequences for . . . sound immigration policy," by "encourag[ing] future surges in illegal migration at sea."[32] It is unclear how broadly *Matter of D-J-* applies. To begin with,

27. Matter of Guerra, 24 I&N Dec. 37, 40 (BIA 2006).
28. Singh v. Holder, 638 F.3d 1196, 1206 (9th Cir. 2011).
29. *See* Matter of Guerra, 24 I&N Dec. 37, 40 (BIA 2006).
30. INA § 236(a)(2)(A).
31. 23 I&N Dec. 572, 579 (A.G. 2003).
32. *Id.*

while there is no denying that the Attorney General can override BIA decisions, Ashcroft's decision conflicts with numerous BIA decisions before and after 2003 repeating flight risk and dangerousness as the controlling considerations regarding discretionary detention. Second, by its terms, the decision seems limited to instances of large-scale unauthorized migration. Admittedly, *Matter of D-J-* involved 216 migrants who entered unlawfully. While this is not a trivial number, it certainly is not massive either. At the same time, the Attorney General's decision stressed concerns among federal law enforcement officials that release would encourage other Haitians to come in a similar manner. These are unspecified and hypothetical migrants, but they were nonetheless sufficiently palpable as to play an important role in Ashcroft's decision.

Despite these questions, *Matter of D-J-* remains an important part of DHS's litigation arsenal. During the summer and fall of 2014, DHS repeatedly relied on Ashcroft's reasoning and holding in its attempts to convince immigration judges to deny bond to detained Central American women and children who arrived during a temporary but substantial uptick in unauthorized migration from the region. ICE attorneys relied on unsubstantiated claims by department officials that release would encourage additional unauthorized migration. Eventually, a federal court concluded that the government could not use national security claims or the desire to deter others from coming to the United States as a basis for detaining mothers and children.[33]

Mandatory Detention

For many migrants, discretionary assessments of dangerousness or flight risk are largely irrelevant. They are instead subject to the INA's so-called mandatory detention provision.[34] Added to the INA in 1996, § 236(c) requires immigration judges to order into custody any migrant whom there is reason to believe is removable for almost every crime-based reason, including crimes involving moral turpitude, controlled substance offenses,

---

33. R.I.L-R et al. v. Johnson, No. 1:15-ev-00011-JEB.mem.op (D.D.C. Feb. 20, 2015), *available at* http://crimmigration.com/wp-content/uploads/2015/02/Memorandum.pdf.
34. INA § 236(c).

and aggravated felonies.[35] No matter how many equities the migrant can point to, an immigration judge cannot consider releasing someone subject to mandatory detention. Such a procedure, the Supreme Court held in *Demore v. Kim*, is constitutionally permissible.[36] There is no question that this is an expansive obligation. It applies to migrants who were taken into criminal custody and released even if they were not sentenced to a term of imprisonment.[37] It may apply even if DHS does not charge the migrant as removable for one of the reasons enumerated in § 236(c).[38] Consequently, attorneys must always consider the possibility of mandatory detention when a migrant is charged as removable due to some criminal activity. An LPR convicted of a minor drug crime, for example, may have been convicted of a controlled substance offense and thus subject to mandatory detention.[39] The same goes for a person who entered without inspection and was convicted of a minor theft offense.[40]

Though § 236(c) is broad, there is plenty of room for strategic representation. Perhaps because it imposes a deprivation of liberty without individualized assessments of risk, much of § 236(c)'s nuances are hotly contested. The Board, for example, takes the position that § 236(c) applies if a migrant is removable for one of the reasons listed in the statute even if she was not taken into ICE custody immediately upon release from criminal custody.[41] According to the Board, this position helps fulfill Congress's intent in enacting § 236(c). "Congress," the Board explained, "was not simply concerned with detaining and removing aliens coming directly out of criminal custody; it was concerned with detaining and removing *all* criminal aliens."[42] One court of appeals agrees with the BIA's position,[43] but a constantly growing number of federal district courts have taken

---

35. *See* IIRIRA, Pub. L. 104-208, Div. C, Title III, Subtitle A, § 303(a), 110 Stat. 3009-585; 63 Fed. Reg. 27444 (explaining the "reason to believe" threshold inquiry).
36. *See* 538 U.S. 510, 524–25, 531 (2003).
37. Matter of West, 22 I&N Dec. 1405, 1409 (BIA 2000); *see* Straker v. Jones, No. 13 Civ. 6915, 2013 WL 6476889, at *15 (S.D.N.Y. Dec. 10, 2013).
38. Matter of Kotliar, 24 I&N Dec. 124, 126 (BIA 2007).
39. *See* INA § 236(c)(1)(B).
40. *See* INA § 236(c)(1)(A) (requiring detention of migrants deemed inadmissible as a result of a conviction for a crime involving moral turpitude, among other reasons).
41. *See* Matter of Rojas, 23 I&N Dec. 117, 122, 124, 127 (BIA 2001).
42. *Id.* at 122.
43. *See* Sylvain v. Atty. Gen., 714 F.3d 150, 157 (3d Cir. 2013).

issue with the Board's conclusion.[44] The Board also takes the position that a conviction is not required to trigger § 236(c). Pre-conviction release is sufficient.[45] Some federal courts disagree with this position as well.[46]

In addition, the BIA itself has identified important limitations to § 236(c)'s reach. First, the provision does not apply to individuals released from physical criminal custody on or before October 8, 1998, the date on which the BIA decided the provision became effective.[47] Second, the BIA takes the position that the criminal custody must be "directly tied to the basis for detention under sections 236(c)(l)(A)-(D) of the Act."[48] Release from criminal arrest for activity that would not result in removal under one of the reasons enumerated in § 236(c) thus cannot lead to mandatory detention. Third, a person deemed mandatorily detainable can avoid detention by showing that it is not "substantially likely" that DHS will ultimately prove that she is removable for one of the enumerated reasons.[49] This is a difficult route to successfully navigate, but it does represent a small check on immigration officials' detention power.

Despite being called the "mandatory detention" provision, § 236(c) actually requires the Justice Department to take migrants who fit these criteria into "custody" rather than "detention." This is an important distinction. Conflating these two words led the BIA to conclude that § 236(c) requires physical confinement in an enclosed space from which they cannot leave, that is, detention.[50] Anything short of this—for example, electronic monitoring through use of an ankle bracelet—will not meet the BIA's interpretation of § 236(c).[51] While custody certainly includes detention, typically custody is not limited to detention. Indeed, in the context of habeas corpus, custody is interpreted much more broadly to mean almost any form of restraint on personal liberty imposed by a court. Had the BIA adopted that position—which is what the immigration

44. *See* Valdez v. Terry, 874 F. Supp. 2d 1262, 1274–75 (D.N.M. 2012) (collecting cases).
45. *See* Matter of Kotliar, 24 I&N Dec. 124, 125 (BIA 2007); Matter of West, 22 I&N Dec. 1405, 1410 (BIA 2000).
46. Straker v. Jones, No. 13 Civ. 6915, 2013 WL 6476889, *11-12 (S.D.N.Y. Dec. 10, 2013).
47. Matter of Adeniji, 22 I&N Dec. 1102, 1116 (BIA 1999).
48. Matter of García Arreola, 25 I&N Dec. 267, 269 (BIA 2010).
49. Matter of Joseph, 22 I&N Dec. 799, 800, 806 (BIA 1999).
50. *See* Matter of Aguilar-Aquino, 24 I&N Dec. 747, 751–53 (BIA 2009).
51. *See id.* at 751.

judge had concluded—the mandatory custody provision (as it ought to be called) would have had an entirely different impact on crimmigration law. Instead of pushing people into prisons, jails, or detention centers, it would have led many into some form of alternative to detention.

Detention after Entry of Removal Order

Not surprisingly, the INA requires detention of migrants ordered removed.[52] According to the statute, DHS is to remove individuals from the United States within ninety days of a removal order becoming final, a window of time called the "removal period."[53] After that ninety-day removal period, a detained migrant may be released under DHS supervision.[54] Through a complicated review process governed by both the statute and regulations, designated immigration officials essentially gauge a detained migrant's likelihood to endanger the public.[55] Naturally, a detainee's criminal record forms a significant part of this assessment.[56]

Individuals removable for a host of reasons—including the principal crime-based grounds—"may be detained beyond the removal period."[57] For many years the INS took the position that it could hold these individuals indefinitely. It appears to have done so with some frequency; one journalist reported that as many as 4,400 migrants were detained indefinitely in 2000 after having been ordered removed for no reason except a lack of diplomatic relations with their country of citizenship.[58] After much litigation, the Supreme Court concluded that such a practice raises serious questions.[59] As the Court explained in *Zadvydas v. Davis*, "Freedom from imprisonment—from government custody, detention, or other forms of physical restraint—lies at the heart of the liberty that [the Fifth Amendment's Due Process] Clause protects."[60] To avoid this problem,

---

52. INA § 241(a)(2).
53. INA § 241(a)(1)(A), (B).
54. INA § 241(a)(3).
55. 8 C.F.R. § 241.4(e)–(f).
56. 8 C.F.R. § 241.4(f)(2).
57. INA § 241(a)(6); 8 C.F.R. § 241.4(a).
58. MICHAEL WELCH, DETAINED: IMMIGRATION LAWS AND THE EXPANDING I.N.S. JAIL COMPLEX 94 (2002).
59. Zadvydas v. Davis, 533 U.S. 678, 696 (2001).
60. *Id.* at 690.

the Court read into the INA "an implicit 'reasonable time' limitation."[61] Specifically, the Court approved post-removal order detention for six months without threat of judicial intervention. After that, the Court held, "once the alien provides good reason to believe that there is no significant likelihood of removal in the reasonably foreseeable future, the Government must respond with evidence sufficient to rebut that showing."[62] A detained migrant who successfully meets this standard is released from detention, but may be taken into detention again at any moment if removal in the reasonably foreseeable future becomes significantly likely.

Prolonged Detention

Despite *Zadvydas*'s clear pronouncement that indefinite detention after entry of a removal order is constitutionally doubtful, migrants continue to find themselves in detention for significant periods of time. In a 2009 report, for example, the former director of DHS's Office of Detention Policy and Planning, Dora Schriro, found that approximately 2,100 migrants had been detained for one year or more.[63] A 2014 investigation by a Boston Globe reporter revealed a handful of far more extreme periods of immigration confinement: twenty years for one, eighteen for another, and seven years for a third.[64]

Developing a creative litigation strategy from *Zadvydas* and *Demore*, migrants have had an increasing amount of success winning release from prolonged detention. All of these cases have relied on the Due Process Clause's promise to act as a bulwark against unchecked detention. Together, they have dramatically reshaped prolonged immigration detention in the aftermath of *Zadvydas* and *Demore*. This section discusses the most notable of these cases, but readers should be aware that many more exist, especially at the district court level.

The Sixth Circuit began the judicial trend of constraining prolonged detention within a year of the Supreme Court issuing *Demore*. In *Ly v.*

---

61. *Id.* at 682.

62. *Id.* at 701.

63. DORA SCHRIRO, IMMIGRATION DETENTION OVERVIEW AND RECOMMENDATIONS 6 (2009).

64. Maria Sacchetti, *Jailed Immigrants Face Long Stays in Federal Cells*, BOSTON GLOBE (Feb. 18, 2014).

Hansen, the Sixth Circuit considered a due process claim by a migrant who had been detained for over 500 days pursuant to INA § 236(c) before the district court ordered his release.[65] Borrowing from *Zadvydas*, the court interpreted § 236(c) as allowing "*limited* civil detention, without bond," but prohibiting "permanent civil detention without a showing of a 'strong special justification' that consists of more than the government's generalized interest in protecting the community from danger."[66] Congress may have a great deal of leeway when it comes to immigration law, but its legislating is always subject to constitutional limitations. In this instance, the Due Process Clause provides migrants with a liberty interest that indefinite detention would impinge.[67] To avoid this constitutional problem, the court imposed a "reasonable time limitation" on detention pursuant to § 236(c).[68]

Similarly, in *Diop v. ICE/Homeland Security* the Third Circuit held that the Due Process Clause prohibits long-term detention pending removal proceedings unless the government can show that the detained migrant presents a danger to the community or is unlikely to appear for removal proceedings.[69] This conclusion was obviously important to migrants detained within the Third Circuit. It resonates more broadly, however, because in it the Third Circuit reconceptualized the legal analysis that the Supreme Court developed in *Zadvydas* and *Demore* by bridging the gap that remained between those two decisions. In *Zadvydas*, the Court imposed a reasonable timeline on detention that had become unlikely to occur in the reasonably foreseeable future.[70] In *Demore*, meanwhile, the Court had upheld mandatory detention without individualized consideration of dangerousness or flight risk in large part because most migrants were detained for a short period of time. "[T]he detention at stake under [INA § 236(c)]," the Court explained, "lasts roughly a month and a half in the vast majority of cases in which it is invoked, and about five months

---

65. 351 F.3d 263, 265 (6th Cir. 2003).
66. *Id.* at 267.
67. *Id.* at 268–69.
68. *Id.* at 270.
69. 656 F.3d 221, 233 (3d Cir. 2011).
70. 533 U.S. 678, 682 (2001).

in the minority of cases in which the alien chooses to appeal."[71] Diop, in contrast, had been detained for thirty-five months pending removal proceedings.[72] On its face, Zadvydas would seem irrelevant to his plight. The Third Circuit, however, thought that the substantial amount of time that Diop had spent imprisoned was more than just a difference between his experience and that of the average detained migrant. Instead, this was a difference of constitutional magnitude. The Due Process Clause may permit mandatory detention for some period of time, but eventually the Clause's deep commitment to personal liberty requires an individualized assessment of dangerousness or flight risk. Importantly, to reach this conclusion the Third Circuit essentially took the reasonable time limit that Zadvydas recognized as applying to detention following entry of a removal order and applied it to pre-removal order detention.[73]

The end result of the Sixth and Third Circuit's approach is to require "a two step-process: a reviewing court must first determine that a detention has been unreasonably long, and following such a determination, must determine whether the unreasonable detention is necessary to fulfill § 1226's [INA § 236(c)'s] purposes."[74] In practice, this means that a federal district court hearing a detained migrant's habeas challenge to continued detention must first conclude that detention has become unreasonably long. After that, a federal judge or immigration judge must decide whether continued detention is necessary to ensure the migrant's appearance for removal hearings or to protect public safety.

A key question remaining in the Sixth and Third Circuits after Ly and Diop is what constitutes a reasonable period of detention. Unfortunately, neither court defined reasonableness.[75] Both in fact eschewed a bright-line pronouncement.[76] To determine whether detention has become so long as to be unreasonable, both circuits instead require "a fact-dependent

---

71. Demore v. Kim, 538 U.S. 510, 530 (2003).

72. Diop, 656 F.3d at 234.

73. Id. at 231.

74. Leslie v. Attorney General, 678 F.3d 265, 269–70 (3d Cir. 2012).

75. Farrin R. Anello, Due Process and Temporal Limits on Mandatory Immigration Detention, 65 HASTINGS L.J. 363, 388–89 (2014).

76. See Diop, 656 F.3d at 233; Ly v. Hansen, 351 F.3d 263, 271 (6th Cir. 2003).

inquiry that will vary depending on individual circumstances."[77] Applied to Diop's thirty-five month confinement, the Third Circuit concluded that his continued detention without an individualized assessment was unreasonable.[78] The same goes for a migrant detained almost four years despite the fact that part of the reason his detention was so long was that he appealed a few decisions and requested a few continuances to deal with medical problems that developed while his removal case was pending.[79] The Sixth Circuit likewise concluded that Ly's eighteen-month detention was unreasonably long.[80]

Following the trajectory that the Sixth and Third Circuits began, a California federal district court, ultimately with the Ninth Circuit's support, took a stronger position. In *Rodriguez v. Robbins*, the district court entered a preliminary injunction requiring DHS to grant bond hearings to a class consisting of all migrants detained six months or more.[81] On appeal, the Ninth Circuit affirmed the district court's order.[82] Relying on *Zadvydas* and *Demore*, the Ninth Circuit explained, "Thus, it is clear that while mandatory detention under § 1226(c) [INA § 236(c)] is not constitutionally impermissible *per se,* the statute cannot be read to authorize mandatory detention of criminal aliens with no limit on the duration of imprisonment."[83] Instead, these cases allow for a "relatively brief[] period of detention" without individualized review.[84] After that relatively brief period, § 236(c) ceases to apply. At that point detention remains permissible under § 236(a), the statute's discretionary detention provision, which requires an individualized assessment of flight risk and dangerousness.[85] Because it had previously concluded in a different case that detention lasting six months or more was presumptively prolonged and thus constitutionally suspect, the Ninth Circuit affirmed the district court's bright-line six-month rule: anyone detained six months deserves

77. *Diop,* 656 F.3d at 233; *see Ly,* 351 F.3d at 271.
78. *Diop,* 656 F.3d at 234.
79. Leslie v. Attorney General, 678 F.3d 265, 271 (3d Cir. 2012).
80. *Ly,* 351 F.3d at 270.
81. 715 F.3d 1127, 1130 (9th Cir. 2013).
82. *Id.* at 1131.
83. *Id.* at 1137.
84. *Id.* at 1138.
85. *Id.*

an audience before an immigration judge.[86] At that bond hearing, the government carries the burden of showing that continued detention is necessary to ensure the migrant's appearance at future court dates or to avoid endangering the public.[87]

There is much to say for the Ninth Circuit's position. First, it has the benefit of clarity. Immigration courts in the Ninth Circuit must provide detained migrants with a bond hearing once they have been detained six months without exception. Unlike the processes required in the Sixth and Third Circuits, no fact-specific (and labor intensive) inquiry concerning the reasonableness of detention is needed. Second, the Ninth Circuit's rule is easy to follow. Immigration courts simply need to keep track of how long a migrant has been detained under INA § 236(c). Once month six comes around, the immigration court must provide the migrant with a bond hearing. The reasonableness inquiry required by the Sixth and Third Circuits, in contrast, requires a migrant to file a petition for writ of habeas corpus with a federal district court, the district court then has to consider whether the detention length is reasonable, and, if the court decides that detention is not reasonable, a bond hearing has to be scheduled at which an immigration judge must assess the migrant's dangerousness and flight risk. If the federal court decides that detention is reasonable, the migrant remains confined, always capable of repeating this protracted process. Third, a bright-line rule avoids inconsistent results that arise when different district court judges consider factually similar situations and come to conflicting positions about whether detention is reasonable.

Borrowing much from the Ninth Circuit's analysis, a federal district court in Massachusetts certified a class of migrants who have been or will be detained pursuant to INA § 236(c) for more than six months without an individualized bond hearing.[88] As in *Ly*, *Diop*, and *Rodriguez*,

---

86. *Id.* at 1139 (discussing Diouf v. Napolitano, 534 F.3d 1081, 1091 (9th Cir. 2011)); *see* Rodriguez v. Robbins, 2012 WL 7653016, at *1 (C.D. Cal. Sept. 13, 2012) (requiring a bond hearing before an immigration judge).

87. Casas-Castrillon v. DHS, 535 F.3d 942, 951 (9th Cir. 2008) (quoting Tijani v. Willis, 430 F.3d 1241, 1242 (9th Cir. 2005)).

88. Reid v. Donelan, 297 F.R.D. 185, 194 (D. Mass. 2014).

the district court took this position after concluding that *Zadvydas* and *Demore* require reading a reasonableness limit to § 236(c) so as to avoid due process problems.[89]

Further Reading

Farrin R. Anello, *Due Process and Temporal Limits on Mandatory Immigration Detention*, 65 HASTINGS L.J. 363 (2014).

Mark Noferi, *Cascading Constitutional Deprivation: The Right to Appointed Counsel for Mandatorily Detained Immigrants Pending Removal Proceedings*, 18 MICH. J. RACE & LAW 63 (2012).

---

89.   Reid v. Donelan, 991 F. Supp. 2d 275, 278 (D. Mass. 2014).

MIGRANTS IN THE CRIMINAL JUSTICE SYSTEM

Immigration law is no longer confined to immigration courtrooms. Today it is a feature of criminal proceedings in almost every state and federal courthouse in the United States. After focusing on the immigration law consequences of criminal activity in Part 1, the following three chapters turn to various ways in which migrants are treated differently from United States citizens in criminal proceedings.

Part 2 begins in chapter 5 by delving into that most foundational of protections that the Constitution provides criminal defendants: the right to counsel. In recent years, right to counsel case law has experienced a sea change. Once thought to have little or no bearing on immigration law, the Supreme Court clarified in 2010 that the right to counsel requires criminal defense attorneys to advise their migrant clients about the immigration consequences of conviction. Chapter 5, therefore, focuses on that 2010 decision, *Padilla v. Kentucky*[1] and the line of cases that has

---

1. 559 U.S. 356 (2010).

developed since then, including the Court's 2013 return to criminal defense attorneys' immigration law obligations in *Chaidez v. United States*.[2]
The chapter closes with a careful discussion of how criminal defense attorneys should respond to these judicial developments so that they do
more than merely meet the minimum requirements of constitutional competency, but instead provide defendants with the information that they
need to make sound decisions about how to proceed in criminal cases.

From chapter 5's concern about constitutional rights, the following
two chapters shift attention to substantive criminal law and procedures
used to prosecute immigration crimes in the federal and state systems.
Chapter 6 is devoted to federal crimes related to immigration, with a
special concern for two of the most commonly prosecuted offenses: illegal entry and illegal reentry. This chapter includes a discussion of legal
issues created by two policy initiatives that result in many immigration
crime convictions, Operation Streamline and fast-track plea agreements.
Part 2's final chapter, chapter 7, hones in on immigration-related criminal prosecutions in state courts. This chapter addresses substantive state
crimes specially targeting migrants as well as state criminal procedures
that apply exclusively to migrants. The chapter includes a discussion of
state-level attempts to regulate migration through their criminal justice
systems that have been deemed unconstitutional.

---

2. 133 S. Ct. 1103 (2013).

CHAPTER 5

Right to Counsel

"In an adversary system of criminal justice, there is no right more essential than the right to the assistance of counsel," the Supreme Court explained in 1978.[1] By that measure, the right to counsel's vitality provides a measure of the criminal justice system's health. Without counsel, the typical defendant is left to fend off the state's impressive power to punish without the tools needed to navigate legal processes. To remedy this, the right to counsel "embodies a realistic recognition of the obvious truth that the average defendant does not have the professional legal skill to protect himself when brought before a tribunal with power to take his life or liberty, wherein the prosecution is presented by experienced and learned counsel."[2] In only a few words, the Sixth Amendment ensures that every criminal defendant who so chooses can rely on an attorney to advocate on her behalf. "In all criminal prosecutions," the Sixth Amendment states,

---

1. Lakeside v. Oregon, 435 U.S. 333 (1978).
2. Johnson v. Zerbst, 304 U.S. 458, 462–63 (1938).

"the accused shall enjoy the right . . . to have the assistance of counsel for his defence." With this "guiding hand of counsel," as the Court once described the attorney's value to a defendant, the Sixth Amendment ensures that criminal prosecutions do not become "a sacrifice of unarmed prisoners to gladiators."[3] Rather, the attorney could act, as one commentator wrote, "as both an offensive 'sword' and a defensive 'shield' for the defendant."[4]

Doctrinal Evolution

But, as is often the case in constitutional criminal procedure, the Counsel Clause's history is much more complicated. Indeed, the right to counsel touches some of the worst moments in the history of the United States' criminal justice system and some of the best moments in our Constitution's constant evolution. As originally enacted, the Sixth Amendment right to counsel was intended to allow anyone who wished to hire an attorney to do so. The clause simply ensured that the government could not deny a criminal defendant this opportunity, as had traditionally occurred in Britain. Moreover, the clause was not considered to have any quality control mechanism. It was, essentially, a caveat emptor guarantee: the criminal defendant who wanted to retain counsel and could afford to do so was saddled with the consequences of that representation.

Beginning in the early twentieth century and stretching through *Padilla* and its progeny, the Supreme Court began to make the right to counsel more vibrant. This profound evolution that created today's right to counsel started in the throes of the Jim Crow South when a group of young black men were convicted of raping two white women. The Scottsboro Boys, as these defendants came to be known, had been appointed every member of the local bar. None of these attorneys proved particularly dedicated to their assignment. One of the attorneys—whose usual job was to represent the local electricity company—reportedly said that his employer "had enough juice to burn all nine of the defendants."[5] Clearly this was not someone

---

3. United States v. Cronic, 466 U.S. 648, 657 (1984); Powell v. Alabama, 287 U.S. 45, 69 (1932).

4. James J. Tomkovicz, The Right to the Assistance of Counsel: A Reference Guide to the United States Constitution 49 (2002).

5. Edmund Wilson, *The Freight-Car Case* 38, 39 (New Republic Aug. 26, 1931).

invested in his client's well-being. On appeal, the Supreme Court concluded in *Powell v. Alabama* that the young men had been denied the "effective and substantial aid" that the Sixth Amendment requires.[6] Though focused on the Fourteenth Amendment's Due Process Clause instead of the Sixth Amendment's Counsel Clause, the Court explained that the trial attorneys had not evidenced the "consultation, thorough-going investigation, and preparation" necessary to provide "the aid of counsel in any real sense."[7] Instead, the Court implied, the attorneys had been little more than empty vessels standing alongside the defendants. Six years later, the Court built on *Powell* in *Johnson v. Zerbst* by acknowledging that most defendants simply lack the understanding of legal processes necessary to act as an actual adversary to the professional prosecutor wielding the power and authority of the state.[8]

Despite the Court's recognition that defendants are usually ill equipped to represent themselves, it did nothing to remedy this problem until 1963 when it issued *Gideon v. Wainwright*, the Court's best known right to counsel decision.[9] In *Gideon*, the Court took an enormous leap forward by holding that the right to counsel does more than provide defendants an opportunity to retain counsel; it actually requires appointment of counsel if a defendant cannot afford to pay for one.[10] Even then, though, the Court made no mention of a quality-control component to the Counsel Clause (later the Court added that appointed counsel is only available to defendants facing the possibility of imprisonment[11]). That would not come until 1970 when the Court included an unassuming footnote in *McMann v. Richardson* explaining "that the right to counsel is the right to effective assistance of counsel."[12] That footnote has come to define modern right to counsel jurisprudence. Today, the Sixth Amendment is indisputably understood to ensure, first, that criminal defendants are provided an opportunity to hire an attorney or have one appointed, and second, no matter how the attorney–client relationship develops, the

---

6. 287 U.S. 45, 49, 53 (1932).
7. *Id.*
8. Johnson v. Zerbst, 304 U.S. 458, 462–63 & n.10 (1938).
9. 372 U.S. 355 (1963).
10. *Id.* at 344.
11. Argersinger v. Hamlin, 407 U.S. 25, 37–38 (1972).
12. 397 U.S. 759, 771 n.14 (1970).

attorney is required to use a minimum level of competency as the defendant's advocate.

Identifying the appropriate measure of constitutional competency took some time and resulted in a hodgepodge of judicial tests, but eventually the Supreme Court clarified things in *Strickland v. Washington*.[13] There the Court announced the two-part test that continues to govern whether an attorney provided the effective assistance that the Sixth Amendment requires:

> First, the defendant must show that counsel's performance was deficient. This requires showing that counsel made errors so serious that counsel was not functioning as the "counsel" guaranteed the defendant by the Sixth Amendment. Second, the defendant must show that the deficient performance prejudiced the defense. This requires showing that counsel's errors were so serious as to deprive the defendant of a fair trial, a trial whose result is reliable. Unless a defendant makes both showings, it cannot be said that the conviction or death sentence resulted from a breakdown in the adversary process that renders the result unreliable.[14]

To gauge deficient performance—the *Strickland* test's first prong—courts must ask "whether counsel's assistance was reasonable considering all the circumstances."[15] For guidance as to what constitutes reasonable performance in a given situation, courts consult "[p]revailing norms of practice" articulated in treatises, attorney training materials, and academic publications, among other sources.[16] Measuring prejudice—*Strickland*'s second prong—meanwhile requires that the defendant "show that there is a reasonable probability that, but for counsel's unprofessional errors, the result of the proceeding would have been different."[17]

Whether it makes sense for a convicted individual to pursue an ineffective assistance of counsel claim requires a delicate calculus. On the one

---

13. 466 U.S. 668 (1984).
14. *Id.* at 687.
15. *Id.* at 688.
16. *Id.* at 688–89.
17. *Id.* at 694.

hand, it carries the significant potential benefits of vacating a conviction. On the other hand, vacating a conviction means that the criminal process can begin anew. If so inclined, a prosecutor can reinitiate a criminal case. Any favorable plea that the defendant may have obtained the first time around may be off the table the second time around. Complicating this analysis a bit more, it is entirely possible that a prosecutor will not exercise her prerogative to refile a criminal case. Perhaps prosecutorial priorities have shifted, evidence may have been lost, or witnesses become unavailable. All of these would make reprosecuting a case more difficult.

Importantly, neither the Supreme Court nor any lower court has ever attempted to identify best practices for criminal defense attorneys. The robust body of caselaw that has developed around the effective assistance of counsel requirement, including the cases discussed below, identifies the least amount of legal competency required by the Constitution. Attorneys, of course, can and should aspire for much more.

Right to Counsel and Immigration Consequences before *Padilla*

All the while that the right to counsel was evolving, courts almost universally concluded that it had little if anything to say about potential immigration consequences that a defendant might face upon conviction. In case after case, state and federal courts concluded that immigration consequences were "collateral" to a criminal prosecution, and the Sixth Amendment right to counsel only concerns itself with "direct" consequences of conviction.[18] In practice, this meant that defense attorneys were required to provide effective representation when it came to questions of guilt or the sentence that might be meted out by a sentencing judge at the conclusion of a criminal proceeding. But because immigration judges sitting wholly outside the state or federal criminal court systems hand down immigration consequences, the right to counsel simply did not apply.

The direct/collateral consequence distinction led to problems that were as predictable as they were serious. Time after time, migrants entered guilty

---

18. *See, e.g.*, Broomes v. Ashcroft, 358 F.3d 1251, 1257 (10th Cir. 2004), *abrogated by* Padilla v. Kentucky, 559 U.S. 356 (2010); State v. Rojas-Martinez, 125 P.3d 930, 935 (Utah 2005), *abrogated by* Padilla, 559 U.S. 356.

or nolo contendere pleas without a clue that they would later face removal. Amadeo Santelises, for example, received no advice about immigration consequences.[19] The defense attorney for Sabino Del Rosario considered the possibility that Del Rosario would be deported but did not bother to research the issue thoroughly.[20] José Padilla, the petitioner in *Padilla v. Kentucky*, presents a more glaring picture: he asked about the possibility of removal, his attorney incorrectly told him he had nothing to worry about, and the Kentucky courts concluded that he was without recourse.[21] With knowledge of the immigration consequences facing them, these and many others would have undoubtedly pursued a different path—perhaps aimed for a different plea that avoids removal or, as a last ditch effort, gone to trial.

Recognizing that removal from the United States is an enormous consequence and that a criminal defense attorney's guidance may be the best opportunity a migrant has to avoid removal, some courts took a more humanitarian approach to the right to counsel. A number of courts distinguished between instances in which a defense attorney kept silent about potential immigration consequences and those in which the attorney affirmatively misadvised a client. Silence, those courts insisted, did not violate the Sixth Amendment, but affirmative misrepresentations were objectively unreasonable, thereby violating *Strickland*'s first prong.[22]

Two state courts presciently took a more expansive view of the right to counsel. In 1987, the Colorado Supreme Court held that the Sixth Amendment right to counsel applies to immigration consequences of conviction.[23] Coming only three years after *Strickland*, the Colorado court announced a uniform standard by which to measure the competency of

19. United States v. Santelises, 509 F.2d 703, 704 (2nd Cir. 1975), *abrogated by Padilla*, 559 U.S. 356.

20. United States v. Del Rosario, 902 F.2d 55, 57 (D.C. Cir. 1990), *abrogated by Padilla*, 559 U.S. 356.

21. Commonwealth v. Padilla, 253 S.W.3d 482, 485 (Ky. 2008), *overruled by Padilla*, 559 U.S. 356.

22. *See, e.g.*, United States v. Kwan, 407 F.3d 1005, 1015 (9th Cir. 2005), *abrogated by Padilla*, 559 U.S. 356; United States v. Cuoto, 311 F.3d 179, 188 (2nd Cir. 2002), *abrogated by Padilla*, 559 U.S. 356; State v. Rojas-Martinez, 125 P.3d 930, 935 (Utah 2005), *abrogated by Padilla*, 559 U.S. 356; Matter of Resendiz, 19 P.3d 1171, 1177 (Cal. 2001), *abrogated by Padilla*, 559 U.S. 356.

23. People v. Pozo, 746 P.2d 523 (Colo. 1987) (en banc).

a criminal defense attorney's advice. A reasonably competent attorney, the Court explained in *People v. Pozo*, would investigate any area of law if "the body of law was relevant to the circumstances of the client and the matters for which the attorney was retained."[24] This duty, the court added, derives from the "fundamental principle that attorneys must inform themselves of material legal principles that may significantly impact the particular circumstances of their clients."[25] Immigration law is no exception. To determine whether immigration law consequences are relevant to a particular client, the court held that there must be "sufficient information to form a reasonable belief that the client was in fact an alien."[26] If that threshold requirement is met, then Colorado defense attorneys were constitutionally obligated to advise about immigration law consequences of conviction.

Seventeen years later the New Mexico Supreme Court took a similar approach. In *State v. Paredez*, the court not only held that affirmative misadvice was objectively unreasonable but also "h[e]ld that an attorney's non-advice to an alien defendant on the immigration consequences of a guilty plea would also be deficient performance."[27] Anything less, the court implied, would deny the reality that most defendants cannot navigate the complexity of immigration law consequences alone.[28] Like the Colorado Supreme Court in *Pozo*, the *Paredez* court obligated defense attorneys "to determine the immigration status of their clients."[29] If this inquiry leads to the conclusion that the client is not a United States citizen, the defense attorney must advise the client about immigration consequences of conviction.[30] Going beyond the Colorado court's opinion, the New Mexico court also addressed *Strickland*'s prejudice prong. A migrant claiming she was denied her Sixth Amendment right to effective assistance of counsel on the basis of no advice or faulty advice about immigration consequences, the court held, "must show 'he would not have

---

24. *Id.* at 527.
25. *Id.* at 529.
26. *Id.*
27. 101 P.3d 799, 804–06 (N.M. 2004).
28. *See id.* at 805.
29. *Id.*
30. *Id.*

entered into the plea agreement if he had been given constitutionally adequate advice about the effect that his guilty plea would have on his immigration status.'"[31] Though in some instances, the court acknowledged, a defendant may choose removal over prison time, in other instances the opposite may be true.[32]

Padilla v. Kentucky

Out of this history arose *Padilla v. Kentucky*.[33] In that decision, the Supreme Court for the first time recognized that the Sixth Amendment right to counsel does apply to the advice that a criminal defense attorney provides a client who is not a United States citizen. To do this, it began by first reviewing key changes in the relationship between immigration law and criminal law that occurred since roughly 1990. Congress, the Court recounted, has vastly expanded the number and types of crimes that can result in removal, stripped state and federal judges of a longstanding power to preclude removal on the basis of a particular conviction, and limited the ability of immigration judges to exercise discretion to waive removal.[34] Combined, these changes have made immigration law so deeply intertwined with criminal law "that, as a matter of federal law, deportation is an integral part—indeed, sometimes the most important part—of the penalty that may be imposed on noncitizen defendants who plead guilty to specified crimes."[35] For this reason, the Court added, "we find it 'most difficult' to divorce the penalty from the conviction in the deportation context."[36] Without explicitly saying so, the Court essentially acknowledged crimmigration law's development and significant impact on legal proceedings, the work of criminal and immigration attorneys, and, of course, migrants.

Recognition of this new reality led the Court to reject the direct/collateral consequence distinction that so many lower courts had relied upon to conclude that the right to counsel was inapplicable to the

---

31. *Id.* (quoting Gonzalez v. State, 83 P.3d 921, 925 (Or. Ct. App. 2004)).
32. *See* State v. Paredez, 101 P.3d 799, 806 (N.M. 2004).
33. 559 U.S. 356 (2010).
34. Padilla v. Kentucky, 559 U.S. 356, 360–64 (2010).
35. *Id.* at 364.
36. *Id.* at 366.

immigration consequences of conviction. Instead of using the direct/ collateral distinction to artificially segregate criminal law and immigration law for purposes of the advice required by the Sixth Amendment's right to counsel, the Court instead grounded itself in a realistic appreciation of the law that applies to migrants who find themselves in criminal proceedings. Removal has become "intimately related to the criminal process" such that, for many migrants, the Court noted, "recent changes in our immigration law have made removal nearly an automatic result for a broad class of noncitizen offenders."[37] As a result, it concluded that "[t]he collateral versus direct distinction is thus ill suited to evaluating a *Strickland* claim concerning the specific risk of deportation. *Strickland* applies to Padilla's claim."[38]

Announcing that the right to counsel has something to say about immigration consequences of conviction would have been monumental in-and-of-itself. The Court could have stopped there and let lower courts experiment with various standards by which to measure whether an attorney met the constitutional requirement. That is exactly what the Court did between *McMann*, the case in which the Court dropped a footnote stating that "that the right to counsel is the right to effective assistance of counsel,"[39] and *Strickland*. The lower courts had been busy developing and applying various tests to measure constitutional effectiveness until the Court became involved in 1984 in the *Strickland* decision.

The *Padilla* Court, however, skipped the experimentation stage and instead announced a two-part test that gauges whether a criminal defense attorney provided the advice about immigration consequences of conviction that the right to effective assistance of counsel requires. Sometimes, the Court explained, "the terms of the relevant immigration statute are succinct, clear, and explicit in defining the removal consequence."[40] In Padilla's situation, for example, the immigration consequences of his plea "could easily be determined from reading the removal statute": his removal under INA § 237(a)(2)(B)(i), the controlled substance offense provision, was "presumptively mandatory."[41] Other times, however, the "consequences

---

37. *Id.* at 365–66.
38. *Id.* at 366.
39. McMann v. Richardson, 397 U.S. 759, 771 n.14 (1970).
40. *Padilla*, 559 U.S. at 368.
41. *Id.* at 369.

of a particular plea are unclear or uncertain."[42] Accordingly, "when the
deportation consequence is truly clear . . . the duty to give correct advice
is equally clear," but "[w]hen the law is not succinct and straightforward
. . . a criminal defense attorney need do no more than advise a noncitizen
client that pending criminal charges may carry a risk of adverse immigration consequences."[43] Under no circumstance is silence an option.[44] Nor is
it enough to keep from affirmatively misleading a defendant.[45] "[T]here is
no relevant difference between an act of commission and an act of omis-
sion in this context," the Court noted, so a criminal defense attorney must
speak up about immigration consequences of conviction and make sure
that whatever she says accurately reflects the state of immigration law.[46]
Though not part of the *Padilla* decision's holding, the two-part framework that the Court announced has become a central component of lower
courts' application of the Sixth Amendment right to effective assistance of
counsel, as the following section illustrates.

What Advice Is Required Under *Padilla*?

As an interpretation of the Sixth Amendment right to effective assistance
of counsel, *Padilla* sets a floor and not a ceiling. That is, it marks the
least amount of assistance that criminal defense attorneys can provide
and still comply with the Constitution. It does not identify anything near
best practices so it should not be read as a decision that sets out a model
of representation.

Though it interprets the constitutionally permissible floor for criminal defense representation only, it is nonetheless helpful to know where
the bottom is. As is so often true of Supreme Court decisions, Justice
Stephens' majority opinion in *Padilla* provides broad guidance but leaves
many questions unanswered. It is up to the lower courts to fill in those
gaps. In the years since *Padilla* was issued, the state and federal courts
have done just that in case after case in which a convicted migrant attempts to avoid adverse immigration consequences by challenging the

---

42. *Id.*
43. *Id.*
44. *Id.* at 370.
45. *Id.*
46. *Id.* (internal quotations omitted).

constitutional validity of the underlying conviction. Naturally, this has created substantial variation from jurisdiction to jurisdiction. In some instances, there is even disagreement for a time within a single state as legal issues take their time moving up the appellate process.

Despite that variation, some trends have emerged that attorneys and courts can use to determine what is constitutionally required representation. On its face, *Padilla*'s two-tiered test appears rather straightforward. When a client will clearly face presumptively mandatory removal upon conviction, her criminal defense attorney must advise her as such. But when it is not clear what will happen once the defendant enters immigration court, the attorney is constitutionally obligated to do no more than flag removal as a possibility. How are attorneys—and the courts that review claims of ineffective assistance of counsel—to know whether removal is clearly going to result or whether there is a question mark lingering over a criminal defense client's immigration future? The *Padilla* Court did not explicitly address this so some disagreement remains, but its analysis provides a wealth of guidance.

As a threshold matter, the Court's opinion suggests that a criminal defense attorney must determine her client's citizenship status—a United States citizen after all is immune from immigration law problems. The majority opinion grounds its holding in a concern for "a class of clients least able to represent themselves."[47] The complexities of criminal law's intersection with immigration law are beyond the reach of most migrants facing criminal charges, the Court suggested. There is no reason to think that the Court took a different view of citizenship. Whether or not a person is a United States citizen is a legal determination that requires investigating a subfield of law that is complicated and convoluted. As a result, it is not at all unusual for individuals, because of no fault of their own, not to know that they are not United States citizens or even that they are United States citizens despite having believed that they are not. Luis Fernando Juárez, for example, was certain that he was not a United States citizen. He knew he had been born in México and come to the United States as a six-year old with his mother who appears to have lacked authorization to be in the United States at that time. Years later Juárez was

---

47. *Id.* at 371.

convicted of drug possession and deported. He returned without authorization and eventually pleaded guilty to lying about being a United States citizen on a firearms purchase application and illegal reentry.[48] Juárez, these events suggest, had no doubt that he was not a United States citizen. Except that apparently he might have been. A statute repealed six years before he pleaded guilty to lying about his citizenship status and illegal reentry might have conferred citizenship status upon him the moment his mother naturalized, the result of a particularly messy area of citizenship law called "derivative citizenship."[49] At the very least, the Fifth Circuit concluded, Juárez's criminal defense attorney had a duty to explore the possibility that Juárez might be immune from conviction because he was a United States citizen. The fact that the attorney had "never heard of derivative citizenship" did not release him from his "duty to independently research the law and investigate the facts surrounding Juarez's case."[50] The attorney's failure to do so rendered his performance constitutionally defective and prejudicial, satisfying *Strickland*'s two prongs.

Similarly, the concurring opinion that Justice Alito wrote, and which Chief Justice Roberts joined, also suggests that criminal defense attorneys must delve into their client's citizenship status. According to Justice Alito, a *Padilla* duty arises "[w]hen a criminal defense attorney is aware that a client is an alien."[51] Justice Alito does not explain whose duty it is to bring this awareness to the attorney, but the Court has consistently placed legal determinations into the hands of attorneys, not clients, so it is difficult to see why citizenship would be any different. Similarly, the American Bar Association's Criminal Justice Standards—a common measure of what is expected of the reasonably competent attorney for ineffective assistance purposes—requires that when it comes to the consequences of a conviction "defense counsel should be active, rather than passive, taking the initiative . . . rather than waiting for questions from the defendant."[52]

48. *See* United States v. Juarez, 672 F.3d 381, 384–85 (5th Cir. 2012).
49. *Id.* at 386 n.2.
50. *Id.* at 387.
51. Padilla v. Kentucky, 559 U.S. 356, 387 (2010) (Alito, J., concurring).
52. AM. BAR ASSOC., ABA STANDARDS FOR CRIMINAL JUSTICE § 14-3.2(f) cmt. (1999).

Requiring attorneys to determine a client's citizenship status is consistent with the two most relevant lower court decisions that the Supreme Court did not abrogate: Colorado's *People v. Pozo* and New Mexico's *State v. Paredez*. Both courts recognized that citizenship status is a threshold issue for providing effective assistance when it comes to immigration consequences of conviction. The Colorado Supreme Court held that defense attorneys must investigate immigration consequences of a conviction when they have "sufficient information to form a reasonable belief that the client was in fact an alien."[53] The Kansas Supreme Court adopted a similar position in 2002 when it held that a criminal defense attorney has a "duty to investigate [a client's] immigration status" if she "knew or should have known that [the client] was an alien."[54] New Mexico's Supreme Court took an even stronger position on the defense attorney's obligation to learn the defendant's immigration status: "We hold that criminal defense attorneys are obligated to determine the immigration status of their clients. If a client is a noncitizen, the attorney must advise that client of the specific immigration consequences of pleading guilty, including whether deportation would be virtually certain."[55] Despite the variation among these opinions, it is clear that in some situations these state courts—two of which the *Padilla* Court cited approvingly—have expected a defense attorney to investigate a client's immigration status for many years.

This context clarifies that a criminal defense attorney who assumes that a client is a United States citizen or simply fails to ask questions that would lead a reasonable attorney to conclude that a client might not be a United States citizen provides constitutionally deficient representation. "[C]ounsel has a duty to make reasonable investigations or to make a reasonable decision that makes particular investigations unnecessary," the *Strickland* Court announced.[56] In a similar vein, the ABA's Model Rules

---

53. People v. Pozo, 746 P.2d 523, 529 (Colo. 1987).

54. State v. Muriithi, 46 P.3d 1145, 1151 (Kan. 2002), *abrogated in part by* Padilla v. Kentucky, 559 U.S. 356 (2010).

55. State v. Paredez, 101 P.3d 799, 805 (N.M. 2004); *see* State v. Favela, 343 P.3d 178, 184 (N.M. 2015).

56. Strickland v. Washington, 466 U.S. 668, 691 (1984).

of Professional Conduct explain that "[p]erhaps the most fundamental legal skill" indicative of competent representation "consists of determining what kind of legal problems a situation may involve."[57] Keeping silent about citizenship questions that might raise further immigration law questions will not do.

Once immigration law is identified as a relevant concern for a defendant due to not being a United States citizen, a criminal defense attorney must then analyze immigration law to determine whether the INA clearly calls for presumptively mandatory removal if convicted. Ignoring possible immigration consequences entirely is unquestionably deficient performance.[58] Often, however, courts reviewing claims of ineffective assistance of counsel are not faced with a defense attorney who did nothing. They are instead faced with a defense attorney who provided some advice about immigration consequences and the court must determine whether that comported with *Padilla's* broadly worded obligations. Gauging what advice is required in the first place is no simple feat for attorneys. As Justice Alito pointed out in his concurring opinion in *Padilla*, "providing advice on whether a conviction for a particular offense will make an alien removable is often quite complex."[59] It is, however, entirely manageable. Just as immigration attorneys have long engaged the intricacies of criminal law and procedure, criminal defense attorneys must now engage with immigration law.

The first order of business is to determine whether the INA is "truly clear" that "presumptively mandatory" removal will result. Despite the *Padilla* Court's failure to explain what "truly clear" means, the Court did provide one example: the controlled substance offense provision that it repeatedly noted would lead to immigration law troubles for Padilla himself. "Padilla's crime," the Court explained, "like virtually every drug offense except for only the most insignificant marijuana offenses, is a deportable offense under 8 U.S.C. § 1227(a)(2)(B)(i)," the statutory provision in which the controlled substance offense is codified.[60] In a different passage, the Court explained that the INA succinctly, clearly,

57. AM. BAR ASSOC., MODEL RULES OF PROF'L CONDUCT R. 1.1 cmt (2007).
58. Zemene v. Clarke. 768 S.E.2d 684, 690 (Va. 2015)
59. *Padilla*, 559 U.S. at 377 (2010) (Alito, J., concurring).
60. *Id.* at 359 n.1.

and explicitly requires Padilla's removal, then, for support, immediately cites the controlled substance offense provision and quotes it almost in its entirety.[61] This discussion strongly suggests that the Court thinks of the controlled substance offense provision as an example of the INA clearly calling for presumptively mandatory removal. Accordingly, a criminal defense attorney must determine whether a client is facing a charge that will constitute a controlled substance offense and, if so, advise that conviction will result in presumptively mandatory removal. The Court's discussion of the controlled substance offense provision means lower courts must also adopt this view, and indeed some have had occasion to do so.[62]

In a separate, single-sentence passage, the Court referenced the illicit trafficking in a controlled substance subsection of the aggravated felony definition. "Subject to limited exceptions," the Court wrote, "this discretionary relief is not available for an offense related to trafficking in a controlled substance. See § 1101(a)(43)(B); § 1228."[63] Some courts have read this sentence to be the Court's assessment that Padilla was convicted of an aggravated felony.[64] To do so is to decontextualize this sentence in two ways: one literary and the other doctrinal. First, this sentence does not refer to Padilla's particular plight. Instead, it appears within an eight-paragraph section spanning four of the majority opinion's 19 pages that chronicles almost a century's worth of immigration law history.[65] This section's purpose, as the Court states in its opening line, is to chart how "[t]he landscape of federal immigration law has changed dramatically over the last 90 years."[66] It is by its nature a generalized overview of the shifting legal sands that have produced crimmigration law and that justified the Court's landmark holding. One of those changes has been Congress's decision to prohibit immigration judges from exercising

---

61. *Id.* at. 368.
62. *See, e.g.*, Comm. v. Clarke, 949 N.E.2d 892, 905 (Mass. 2011), *abrogated on other grounds by* Chaidez v. United States, 133 S. Ct. 1103 (2013); United States v. Hubenig, 2010 WL 2650625, at *8-*9 (E.D. Cal. July 1, 2010) (unpublished); People v. Picca, 947 N.Y.S.2d 120, 125 (N.Y. App. Div. 2012); State v. Martinez, 253 P.3d 445, 447 (Wash. Ct. App. 2011).
63. *Padilla*, 559 U.S. at 364.
64. *See* Ex Parte Isabel Rodriguez, 378 S.W.3d 486, 489 (Tex. Ct. App. 2012).
65. *Padilla*, 559 U.S. at 360–64.
66. *Id.* at 360.

the discretion to waive removal for someone convicted of an aggravated felony, including illicit trafficking offenses, in all but a limited number of exceptions, as the Court correctly notes. This, though, is only one of several entanglements of criminal law and immigration law that have raised the stakes of criminal proceedings for migrants, many of which the Court discusses in this section. To read this sentence as a statement of Padilla's specific situation, therefore, is to read it out of its decisional context.

Second, the Court's understanding of the illicit trafficking type of aggravated felony belies any claim that this sentence can be read as the Court's implicit claim that it thinks Padilla was convicted of an illicit trafficking offense. In the four terms leading to and including the term in which it issued *Padilla*, the Court directly grappled with the illicit trafficking provision three times, including one decision issued roughly ten weeks later.[67] Only one of the Court's justices changed during this period: Justice Souter retired and Justice Sotomayor took the bench. The justices who took part in the *Padilla* decision, therefore, knew quite well that "trafficking" is a term with an intricate meaning not to be used lightly. Because of their keen familiarity with the term's meaning and the significance of an aggravated felony conviction, they surely knew that both of those other two illicit trafficking decisions, *Lopez v. Gonzales*[68] and *Carachuri-Rosendo v. Holder*,[69] bore down on Padilla's convictions: two drug possession offenses and one marijuana trafficking crime.[70] Combined, those two decisions almost certainly foreclose the possibility that Padilla's possession convictions could be considered illicit trafficking. Illicit trafficking, the Court held in *Lopez*, ordinarily involves commercial dealing and possession does not.[71] If an exception is to be made for multiple possession convictions, the Court added in *Carachuri-Rosendo*, it can come only by way of a criminal prosecution under the state's recidivist

---

67. *See* Carachuri-Rosendo v. Holder, 560 U.S. 563 (2010); Lopez v. Gonzales, 549 U.S. 47 (2006).
68. 549 U.S. 47 (2006).
69. 560 U.S. 563 (2010).
70. Petition for Writ of Certiorari at 3, Padilla v. Kentucky, 559 U.S. 356 (2010) (No. 08-651).
71. 549 U.S. at 53–54.

offender process, something that does not appear to have happened in Padilla's situation.[72]

The only possibility that remains, then, is that Padilla's marijuana trafficking conviction constitutes illicit trafficking. Here the Court's extensive categorical approach jurisprudence governs (see chapter 2). Padilla was convicted of "possessing with intent to sell or transfer" marijuana.[73] Kentucky statutorily defines "sell" to include commercial activity but explicitly defines "transfer" as "without consideration and not in furtherance of commercial distribution."[74] Under the categorical or modified categorical approach, it is anything but clear that Padilla was convicted of "illicit trafficking" for immigration law purposes. To conclude that the Court's singular reference to illicit trafficking means that it concluded that Padilla was convicted of illicit trafficking despite its familiarity with the complicated definition of illicit trafficking and the narrow reach of the categorical analysis would be to read this sentence out of its doctrinal context. The Court is not prone to such facile assumptions.

Though the Court's analysis does not cast Padilla's convictions as aggravated felonies, it does do more than simply speak about the controlled substance offense provision. Indeed, its analysis provides concrete guidance about how to interpret other crime-based grounds of removal. The controlled substance offense, as the *Padilla* Court put it, "commands removal for all controlled substances convictions except for the most trivial of marijuana possession offenses."[75] Of course, not all drugs are "controlled substances" as defined by federal law (see chapter 2). That important nuance aside, the controlled substance offense provision undeniably sweeps quite broadly across the range of state and federal drug crimes: most but not all are included. A defense attorney representing a client in immigration proceedings needs to delve deeply into the applicable state and federal statutes to determine whether a client's conviction is one that

72. 560 U.S. at 582.
73. Commonwealth of Kentucky v. Padilla, Indictment No. 01-CR-00517 count 3 (Ky. Hardin Circuit Ct. Oct. 31, 2001); Commonwealth of Kentucky v. Padilla, Order, No. 01-CR-00517 (Ky. Hardin Circuit Ct. Sept. 6, 2002).
74. KY. REV. STAT. ANN. §§ 218A.010(37), (43).
75. Padilla v. Kentucky, 559 U.S. 356, 368 (2010).

does not fall within the controlled substance offense provision's reach, but the *Padilla* Court's analysis indicates that a criminal defense attorney preparing to advise a client about the immigration law consequences of conviction does not have to do this.

This analysis carries important implications for criminal defense attorneys whose clients are facing charges that might fall into other crime-based grounds of removal. Attorneys, the Court's analytical approach suggests, should look to the core of the offenses captured by a particular crime-based ground. Just as the controlled substance offense provision includes most but not all drug crimes, criminal defense attorneys should advise that presumptively mandatory removal will result from conviction for crimes that fall within the center of offenses that a particular removal provision targets even if it might fall off the periphery under the microscopic scrutiny required of immigration attorneys. One court, for example, concluded that a criminal defense attorney should have advised that aggravated sexual assault is clearly rape or sexual abuse of a child, a type of aggravated felony, without engaging in any analysis of how rape or sexual abuse of a child are defined for immigration law purposes.[76] Another, in contrast, held that an attorney could satisfy the right to counsel obligation by providing general advice to a client facing conviction for a crime that might constitute a crime involving moral turpitude. Because it is notoriously difficult to pin down what constitutes a crime involving moral turpitude, determining whether conviction would result in removal under this provision "is not as simple as reading the text of the INA," the court explained.[77]

The *Padilla* Court's discussion is also helpful to our understanding of the relevance of relief from removal to a criminal defense attorney's Sixth Amendment obligation. Migrants convicted of controlled substances offenses remain eligible for cancellation of removal and other forms of relief. That the Supreme Court takes the position that Padilla, having been convicted of what the Court characterized as a controlled substance offense, should have been told that a conviction would render his removal virtually

76. Ex Parte Romero, 351 S.W.3d 127, 130 (Tex. App. 2011), *vacated on other grounds by* 393 S.W.3d 788 (Tex. Crim. App. 2013); *see also* State v. Sandoval, 249 P.3d 1015, 1019–20 (Wash. 2011) (en banc).

77. Lopez-Penaloza v. State, 804 N.W.2d 537, 545–46 (Iowa Ct. App. 2011).

automatic suggests that the mere possibility that relief will be available in immigration proceedings does not free the attorney from providing the higher level of advice *Padilla* contemplates: removal will be presumptively mandatory if convicted.

As it is, because *Padilla* addresses only the least effective representation that is constitutionally permissible, it would be misguided to think of it as a standard-bearer. This discussion should not be interpreted as such either. Attorneys should aspire to provide much more zealous representation than *Padilla* requires. This is important because relief from removal is almost always available in theory. Even migrants convicted of aggravated felonies can seek certain types of relief. Had the Court concluded that the possibility of relief means that a criminal defense attorney need only advise that "pending criminal charges may carry a risk of adverse immigration consequences,"[78] criminal defense attorneys would almost never be held to the higher duty of providing specific advice about immigration consequences.

Padilla *Prejudice*

Even if a criminal defense attorney provided constitutionally deficient advice, the ineffective assistance analysis is not over. *Strickland*'s second prong requires that the migrant show that her criminal defense attorney's unreasonable advice prejudiced her. To do this, the *Strickland* Court explained that "[t]he defendant must show that there is a reasonable probability that, but for counsel's unprofessional errors, the result of the proceeding would have been different. A reasonable probability is a probability sufficient to undermine confidence in the outcome."[79] (The "reasonable probability" standard is thought to be "somewhat lower" than the preponderance of the evidence standard that arises in many civil contexts.[80]) In a later case, *Hill v. Lockhart*, the Court explained that the prejudice prong

focuses on whether counsel's constitutionally ineffective performance affected the outcome of the plea process. In other words,

---

78. Padilla v. Kentucky, 559 U.S. 356, 369 (2010).
79. Strickland v. Washington, 466 U.S. 668, 694 (1984).
80. *See id.*

in order to satisfy the 'prejudice' requirement, the defendant must show that there is a reasonable probability that, but for counsel's errors, he would not have pleaded guilty and would have insisted on going to trial.[81]

Like the deficient performance prong, the prejudice prong requires an objective analysis. To successfully argue prejudice, the *Padilla* Court explained, "a petitioner must convince the court that a decision to reject the plea bargain would have been rational under the circumstances."[82] In some instances, the Court noted, a client may be more concerned about remaining in the United States than avoiding imprisonment.[83] Counsel informed of a client's goals and armed with knowledge of the immigration consequences of conviction "may be able to plea bargain creatively with the prosecutor in order to craft a conviction and sentence that reduce the likelihood of deportation."[84] Because the Kentucky Supreme Court did not decide whether Padilla was prejudiced by his defense attorney's advice, the Supreme Court did not clearly explain how the prejudice prong applies in Padilla's situation. It has yet to take this up in a subsequent case, thus there remains some doubt about what these strands of explanatory dicta mean.

In the absence of clear direction from the Supreme Court, lower federal and state courts have begun filling the prejudice prong vacuum in *Padilla* claims. True to their nature, the lower courts have adopted a variety of approaches that are sometimes at odds with each other. Though this complicates attorneys' obligations, it also presents an opportunity for creative, skillful representation. Some courts have held that no rational defendant would have turned down a plea offer when the evidence of guilt was quite strong and conviction after trial would have potentially resulted in much more jail time than pleading.[85] As the Rhode Island Supreme Court

---

81. 474 U.S. 52, 59 (1985); *see* Premo v. Moore, 131 S. Ct. 733, 744 (2011).

82. *Padilla*, 559 U.S. at 372; *see* Commonwealth v. Marinho, 981 N.E.2d 648, 661 (Mass. 2013).

83. *See Padilla*, 559 U.S. at 367 (quoting INS v. St. Cyr, 533 U.S. 289, 323 (2001)).

84. *Padilla*, 559 U.S. at 373.

85. *See, e.g.*, Pilla v. United States, 668 F.3d 368, 373 (6th Cir. 2012); United States v. Shin, 891 F. Supp. 2d 849, 857–58 (N.D. Ohio 2012); Neufville v. State, 13 A.3d 607, 614 (R.I. 2011).

explained its position, "when counsel has secured a shorter sentence than what the defendant could have received had he gone to trial, the defendant has an almost insurmountable burden to establish prejudice."[86] Given that reduced sentences are a typical part of pleas, such reasoning poses enormous obstacles to migrants trying to bring *Padilla* claims. It also conflicts with the Supreme Court's recent encouragement of plea bargaining by presuming that what matters most to defendants is a shorter jail sentence. If the *Padilla* decision stands for anything, it is that deportation is at least as significant to many defendants as the possibility of imprisonment.

Recognizing the unique concerns presented by a choice between more jail time and the possibility of avoiding removal, however, other courts have taken a more nuanced approach to *Strickland*'s prejudice prong in the context of *Padilla* claims.[87] Building off the *Hill* Court's command that the proper focus of the prejudice inquiry is whether the defendant would have gone to trial, Maryland's highest court acknowledged "that many noncitizens might reasonably choose the possibility of avoiding deportation combined with the risk of a greater sentence over assured deportation combined with a lesser sentence."[88] In that vein, the Third Circuit explained that ten years in jail might pale in comparison to the "near-certainty of multiple decades of banishment from the United States" for a twenty-seven-year-old lawful permanent resident.[89] Likewise, the Washington Supreme Court, sitting en banc, held that a lawful permanent resident who had "made this country his home . . . would have been rational to take his chances at trial" even though he would have

---

86. *Neufville*, 13 A.3d at 614.

87. *See* United States v. Orocio, 645 F.3d 630, 645 (3d Cir. 2011), *abrogated on other grounds by* Chaidez v. United States, 133 S. Ct. 1103 (2013); Zemene v. Clarke, 2015 WL 798753 (Va. 2015); People v. Guzman-Ruiz, 6 N.E.3d 806, 811–12 (Ill. Ct. App. 2014); People v. Guzman, 2014 IL App (3d) 090464, ¶ 35 (Jan. 23, 2014) (unpublished); State v. Sandoval, 249 P.3d 1015, 1021–22 (Wash. 2011); Denisyuk v. State, 30 A.3d 914, 929–30 (Md. 2011), *abrogated on other grounds by* Chaidez, 133 S. Ct. 1103, *rev'd on other grounds by* Miller v. State, 77 A.3d 1030 (Md. 2013); State v. Yahya, 2011-Ohio-6090, 2011 WL 5868794, ¶ 22 (Ohio Ct. App. 2011); Campos v. State, 816 N.W.2d 480, 506–07 (Minn. 2012) (Page, J., dissenting); State v. Mendez, 847 N.W.2d 895, 899-900 (Wis. Ct. App. 2014).

88. Denisyuk, 30 A.3d at 929, *abrogated on other grounds by* Chaidez, 133 S. Ct. 1103, *rev'd on other grounds by* Miller v. State, 77 A.3d 1030.

89. *See* Orocio, 645 F.3d at 645, *abrogated on other grounds by* Chaidez, 133 S. Ct. 1103.

faced as much as life imprisonment instead of the six to twelve months he obtained by pleading.[90]

A pair of 2012 Supreme Court decisions complicates the prejudice analysis a bit more. In *Missouri v. Frye*, the Court considered a situation in which a defendant was offered two favorable plea deals, but his criminal defense attorney did not inform him of either.[91] The same day, the Court issued its opinion in *Lafler v. Cooper* in which it considered an ineffective assistance claim brought by a defendant who rejected a plea offer after having been given blatantly incorrect advice (that the prosecution would not be able to prove intent to murder because the victim had been shot below the waist).[92] In both decisions, the Court held that the convicted individuals could raise ineffective assistance of counsel claims despite having been afforded a trial. Merely going to trial, in other words, doesn't cure all potential ineffective assistance.

Federal courts of appeals have been slow to address *Lafler* or *Frye*'s significance to *Padilla* claims. In *Kovacs v. United States*, the Eleventh Circuit became the first to do so when it considered an ineffective assistance claim where the deficient performance prong was not difficult—the petitioner's trial attorney repeatedly and incorrectly said, on the record, that conviction would not lead to removal.[93] Turning to *Strickland*'s prejudice prong, the court identified two routes through which Kovacs could succeed: by showing that there was a "reasonable probability" that he "could have negotiated a plea that did not impact immigration status or that he would have litigated an available defense" or by showing that he had a "viable and sufficiently promising" defense that he would have litigated at trial to avoid immigration consequences. Though it provides migrants convicted after receiving constitutionally unsound advice two avenues for moving forward with ineffective assistance claims, the Eleventh Circuit's formulation of the prejudice inquiry is potentially problematic because it seems to turn an objective inquiry into one that is subjective. That is, instead of

---

90. State v. Sandoval, 249 P.3d 1015, 1021–22 (Wash. 2011).
91. 132 S. Ct. 1399, 1404–05 (2012).
92. 132 S. Ct. 1376, 1383 (2012).
93. 744 F.3d 44, 50 (11th Cir. 2014).

asking whether a reasonable defendant who received accurate advice would have negotiated for an immigration-safe plea or litigated an available defense, the court places a great deal of emphasis on the fact that Kovacs himself actually did so.

For their part, state courts have considered a variety of factors as part of the prejudice analysis required after *Padilla*, *Lafler*, and *Frye*. The Massachusetts Supreme Judicial Court, for example, held that it is simply insufficient to claim ineffective assistance on the basis of a defense attorney's failure to engage in plea negotiations without offering evidence that, had negotiations occurred, a favorable plea deal acceptable to the prosecutor and judge would have resulted.[94] It also expressed skepticism that an unauthorized migrant could be prejudiced by his counsel's advice given that his removability arises from his unauthorized status not his conviction.[95] In contrast, a New York trial court held that unauthorized status is not controlling of prejudice since "[t]o establish that he was prejudiced . . . defendant need not demonstrate that he would have been certain to avoid the possibility of deportation had he rejected the plea and proceeded to trial. All that need be shown is that the choice to fight the case would have been a rational one."[96]

Judicial Admonishments

Courts routinely inform defendants that pleading guilty or nolo contendere will or may have severe consequences. Traditionally these admonishments have alerted the defendant that pleading requires waiving constitutionally protected rights or informed the defendant about the maximum sentence that the judge can issue. The goal of requiring a judge to run through these concerns with the defendant is to ensure that a defendant enters a plea knowingly, voluntarily, and intelligently, a fundamental component of the Due Process Clause.[97] As the Supreme Court explained in *Boykin v. Alabama*, for a plea "to be valid under the Due Process Clause, it must

---

94. Commonwealth v. Marinho, 981 N.E.2d 648, 661–62 (Mass. 2013).
95. *Id.* at 663.
96. People v. Burgos, 950 N.Y.S.2d 428, 447 (N.Y. Sup. Ct. 2012).
97. Brady v. United States, 397 U.S. 742, 748 (1970); *see* Fed. R. Crim. P. 11(b)(1), (2).

be 'an intentional relinquishment or abandonment of a known right or privilege.'"[98] A number of states have taken similar positions with regard to their own judicial admonishment provisions.[99]

In recent decades it has become standard practice in state courts across the country for judicial admonishments to include a few words about possible immigration consequences of conviction. The *Padilla* Court counted twenty-two states that impose this duty on judges either by statute or court rule: Alaska, California, Connecticut, Florida, Georgia, Hawaii, Iowa, Maryland, Massachusetts, Minnesota, Montana, New Mexico, New York, North Carolina, Ohio, Oregon, Rhode Island, Texas, Vermont, Washington, Washington, D.C., and Wisconsin.[100] This is not a comprehensive list since other states have amended their statutes or rules of criminal procedure after *Padilla* was decided—indeed, often in response to *Padilla*.[101] Though the exact wording varies, Rhode Island's statute is illustrative of the bare bones obligation such rules impose on judges. It requires: "Prior to accepting a plea of guilty or nolo contendere in the district or superior court, the court shall inform the defendant that if he or she is not a citizen of the United States, a plea of guilty or nolo contendere may have immigration consequences, including deportation, exclusion of admission to the United States, or denial of naturalization pursuant to the laws of the United States."[102] Though the Federal Rules of Criminal Procedure had long avoided imposing such a requirement on federal judges, that changed after *Padilla*. Rule 11(b)(1)(O) of the Federal Rules of Criminal Procedure was updated in 2013 to require federal judges to inform defendants prior to accepting a plea "that, if convicted, a defendant who is not a United States citizen may be removed from the United States, denied citizenship, and denied admission to the United States in the future."

98. 395 U.S. 238, 243 n.5 (1969) (citing Johnson v. Zerbst, 304 U.S. 458, 464 (1938)).

99. *See, e.g.*, Smith v. State, 857 S.W.2d 71, 73–74 (Tex. Ct. App. 1993) (regarding Tex. Code Crim. Proc. Ann. art. 26.13b (West 2011)); State v. Williams, 404 A.2d 814, 818 (R.I. 1979) (regarding Rule 11 of Rhode Island's Rules of Criminal Procedure).

100. Padilla v. Kentucky, 559 U.S. 356, 374 n.15 (2010).

101. *See, e.g.*, Me. R. Crim. P. § 11(h); Tenn. R. Crim. P. § 11(b)(1)(J).

102. R.I. Gen. L. Ann. § 12-12-22(b).

Without question, these are significant requirements. They represent a desire by legislatures and courts to flag for defendants the possibility of unforeseen effects of pleading guilty or nolo contendere. In this sense, judicial admonishments about the possibility of immigration consequences reflect the Due Process Clause's important goal of providing defendants with the information necessary to ensure that any plea they enter is knowing and voluntary. "[I]f a defendant's guilty plea is not equally voluntary and knowing," the Supreme Court noted, "it has been obtained in violation of due process and is therefore void."[103]

After *Padilla*, state and federal courts have been grappling with the effect that a judicial admonishment about potential immigration consequences has on an ineffective assistance of counsel claim's prejudice prong. How does the prejudice analysis change if the trial court judge presiding over the plea hearing informed the defendant that pleading guilty or nolo contendere might lead to immigration difficulties down the road? A handful of courts have concluded that a judicial admonishment can cure an attorney's prejudicial conduct.[104] Despite that, the dominant trend—including two federal circuits and three state supreme courts— has emerged concluding that a judicial admonishment that includes a statement about potential immigration consequences is alone insufficient to cure an attorney's deficient performance.[105]

The key lies in the different constitutional foundations of judicial admonishments versus the prejudice requirement. While judicial

---

103. Boykin v. Alabama, 395 U.S. 238, 243 n.5 (1969).

104. *See, e.g.*, Mendoza v. United States, 774 F. Supp. 2d 791, 799 (E.D. Va. 2011) (concluding that the "petitioner's sworn acknowledgement" that she understood the trial court's "explicit[] advis[al] in the course of the Rule 11 colloquy that her guilty plea would render her subject to deportation . . . is, by itself, dispositive of the prejudice analysis"); State v. Martinez, 729 S.E.2d 390, 392 (Ga. 2012) (holding that a trial court's admonishment "especially where, as here, the defendant affirmatively acknowledges his understanding that he is certain or almost certain to face deportation" can cure any prejudice caused by an attorney's deficient performance).

105. *See, e.g.*, United States v. Urias-Marrufo, 744 F.3d 361, 369 (5th Cir. 2014); Miranda v. State, 2013 WL 2295839, at *3 (Vt. Super. Ct. 2013); State v. Favela, 343 P.3d 178, 184 (N.M. 2015) (quoting State v. Favela, 311 P.3d 1213, 1221–22 (N.M. Ct. App. 2013); State v. Ortiz, 44 A.3d 425, 513–14 (N.H. 2012); Hernandez v. State, 124 So.3d 757, 759 (Fla. 2012); United States v. Akinsade, 686 F.3d 248, 253–54 (4th Cir. 2012); People v. Kazadi, 284 P.3d 70, 74 (Colo. Ct. App. 2011), *aff'd*, 291 P.3d 16 (Colo. 2012).

admonishments are intended to realize the Due Process Clause's concerns that the defendant entered a plea knowingly, voluntarily, and intelligently, the *Strickland* prejudice requirement is one part of the Sixth Amendment right to effective assistance of counsel.[106] These are distinct constitutional provisions that should fall or stand largely on their own.[107] The first obligation falls on courts; the second falls on defense attorneys. While defendants certainly benefit from having the court flag immigration issues as a concern, no one seriously advocates that judges should take the place of attorneys in strategically guiding defendants through the criminal process. Judges do not have the time to do this. Even if judicial resources were not limited, in an adversarial system of justice judges should not take the role of one party's advocate—effectively what it means to allow them to step in to correct a defendant's constitutionally deficient advice. Explaining this reasoning succinctly, the Fifth Circuit wrote,

> It is counsel's duty, not the court's, to warn of certain immigration consequences, and counsel's failure cannot be saved by a plea colloquy. Thus, it is irrelevant that the magistrate judge asked Urias whether she understood that there *might* be immigration consequences and that she and her attorney had discussed the *possible* adverse immigration consequences of pleading guilty.[108]

Not only are the judge's responsibilities distinct from those of the defense attorney, they are different in substance as well. The judge, as the Fifth Circuit pointed out, is not obligated to advise a defendant facing almost certain removal that removal will be presumptively mandatory upon conviction, as *Padilla* makes clear the Sixth Amendment requires of criminal defense attorneys. Instead, as the Florida Supreme Court noted in holding that a judicial admonishment cannot cure an attorney's prejudice, the

---

106. *See Ortiz*, 44 A.3d at 513–14.

107. *See* Soldal v. Cook County, 506 U.S. 56, 70 (1992) ("[W]e are not in the habit of identifying as a preliminary matter the claim's dominant character. Rather, we examine each constitutional provision in turn."); Lyons v. Pearce, 694 P.2d 969, 971 (Or. 1985) (separately analyzing "whether petitioner's guilty plea was knowing and voluntary, and whether petitioner was denied effective assistance of counsel").

108. United States v. Urias-Marrufo, 744 F.3d 361, 369 (5th Cir. 2014).

burden imposed on judges is lower than that imposed on criminal defense attorneys.[109] Simply raising the issue of potential immigration consequences is enough to meet the court's obligation that a plea is entered knowingly and voluntarily. This is a far cry from the zealous advocacy that the Sixth Amendment requires of criminal defense attorneys. Furthermore, the plea colloquy between a judge and defendant tends to be fairly pro forma. It is, as one commentator wrote, "largely ceremonial and takes place directly before the defendant enters her plea, after she has made that choice."[110] There is little real opportunity for actual decision-making after the plea colloquy. By constitutional design and courtroom practice, therefore, the discussion between judge and defendant is not intended to and does not substitute for the strategic counsel required of a defense attorney.

Retroactivity

Aside from the substantive merits of a potential *Padilla* claim, attorneys need to consider a host of procedural issues that regularly arise. None is more contentious than whether *Padilla*'s holding applies retroactively. It took barely a year after the Supreme Court announced its decision before federal circuit courts and state high courts began to issue decisions on retroactivity. A split among the lower courts developed almost as quickly.[111]

Less than three years after issuing *Padilla*, the Supreme Court largely settled the question in *Chaidez v. United States*: the landmark holding does not apply to convictions that had become final before March 31, 2010, the date *Padilla* was issued. Instead, it applies only to those cases that were pending or not yet initiated on or after March 31, 2010.[112] The Court came

---

109. *See* Hernandez v. State, 124 So.3d 757, 759 (Fla. 2012).
110. Danielle M. Lang, Note, Padilla v. Kentucky: *The Effect of Plea Colloquy Warnings on Defendants Ability to Bring Successful Padilla Claims*, 121 YALE L.J. 944, 985 (2012).
111. *Contrast* Commonwealth v. Clarke, 949 N.E.2d 892, 903 (Mass. 2011), *abrogated by* Chaidez v. United States, 133 S. Ct. 1103 (2013) (applying retroactively), *and* United States v. Orocio, 645 F.3d 630, 641 (3d Cir. 2011), *abrogated by Chaidez*, 133 S. Ct. 1103 (same), *with* Chaidez v. United States, 655 F.3d 684, 689 (7th Cir. 2011) (not retroactive), *and* United States v. Hong, 671 F.3d 1147, 1150 (10th Cir. 2011) (same).
112. Chaidez v. United States, 133 S. Ct. 1103, 1107 (2013).

to this conclusion because *Padilla*, the majority decided, announced a new constitutional rule of criminal procedure. Under the Court's existing retroactivity analysis framework, governed by *Teague v. Lane*, "a case announces a new rule if the result was not *dictated* by precedent existing at the time the defendant's conviction became final. And a holding is not so dictated . . . unless it would have been 'apparent to all reasonable jurists.'"[113] A case does not announce a new rule, however, when it merely applies an established principle to a new set of facts.[114] While a new rule applies only to cases that were not yet initiated or were on direct review on the date the new rule was announced, an old rule applies to all cases including those that have long been final.[115] Chaidez, whose conviction became final in 2004, could therefore only benefit from *Padilla* if the Court concluded that *Padilla* simply extended an existing principle (i.e., *Strickland*'s ineffective assistance of counsel analysis) to a new set of facts (i.e., immigration law consequences of conviction). Unfortunately for her, the Court decided that *Padilla* announced a new rule. Had the *Padilla* opinion done no more than recognize that the right to effective assistance of counsel requires advice about immigration consequences of conviction, Justice Elena Kagan's majority opinion in *Chaidez* implied, it might have stayed within *Strickland*'s well-worn confines. "But *Padilla* did something more," the Court explained.

> [P]rior to asking *how* the *Strickland* test applied ("Did this attorney act unreasonably?"), *Padilla* asked *whether* the *Strickland* test applied ("Should we even evaluate if this attorney acted unreasonably?"). And . . . that preliminary question about *Strickland*'s ambit came to the *Padilla* Court unsettled—so that the Court's answer ("Yes, *Strickland* governs here") required a new rule.[116]

Padilla is thus largely irrelevant to migrants convicted of federal crimes whose convictions became final prior to March 31, 2010. Because many states use the *Teague* retroactivity analysis used by the federal courts, the

---

113.   489 U.S. 288, 301 (1989) (quoting Lambrix v. Singletary, 520 U.S. 518, 527–28 (1997)).
114.   *See Teague*, 489 U.S. at 307.
115.   Griffith v. Kentucky, 479 U.S. 314, 328 (1987).
116.   *Chaidez*, 133 S. Ct. at 1108.

same is true for convictions in many state courts.[117] Other states have reached a similar conclusion for independent reasons.[118]

Problem 5.1

Yannick Yuma is a lawful permanent resident who pleaded no contest in a Nebraska state court to removable offenses on March 9, 2010, roughly three weeks before *Padilla* was announced. He was sentenced on April 7, 2010, one week after *Padilla* was announced. He claims that his attorney did not advise him about the immigration consequences of entering no contest pleas. Does *Padilla* even apply to Yuma's situation?

Yes. Because Padilla *applies only to those convictions that were not yet final on March 31, 2010, whether* Padilla *applies to Yuma's situation depends on state law. In Nebraska, where Yuma was convicted, "entry of judgment occurs with the imposition of a sentence. Thus, although Yuma's case was not pending on appeal when* Padilla *was decided, his convictions were not final at the time, and therefore, the new rule announced in* Padilla *applies to him."* State v. Yuma, *835 N.W.2d 679, 683-84 (Neb. 2013).*

Hope has not entirely been extinguished for migrants whose conviction became final prior to March 31, 2010. Following *Chaidez,* a circuit split has developed over whether *Padilla* applies retroactively to instances in which a defendant was provided incorrect advice about immigration consequences as opposed to no advice. The Second Circuit concluded that misadvice was objectively unreasonable well before 2010, thus ineffective assistance claims premised on allegations that a defense attorney provided incorrect advice about immigration consequences can move forward.[119] The Seventh Circuit, in contrast, held that the *Padilla* Court made no distinction between misadvice and no advice, thus the Supreme Court's holding does not apply retroactively to either type of deficient

---

117. *See, e.g.,* Thiersaint v. Comm'r of Corr., 316 Conn. 89 (2015); People v. Baret, 16 N.E.3d 1216 (N.Y. 2014); Ex Parte De Los Reyes, 392 S.W.3d 675, 679 (Tex. Crim. App. 2013); Hamm v. State, 744 S.E.2d 503, 505 (S.C. 2013) (stating that *Padilla* does not apply retroactively and citing to *Chaidez* but not providing independent analysis).

118. *See, e.g.,* State v. Garcia, 834 N.W.2d 821, 826 (S.D. 2013); State v. Osorio, 837 N.W.2d 66, 69–70 (Neb. 2013).

119. Kovacs v. United States, 744 F.3d 44, 50–51 (2nd Cir. 2014).

representation.[120] Defense attorneys obviously can advocate for the narrow reading of *Chaidez* that the Second Circuit took rather than the Seventh Circuit's broader interpretation.

Possibilities also remain available in a number of states where retroactivity analyses do not perfectly overlap with the U.S. Supreme Court's approach. Courts and advocates have identified a number of routes that could potentially lead to a more expansive application of *Padilla* than *Chaidez* adopted. Perhaps the state constitution provides an independent source of the immigration law advice requirement; perhaps the state uses a different retroactivity analysis than do the federal courts; or, as one state court of last resort noted, perhaps the state uses the *Teague* retroactivity analysis but departs from the U.S. Supreme Court's interpretation of that analysis. None of these routes ensure a more migrant-friendly outcome as the example of Maryland reveals. There the Court of Appeals, the state's highest court, repeated that it had no need to adopt the *Teague* retroactivity framework before concluding that there was no independent state law basis for applying *Padilla* retroactively.[121] The Massachusetts Supreme Judicial Court, also the state's highest court, exemplifies the opposite outcome. In *Commonwealth v. Sylvain*, the court acknowledged the utility of *Teague*'s retroactivity analysis, but then departed from the *Chaidez* Court's broad interpretation of the new rule limitation.[122] Rather than focus on whether the *Padilla* Court's holding would have been apparent to all reasonable jurists, as *Teague*'s retroactivity analysis requires and *Chaidez* did, the Massachusetts court concerned itself with whether "Massachusetts precedent at the time *Padilla* was decided would have dictated an outcome contrary to that in *Padilla*."[123] Examining the new rule limitation through the lens of state precedent, the court concluded that *Padilla* did not announce a new rule because "long before

---

120. Chavarria v. United States, 739 F.3d 360, 362–63 (7th Cir. 2014).
121. Miller v. State, 77 A.3d 1030, 1042–44 (Md. 2013); *see also Baret*, 16 N.E.3d 1216 (noting that it is not bound by *Teague*, but performing a *Teague* analysis nonetheless); *Garcia*, 834 N.W.2d at 824–25 (reaffirming its commitment to apply a different retroactivity framework than announced in *Teague*, but nonetheless holding that *Padilla* is not retroactive).
122. 995 N.E.2d 760, 769 (Mass. 2013).
123. *Id.* at 771.

Padilla was decided, it was customary for practitioners in Massachusetts to warn their clients of the possible deportation consequences of pleading guilty."[124] As if to buttress its outcome by identifying an independent state law basis for its conclusion, the court added that *Padilla* is not a new rule under the state constitution's right to counsel clause.[125] Likewise, the New Jersey Supreme Court has clarified that the state constitution provides an independent basis that prohibits attorneys from affirmatively providing incorrect advice.[126] Importantly, the court has recognized this prohibition since July 2009, almost a year before *Padilla* was issued.[127] Also grounding its decision in state law, the New Mexico Supreme Court concluded that *Padilla* is retroactive to 1990, the year in which the court began requiring criminal defense attorneys to advise their clients about a conviction's impact on immigration status.[128]

As the Maryland, Massachusetts, New Jersey, and New Mexico decisions suggest, the *Teague* retroactivity analysis does not have to bind state courts. *Teague*, after all, was intended to curtail federal courts' ability to disturb state court outcomes when reviewing convictions on writs of habeas corpus.[129] The decision's narrow reach is driven by two concerns—comity and finality. The first requires that federal courts respect state court decisions and the second promotes a clear end-date to a legal proceeding. *Teague* was not meant to limit state courts' power to review their own proceedings. Indeed, the Supreme Court explicitly said as much in *Danforth v. Minnesota*: "[*Teague*] was intended to limit the authority of federal courts to overturn state convictions—not to limit a state court's authority to grant relief for violations of new rules of constitutional law when reviewing its own State's convictions."[130] Though states cannot fashion retroactivity rules that trample on the federal constitution, it is difficult to imagine how that could occur even using a more expansive retroactivity formula than articulated in *Teague* and its progeny. Federal

124. *Id.*
125. Id at 771–72.
126. State v. Gaitan, 37 A.3d 339, 1109 (N.J. 2012).
127. *See* State v. Nuñez-Valdez, 975 A.2d 418, 424–25 (N.J. 2009).
128. Ramirez v. State, 333 P.3d 240, 244 (N.M. 2014).
129. Danforth v. Minnesota, 552 U.S. 264, 280 (2008).
130. *Id.* at 280–81.

courts' interest in comity is irrelevant when it comes to state courts reviewing their own decisions. Likewise, when claims of ineffective assistance of counsel are raised on direct appeal or, in states where they can
only be raised in post-conviction motions, at the first possible litigation
stage, the state courts' interest in finality is better handled through other
means. States can and do avoid endless relitigation through numerous
methods. Constitutional claims not raised at the first possible moment,
for example, are frequently considered waived. Res judicata ensures that
claims are not raised repeatedly. The doctrine of laches prevents litigants
from waiting too long to pursue a claim, while statutes of limitations impose a concrete timeline. All of these respond directly to finality concerns
and are much better suited to that goal than *Teague* and its concern for
the complicated relationship between state and federal courts.[131]

The end result is that states have essentially as much flexibility as they
want to apply *Padilla* retroactively. They can bind themselves to *Teague*
or other limitations, as some have chosen to do, but they are not obligated
to do so.[132]

State Elevated Standards

State courts have also deviated from U.S. Supreme Court guidance by
building on the foundational principle of constitutional law that the federal constitution sets a floor but not a ceiling. That is, states are free to
provide additional protections from those guaranteed by the U.S. Constitution. This principle is rooted in the fact that the federal and state
governments operate as independent sovereigns so state-level experimentation is constitutionally permissible when they adopt complementary
or supplementary requirements. It is only when the states try to provide
fewer or competing protections than afforded by the federal constitution

---

131. *See* Christopher N. Lasch, *Redress in State Postconviction Proceedings for Ineffective Crimmigration Counsel*, 63 DEPAUL L. REV. 959, 1003–05 (2014).

132. *See, e.g.*, People v. Baret, 16 N.E.3d 1216 (N.Y. 2014) ("*Danforth* frees us to interpret *Teague* more broadly than the Supreme Court when addressing retroactivity in the
context of state collateral review."); Luurtsema v. Commissioner of Correction, 12 A.3d
817, 826 n.14 (Conn. 2011) ("the restrictions *Teague* imposes on the fully retroactive application of new procedural rules are not binding on the states.").

that the Supremacy Clause kicks in to preempt state divergence (for a detailed discussion of preemption, see chapter 7).

A handful of states have used their power to expand constitutional protections provided to criminal defendants to elevate the *Padilla* obligation. In Colorado, for example, criminal defense attorneys remain obligated to inquire about a client's citizenship status when the attorney "had sufficient information to form a reasonable belief that the client was in fact an alien."[133] For its part, the Massachusetts Supreme Judicial Court held that informing a client who was to face presumptively mandatory removal upon conviction that he would be "eligible for deportation" and "face deportation" was not sufficiently clear to meet *Padilla*'s higher specific advice requirement.[134]

State Procedure Concerns

While the U.S. Supreme Court dominates the development of substantive case law regarding ineffective assistance of counsel claims, states control their own procedures. At bottom, procedural standards are the rules of legal proceedings and, as in any contest, how the rules are written affects which party is advantaged and which disadvantaged. In practice, this means that state courts have a good deal of flexibility in bringing *Padilla* to life, as the review of state options regarding retroactivity illustrated. Given that state courts adjudicate the vast majority of criminal proceedings and civil post-conviction relief claims, state procedures are immensely important. As such, attorneys must keep a close eye on the development of critical procedural devices necessary to bring and win *Padilla* claims in the states.

Several states have interpreted their procedural rules in such a way as to pose significant obstacles to migrants interested in raising *Padilla* claims. A number of states have interpreted alternative criminal dispositions that are quite popular among defendants, attorneys, and courts in such a way as to create difficult and sometimes disastrous results for migrants convicted in violation of their right to effective assistance of counsel. The Colorado

---

133. People v. Pozo, 746 P.2d 523, 529 (Colo. 1987) (en banc); *see* Kazadi v. People, 291 P.3d 16, 25 (Colo. 2012) (reaffirming *Pozo*).

134. *See* Commonwealth v. DeJesus, 9 N.E.3d 789, 796 (Mass. 2014).

Supreme Court, for example, concluded that a defendant who receives a "deferred judgment," a disposition that the court described as "a continuance of the defendant's case in lieu of the imposition of sentence," has not been convicted under state law, and a defendant who has not been convicted cannot utilize the state's principal post-conviction relief route to try to vacate the conviction.[135] The problem for migrants, of course, is that a person who has been granted deferred judgment in Colorado is required to plead guilty and submit to probation, enough to satisfy the INA's definition of "conviction."[136] Deferred judgment in Colorado therefore results in a conviction for purposes of immigration law, but not state law. Consequently, a migrant can be removed but cannot challenge removal by arguing that the immigration law conviction resulted from unconstitutionally poor representation. Instead, a defendant who received a deferred judgment must attempt to withdraw the plea, a much more difficult path that involves showing that the state will not be prejudiced by withdrawal.[137] The Tennessee Supreme Court, meanwhile, concluded that the state's post-conviction procedures are inapplicable to a judicial diversion that was successfully completed then expunged.[138] As with the Colorado example, the problem for migrants arises from the interaction of state procedures with the INA's definition of "conviction." According to the Tennessee court, the term "conviction" as used for state-law post-conviction proceedings requires an adjudication of guilt by a court and the formal entry of a judgment.[139] No judgment is entered, the court concluded, when a defendant successfully abides by the terms of judicial diversion.[140] As such, there is no conviction for a state court to review in a post-conviction proceeding.[141] There is, however, both a guilty or nolo contendere plea and court-imposed supervision, including fees, enough to meet the immigration law definition

---

135. *See Kazadi*, 291 P.3d at 22–23.

136. *See* COLO. REV. STAT. ANN. § 18-1.3-102(1)(a), (2); Matter of Chairez, 21 I&N Dec. 44, 49 (BIA 1995).

137. *Kazadi*, 291 P.3d at 29 (Bender, C.J., dissenting).

138. *See* Rodriguez v. State, 437 S.W.3d 450, 455–56 (Tenn. 2014).

139. *Id.* at 455.

140. *Id.* at 457.

141. *Id.* at 455.

of "conviction."[142] Other courts have reached similar conclusions under their own criminal adjudication alternatives.[143]

Still other states have taken harsh views of deadlines imposed for pursuing post-conviction relief. The Arkansas Supreme Court, for example, took the position that the deadlines for filing post-conviction motions to vacate convictions obtained through unconstitutional proceedings are jurisdictional and thus cannot be waived.[144] On its face this is not particularly problematic. The problem arises from the fact that the state post-conviction statute requires that post-conviction challenges be filed within ninety days of the state trial court's judgment or sixty days of a state appellate court's decision.[145] Many—perhaps most—migrants denied effective assistance of counsel do not learn about potential constitutional deficiencies in their criminal cases until ICE notifies them that they are suspected of being removable. For lawful permanent residents in particular, this often happens many years after being convicted when they are returning to the United States from an otherwise ordinary trip abroad. The unfortunate mix of state procedural limitations and immigration law, however, means that the time to challenge an unconstitutional conviction has long since passed.

Further Reading

César Cuauhtémoc García Hernández, Strickland-*Lite: Padilla's Two-Tiered Duty for Noncitizens*, 72 MD. L. REV. 844 (2013).

César Cuauhtémoc García Hernández, *Criminal Defense After* Padilla v. Kentucky, 26 GEO. IMMIGR. L.J. 475 (2012).

KARA HARTZLER, SURVIVING *PADILLA*: A DEFENDER'S GUIDE TO ADVISING NONCITIZENS ON THE IMMIGRATION CONSEQUENCES OF CRIMINAL CONVICTIONS (2011).

Immigrant Defense Project et al., *Practice Advisory: Seeking Post-Conviction Relief Under* Padilla v. Kentucky *After* Chaidez v. U.S. (Feb. 28, 2013), available at http://immigrantdefenseproject.org/wp-content/uploads/2013/03/Chaidez-advisory-FINAL-201302281.pdf.

Christopher N. Lasch, *Redress in State Postconviction Proceedings for Ineffective Crimmigration Counsel*, 63 DEPAUL L. REV. 959, 1003–05 (2014).

---

142. TENN. CODE ANN. § 40-35-313(a)(1)(A)-(B).

143. *See, e.g.*, State v. Kona, 2014-Ohio-1242, 2014 WL 1340566 (Ohio Ct. App. March 27, 2014) (unpublished), *rev. granted by* 15 N.E.3d 883 (Ohio).

144. *See* State v. Tejeda-Acosta, 427 S.W.3d 673, 678–79 (Ark. 2013).

145. Ark. Code Ann. R. 37.2(c).

CHAPTER 6

Federal Immigration Crimes

Though immigration is largely governed by civil law, multiple INA sections use criminal penalties to punish migrants. This chapter touches most of the existing federal immigration crimes but focuses on the two that are most significant: illegal entry and illegal reentry. After decades of going largely unused, illegal entry and illegal reentry now dominate federal court dockets. Combined, immigration law crimes have been the largest category of offenses federal prosecutors have pursued in recent years, with illegal entry and reentry prosecutions leading the way. Because of this historically aberrational prosecutorial trend, the chapter also discusses key policy initiatives that facilitate the federal government's heavy reliance on its criminal law power to police immigration law: Operation Streamline and the growing use of fast-track plea agreements. These trends have done much to criminalize immigration law in recent decades.

Historical Precursors to Illegal Entry and Illegal Reentry

The INA criminally punishes unauthorized entry into the United States through two sections. INA § 275 punishes entering without the federal government's permission, while § 276 punishes doing so after having already been removed. Referred to as illegal entry and illegal reentry, respectively, these federal crimes have existed in roughly the same form since 1929.[1] Before then Congress had never criminalized entering without authorization and had enacted only four statutes criminalizing reentry, all of which were much narrower than the 1929 enactment. The Aliens Act of 1798 criminalized returning to the United States after having been removed upon order of the president, a penalty that appears never to have been applied to anyone.[2] Over a century later, a 1910 statute subjected people deported for involvement in prostitution and subsequently attempted to return to the United States to up to two years imprisonment.[3] Eight years after that another statute threatened migrants deported for being anarchists who subsequently returned or attempted to return with up to five years imprisonment.[4]

The 1929 provision took a broader sweep. Of greatest historical significance, the statute for the first time turned to criminal law to do what Congress had largely thought civil law was well-equipped to handle by itself: regulate cross-border movement without the federal government's permission. Specifically, the new law allowed for up to a year imprisonment for nothing more than entering clandestinely or after lying to an immigration official.[5] Its illegal reentry provisions, meanwhile, targeted anyone who entered or attempted to enter the United States without authorization after having been previously deported.[6] Up to two years imprisonment could be meted out against violators.

---

1. Act of March 4, 1929, Pub. L. No. 70-1018, ch. 690, §§ 1-2, 45 Stat. 1551.
2. Aliens Act of June 25, 1798, ch. 58, § 1, 1 Stat. 570; *see* Gregory Fehlings, *Storm on the Constitution: The First Deportation Law*, 10 TULSA J. COMP. & INT'L L. 63, 105–10 (2002).
3. Act of March 26, 1910, ch. 128, § 3, 36 Stat. 264, 264–65.
4. Act of October 16, 1918, Pub. L. No. 61-107, ch. 186, § 3, 40 Stat. 1012–13.
5. Act of March 4, 1929, Pub. L. No. 70-1018, ch. 690, §2, 45 Stat. 1551.
6. *Id.* at §1.

The 1929 enactment's framework remains largely intact. Illegal entry and illegal reentry remain distinct offenses that mirror the language adopted almost a century ago. The former is punishable as a misdemeanor, while the latter is treated as a felony. Each offense is addressed in turn.

Illegal Entry

Illegal entry, as it currently exists, is fairly straightforward. It targets migrants who engage in any of three activities related to coming to the United States: entering or attempting to enter outside a port-of-entry; eluding examination or inspection by immigration officials; and providing a willfully false or misleading representation or willful concealment of a material fact in order to enter or attempt to enter the United States.[7] A first time offense is punishable by up to six months imprisonment and a subsequent offense can result in as much as two years in prison. The median prison term meted out in fiscal year 2010 was eighteen months.[8]

At bottom, all three prongs prohibit entering the United States clandestinely or as a result of misleading government agents. A person who presents herself to immigration officials and requests permission to proceed into the United States is not subject to an illegal entry conviction. Likewise, a person who is allowed into the United States is not punishable for illegal entry even if government officials later discover that the immigration officer should not have allowed the migrant to proceed so long as the migrant did not lie, misrepresent herself, or conceal material facts about herself. This is, however, almost certainly basis for removal through the immigration courts.[9] Most importantly, a migrant who genuinely obtains a nonimmigrant visa or lawful permanent resident status, presents herself for inspection by an immigration officer, then proceeds into the United States with the officer's permission is not subject to illegal entry even if she does not leave the United States as required by the nonimmigrant visa or commits some removable act (for example, any of the crimes that can result in removal). These actions can all result in removal, but they do not

---

7. INA § 275(a).
8. MARK MOTIVANS, IMMIGRATION OFFENDERS IN THE FEDERAL JUDICIAL SYSTEM, 2010, at 30 (2012, rev. 2013).
9. *See* INA § 237(a)(1)(A).

subject a migrant to criminal prosecution for illegal entry. Though lawful permanent residents and others with authorization to enter the United States are theoretically punishable for illegal entry if they engage in any of the conduct proscribed by INA § 275, the likelihood that they will do so is slim so illegal entry is primarily a concern for individuals who lack lawful means to enter. In effect, illegal entry applies only to people who sneak into the country or lie their way in. It does not apply to individuals who become removable for any other reason, including sticking around longer than allowed or committing a crime.

In many situations, proving the elements of illegal entry is rather simple. For countless individuals, Border Patrol agents can quickly gather the critical evidence necessary for a successful prosecution by doing nothing more than locating the migrants near the border. Watching a person emerge on the Río Grande River's northern bank or trek through a remote desert tends to go a long way in proving that the person entered the United States without appearing at a port-of-entry. Many individuals in this position make little effort to conceal their conduct or identity.

Defenses to illegal entry prosecutions, however, are available. The most important relies on the statute's explicit statement that it applies only to "aliens." United States citizenship is thus an absolute defense. A United States citizen cannot commit illegal entry no matter how flagrantly she eludes immigration officials. Properly identifying an illegal entry defendant's citizenship status is therefore critical. The *Padilla* decision's requirement that, to meet their Sixth Amendment obligation to provide effective assistance of counsel, criminal defense attorneys provide migrant clients with advice about immigration consequences of conviction implies that defense attorneys must query a defendant's citizenship status. Defense attorneys in Colorado, New Mexico, and other states that recognize an obligation to inquire into citizenship have an independent reason for delving into this threshold question.[10] Under either *Padilla* or state court interpretations, failure to ask about citizenship status may lead to ineffective assistance of counsel findings. Even if that were not the case,

---

10. State v. Paredez, 101 P.3d 799, 805 (N.M. 2004); People v. Pozo, 746 P.2d 523, 529 (Colo. 1987).

zealous defense attorneys should explore the possibility that a client is immune to prosecution for this offense. Though the Sixth Amendment does not drive judges' or prosecutors' conduct as it does that of defense attorneys, judges and prosecutors should encourage an inquiry into an illegal entry defendant's citizenship status out of equity and prudential concerns: it is simply unfair and a waste of time and money to investigate, prosecute, detain pending criminal proceedings, and imprison convicted individuals for crimes that they are legally not capable of committing.

Citizenship law can be deceiving. For most people, citizenship is determined by place of birth so it is easily discernible: the Fourteenth Amendment provides that every person born in the United States is a United States citizen. Sometimes, however, that simple factual question—where were you born?—can turn into a convoluted factual answer. Some people cannot document where they were born. Others, including some who are still alive, were born along the border on territory that has literally changed nations.[11] Many others have been led by well-meaning parents to fervently believe that they were born in the United States though they were not. Because an honest answer is not necessarily a legally binding answer, it does not matter that a defendant genuinely believes she was born in the United States. If she was not, the Fourteenth Amendment does not provide her with United States citizenship. Likewise, if she was born in the United States, she is a United States citizen no matter her attachment to the country or knowledge of her birthplace.

All hope of having acquired United States citizenship is not lost for people born outside the United States and facing illegal entry charges. They may have obtained citizenship through United States citizen relatives even if no one knew it. A person born outside the United States to an unmarried United States citizen mother is a United States citizen, but only if the child was born after December 23, 1952, and the mother was physically present in the United States for at least one year prior to the child's birth.[12] Citizenship is also granted to a child born outside the United States to parents who were not United States citizens at the time of the

---

11. *See* Matter of Cantu, 17 I&N Dec. 190, 207–09 (A.G. 1978).
12. INA § 309(c).

child's birth, but who became citizens before the child's eighteenth birthday and subsequently began "residing permanently in the United States" prior to turning eighteen—but only if all this happened before 2000 when this statute was repealed.[13] That year Congress amended the INA to provide citizenship to children under 18 years old whose parent becomes a citizen, but only if the child is living in the United States as a lawful permanent resident with the citizen parent.[14] These are not uncommon occurrences—nor is this a comprehensive list of routes to citizenship. Outside of the Fourteenth Amendment, citizenship law is anything but simple. For the illegal entry defendant, the end result is the same: absolute immunity from conviction. It is difficult to imagine a situation in which the stakes are higher than potential banishment from one's own country of citizenship.

Alienage is not the only available defense to an illegal entry prosecution. The general statute of limitations on federal prosecutions presents another option. In general, federal criminal prosecutions must begin within five years of the crime's commission.[15] Illegal entry falls within this general statute of limitations.[16] The trickier question is on what date the five-year period begins to run. The Supreme Court is clear that statutes of limitations "'normally begin to run when the crime is complete'."[17] Most crimes begin and end within a short period of time. Some, however, may continue on. Conspiracy, the Court explained, "continues as long as the conspirators engage in overt acts in furtherance of their plot."[18] The breadth of the five-year statute of limitations therefore depends on whether illegal entry is a continuing crime or not. If the illegal entry is completed on the date that the migrant crossed the border, then any illegal entry prosecution lodged more than five years later is barred by the statute of limitations. However, if illegal entry is considered a continuing

13. INA § 321 (1999) (repealed by the Child Citizenship Act of 2000, Pub. L. 106-395, § 103, 114 Stat. 1631, 1632).

14. Child Citizenship Act of 2000. Pub L. 106–395, § 101, 114 Stat. 1631 (codified at INA §320).

15. 18 U.S.C. § 3282(a).

16. *See* United States v. Rincon-Jimenez, 595 F.2d 1192, 1193 (9th Cir. 1979).

17. Toussie v. U.S., 397 U.S. 112, 115 (1970) (quoting Pendergast v. United States, 317 U.S. 412, 418 (1943)).

18. *Toussie*, 397 U.S. at 122.

crime, then the five-year statute of limitations period does not begin running while the migrant is present in the United States, thus the statute of
limitations is effectively irrelevant. Courts agree that illegal entry is not
a continuing crime. The Ninth Circuit, for example, concluded that INA
§ 275(a)(2), the provision that punishes a migrant who "eludes examination or inspection by immigration officers," is not a continuing offense
even if the migrant is found years later living in the United States. The
examination and inspection that (a)(2) requires, the court reasoned, "are
to take place at the time of entry, a fixed point in time," thus "suggest[ing]
that the offense described by s. 1325(2) [INA § 275(a)(2)] is consummated
at the time an alien gains entry through an unlawful point and does not
submit to these examinations."[19] A California state court considering
the legality of a police officer's arrest of a person suspected of violating
federal immigration law came to much the same conclusion regarding
the other prongs of INA § 275.[20] More influentially, the Supreme Court
articulated similar reasoning in dicta, noting "'entry' is limited to a particular locality and hardly suggests continuity."[21] It has not, however,
conclusively held as much.

Illegal Reentry

Criminal prosecutions for illegal reentry build on prior civil immigration adjudications. Without an earlier removal, there can be no illegal
reentry. The typical illegal reentry prosecution involves a migrant who
was ordered removed and is subsequently caught trying to enter or having
entered.[22] Other situations involve individuals who were removed then
"found in" the United States.[23]

In its current form, illegal reentry carries a sweeping potential punishment range. Individuals convicted of a first illegal reentry offense
can receive as little as a fine with no jail time or as much as two years

---

19. *Rincon-Jimenez*, 595 F.2d at, 1193–94; *see* United States v. Cavillo-Rojas, 510
Fed. Appx. 238, 249 (4th Cir. 2013) (unpublished).
20. Gates v. Superior Court, 238 Cal. Rptr. 592, 598 (Cal. Ct. App. 1987).
21. United States v. Cores, 356 U.S. 405, 408 n.6 (1958); *see* INS v. Lopez-Mendoza,
468 U.S. 1032, 1057 (1984) (White, J., dissenting).
22. INA § 276(a).
23. INA § 276(a)(2).

imprisonment.[24] Migrants who were removed after having been convicted of an aggravated felony can be sentenced to as much as twenty years imprisonment.[25] It is not necessary for the migrant's conviction to have been deemed an aggravated felony in the removal proceedings that resulted in the earlier removal order.[26] Nor is it necessary for the prosecutor in the illegal reentry case to notify the migrant that the government will request the aggravated felony sentencing enhancement. This provision, the Supreme Court held, is merely a sentencing factor; it is not a separate criminal offense.[27] As such, the government is not required to include any reference to a prior aggravated felony conviction in the indictment.[28] Raising this at the sentencing stage is permissible. Despite the enormous possible sentencing range, the median sentence for all illegal reentry convictions in fiscal year 2010 was fifteen months imprisonment.[29]

Every variety of illegal reentry requires entry of "an order of exclusion, deportation, or removal."[30] Clearly the removal orders issued by immigration judges thousands of times over in recent years fit this description. This is true even for in absentia orders.[31] The same goes for orders of exclusion or deportation that immigration judges regularly issued until 1996. Some confusion exists about dispositions that shortcut the ordinary immigration court process. Voluntary departure, INA § 240B, likely cannot form the basis of an illegal reentry prosecution, but the case law addressing this is poorly developed.[32] In contrast, the courts that have addressed the issue agree that expedited removals under INA § 235(b)(1) suffice to meet the removal requirement of an illegal reentry prosecution.[33]

---

24. *Id.*

25. INA § 276(b)(2).

26. *See* United States v. Ramirez, 731 F.3d 351, 352–53 (5th Cir. 2013) (determining that a crime was an aggravated felony during the sentencing stage of an illegal reentry prosecution); U.S. Sentencing Guidelines Manual § 2L1.2 cmt. n.1(A)(ii) (2013).

27. Almendarez-Torres v. United States, 523 U.S. 224, 235 (1998).

28. *Id.* at 227; *see* United States v. Palomino-Rivera, 258 F.3d 656, 661 (7th Cir. 2001).

29. MOTIVANS, *supra* note 8 at 30.

30. INA § 276(a)(1).

31. United States v. Sanchez, 604 F.3d 356, 359 (7th Cir. 2010); United States v. Ramirez-Carcamo, 559 F.3d 384, 389–90 (5th Cir. 2009).

32. United States v. Ortiz-Lopez, 385 F.3d 1202, 1204 n.1 (9th Cir. 2004).

33. United States v. Barajas-Alvarado, 655 F.3d 1077, 1087–88 (9th Cir. 2011); United States v. Lopez-Vasquez, 227 F.3d 476, 485 (5th Cir. 2000).

The illegal reentry offense presents an important complication not present in illegal entry: the "found in" provision. Added to the statute in 1952, the found in provision expands illegal reentry's reach from those migrants who are caught in the process of crossing the border or soon thereafter to include individuals who have moved well beyond that action without the government's knowledge.[34] Just what constitutes being found in the United States is less than intuitive. The prevailing view is that "found in" is synonymous with "discovered."[35] That is, "'found in' in Section 1326 [INA § 276] applies only to situations in which an alien is discovered in the United States after entering the country surreptitiously by bypassing recognized immigration ports of entry."[36] Curiously, several circuits add that, in order to be "found in" the United States, a migrant must have first entered the United States, and to "enter" for these purposes means a migrant "must be free from official restraint," which "includes surveillance, regardless of the alien's awareness."[37] Mere physical presence in the United States will not satisfy the "found in" requirement.

At what point does the federal government discover that a migrant is present in the United States without authorization after having been removed previously? Courts of appeals have taken distinct positions. Some circuits conclude that a migrant's unauthorized presence in the United States can be imputed on the federal government when it could have discovered the migrant's presence through due diligence.[38] Other circuits

34. *See* Immigration and Nationality Act, Pub. L. 82-414, 66 Stat. 163, at 229, § 276 (1952); *see* United States v. DiSantillo, 615 F.2d 128, 134–35 (3d Cir. 1980).

35. *See* United States v. Zavala-Mendez, 411 F.3d 1116, 1120–21 (9th Cir. 2005); United States v. Clarke, 312 F.3d 1343, 1346 (11th Cir. 2002) (quoting United States v. Canals-Jimenez, 943 F.2d 1284, 1288 (11th Cir. 1991)); United States v. Angeles-Mascote, 206 F.3d 529, 531 (5th Cir. 2000); United States v. Whittaker, 999 F.2d 38, 42 (2nd Cir. 1993); United States v. Gomez, 38 F.3d 1031, 1036 (8th Cir. 1994); United States v. Meraz-Valeta, 26 F.3d 992, 997 (10th Cir. 1994), *overruled on other grounds*, United States v. Aguirre-Tello, 353 F.3d 1199 (10th Cir. 2004) (en banc).

36. United States v. Canals-Jimenez, 943 F.2d 1284, 1288 (11th Cir. 1991).

37. United States v. Muniz-Jaquez, 718 F.3d 1180, 1182 (9th Cir. 2013) (citing United States v. Pacheco-Medina, 212 F.3d 1162, 1164 (9th Cir. 2000)); *see* United States v. Macias, 740 F.3d 96, 99–101 (2nd Cir. 2014); *Angeles-Mascote*, 206 F.3d at 531-32.

38. *See, e.g.*, United States v. Lennon, 372 F.3d 535, 540–41 (3d Cir. 2004) (discussing United States v. DiSantillo, 615 F.2d 128, 135-36 (3d Cir. 1980)); United States v. Clarke, 312 F.3d 1343, 1347 (11th Cir. 2002); United States v. Rivera-Ventura, 72 F.3d 277, 282 (2nd Cir. 1995); United States v. Gomez, 38 F.3d 1031, 1037 (8th Cir. 1994).

have adopted the opposite position: the government cannot be said to have found a migrant in the United States until it actually locates the person here.[39] This is a critical issue because the statute of limitations begins to run only when the crime is completed.[40] Illegal reentry begins upon the migrant's clandestine entry into the United States and is completed when immigration officials discover the migrant in the United States.[41] In circuits that take the position that the government's constructive discovery of a migrant satisfies the "found in" prong, the statute of limitations starts running on the date that a government official should reasonably have known that a particular person was in the United States without authorization after having entered surreptitiously following a removal. On the contrary, in those jurisdictions that view illegal reentry as a continuing offense—and there are many[42]—the statute of limitations does not start running until the migrant is already in the custody of immigration officials. A statute of limitations defense is much more likely to succeed in circuits following the former position.

Illegal reentry's complexity does not end there. Like illegal entry, United States citizenship is a complete bar to an illegal reentry conviction. Only an "alien" can be convicted of this crime.[43] Inquiring into a defendant's citizenship status is very important because of the way that criminal prosecutions interact with civil removal proceedings. Illegal reentry is a federal crime applicable only to people who are not United States citizens and who were previously removed through the civil immigration law system. Unlike criminal prosecutions for immigration crimes, the civil immigration law system does not provide indigents with appointed counsel. This means that many people go through the removal process unrepresented. Without even considering expedited removals, in fiscal year 2013

39. *See, e.g.*, United States v. Uribe-Rios, 558 F.3d 347, 354 (4th Cir. 2009); United States v. Are, 498 F.3d 460, 463–64 (7th Cir. 2007) (quoting United States v. Lopez-Flores, 275 F.3d 661, 663 (7th Cir. 2001)).

40. *See* United States v. Rivera-Ventura, 72 F.3d 277, 281 (2nd Cir. 1995).

41. *See* United States v. Gomez, 38 F.3d 1031, 1034 (8th Cir. 1994).

42. *See* United States v. Mendez-Cruz, 329 F.3d 885, 889 (D.C. Cir. 2003); *Lopez-Flores*, 275 F.3d at 663; United States v. Diaz-Diaz, 135 F.3d 572, 575 (8th Cir. 1998); United States v. Castrillon-Gonzalez, 77 F.3d 403, 406 (11th Cir. 1996); United States v. Guzman-Bruno, 27 F.3d 420, 423 (9th Cir. 1994).

43. INA § 276(a).

over 40 percent of respondents—numbering almost 72,000 people—with immigration court cases were unrepresented. Though substantial, this is actually a significant decrease from just four years earlier when 75 percent of people in immigration court—more than 145,000 people—lacked representation.[44] The lack of counsel that characterizes removal proceedings means many do not question their own citizenship status. Because citizenship law is so complicated, however, attorneys sometimes fail to raise this line of defense or misconstrue potentially helpful law.[45] The end result is that United States citizens are sometimes removed. In those instances in which they have longstanding ties to the United States, they tend to return even if that means hiding from immigration agents. For these individuals the best and sometimes first hope for vindicating their right to live in the United States as a citizen comes in an illegal reentry prosecution assisted by counsel.

Citizenship is a defense to illegal reentry because it is one of the elements of the crime.[46] It is not the only potential defense. A string of other defenses arises from the fact that the Supreme Court affords individuals the possibility of judicial review of civil immigration adjudications before facing criminal penalties. It would violate the Fifth Amendment's Due Process Clause, the Court held in *United States v. Mendoza-Lopez*, to rely on the lax procedures of civil adjudications when imposing criminal liability.[47] As the Court explained, "where a determination made in an administrative proceeding is to play a critical role in the subsequent imposition of a criminal sanction, there must be *some* meaningful review of the administrative proceeding."[48] After the Court announced this conclusion, Congress amended INA § 276 to provide a statutory framework that individuals must follow to collaterally attack a prior removal order. Section 276(d) imposes three requirements that an illegal reentry defendant must meet: that all administrative remedies were exhausted, that the removal

44. U.S. DEP'T OF JUSTICE, EXEC. OFFICE FOR IMMIGR. REV., FY 2013: STATISTICS YEARBOOK F1, fig.10 (2014).

45. *See, e.g.*, United States v. Juarez, 672 F.3d 381, 384–85 (5th Cir. 2012).

46. *See* United States v. Flores-Peraza, 58 F.3d 164, 166 (5th Cir. 1995); United States v. Barragan-Cepeda, 29 F.3d 1378, 1381 (9th Cir. 1994).

47. 481 U.S. 828, 837 (1987).

48. *Id.* at 837-38.

process deprived the defendant of an opportunity for judicial review, and
that the removal order was fundamentally unfair. Each prong imposes its
own unique challenges that, alone and in combination, present a tough
uphill climb for defendants hoping to avoid illegal reentry convictions by
challenging the underlying removal order.

The administrative exhaustion requirement demands that individuals
in removal proceedings take challenges to removal orders through the designated administrative process.[49] For removal orders issued by an immigration judge, that entails appealing to the Board of Immigration Appeals,
the administrative appellate route that the Code of Federal Regulations
provides.[50] Expedited removal orders, by their nature more rushed affairs that do not involve seeing an immigration judge, must be contested
through limited review processes specified in the INA and CFR.[51] Failure
to follow these procedures means a failure to exhaust the administrative
remedies available. The only exception to this default rule applies to situations in which the migrant failed to pursue these administrative routes because she was not properly informed that they were available. Sometimes
this consists of the migrant's attorney's failure to tell the migrant that she
could pursue administrative review processes. For pro se migrants, the
equivalent, in some circuits at least, is a failure of the immigration judge
or immigration officials to provide this information.[52] Astonishingly,
other circuits, in contrast, take the view that migrants can fail to exhaust
administrative remedies even when misled by the immigration judge into
believing none were available. As the Tenth Circuit put it, "Because the
immigration judge was under no legal obligation to inform Mr. Chavez-
Alonso of his eligibility for relief from deportation under § 212(c), Mr.
Chavez-Alonso's wavier was not premised on constitutionally relevant
misinformation."[53] Regardless of the failed messenger, the problem lies
with the failed message: a migrant cannot reach a "considered and intelligent" decision to waive the right to appeal or review a decision if she is

49. United States v. Santiago-Ochoa, 447 F.3d 1015, 1019 (7th Cir. 2006); *see* 8 C.F.R. § 1003.3.
50. *Santiago-Ochoa*, 447 F.3d at 1019 ; *see* 8 C.F.R. § 1003.3.
51. INA § 235(b)(1)(C); 8 C.F.R. § 238.1(c)(1).
52. United States v. Ubaldo-Figueroa, 364 F.3d 1042, 1048 (9th Cir. 2004).
53. United States v. Chavez-Alonso, 431 F.3d 726, 728–29 (10th Cir. 2005).

not properly told about those options, and a waiver that is not considered and intelligent does not comport with the Due Process Clause.[54]

To serve as the basis of an illegal reentry prosecution, a migrant must have also been afforded the opportunity for judicial review of the underlying removal order. In the Tenth Circuit's words, the relevant question is whether the immigration hearing "deprived the alien of the right of judicial review."[55] Though the exact contours of what this entails remain unclear, at a minimum this requires someone informing a migrant that she can appeal an adverse immigration decision. Migrants represented by counsel face a difficult time showing that they were not informed of their right to appeal. Attorneys are presumed to know about judicial review and discuss this option with clients. Even unrepresented migrants face a difficult time given that immigration judges are statutorily required to and usually in fact do inform respondents of their right to appeal to the BIA, at which point, presumably, the BIA would inform them of their right to appeal to the federal courts.[56] Ironically, in many instances those most likely to be able to satisfy the deprivation of judicial review requirement are migrants who were placed in summary removal proceedings such as reinstatement of removal and made their way through immigration proceedings without representation. As the Third Circuit explained before concluding that a migrant had been deprived the opportunity for judicial review, the procedures used for reinstatement of removal are "quite summary," generally do not involve appearing before an immigration judge, and do not inform a migrant of her right to appeal to the federal courts.[57]

Lastly, to successfully defend against an illegal reentry prosecution by challenging the underlying removal, a migrant must show that the underlying removal order was fundamentally unfair. Most circuits gauge fundamental unfairness by querying whether the underlying immigration

54. *Ubaldo-Figueroa*, 364 F.3d at 1048 (United States v. Muro-Inclan, 249 F.3d 1180, 1182 (9th Cir. 2001)); *see* United States v. Fares, 978 F.2d 52, 56 (2nd Cir. 1992).

55. United States v. Wittgenstein, 163 F.3d 1164, 1170–71 (10th Cir. 1998) (quoting United States v. Meraz-Valeta, 26 F.3d 992, 997 (10th Cir. 1994)).

56. INA § 240(c)(5); U.S. Dep't of Justice, Immigration Judge Benchbook, *Advisals* 1, 2 (July 15, 2014), http://www.justice.gov/eoir/vll/benchbook/tools/Advisals.pdf. *See* United States v. Copeland, 376 F.3d 61, 63–64 (2d Cir. 2004).

57. United States v. Charleswell, 456 F.3d 347, 355–56 (3d Cir. 2006) (discussing reinstatement requirements set forth at INA § 241(a)(5) and 8 C.F.R. § 241.8).

proceeding complied with procedural due process obligations.[58] "A removal order is 'fundamentally unfair,'" the Ninth Circuit explained, "if '(1) [the alien's] due process rights were violated by defects in his underlying deportation proceeding, and (2) he suffered prejudice as a result of the defects.'"[59] Clearly this is not an easy requirement to meet. It requires that the migrant show that she was actually harmed by the deficiencies that plagued the removal process. Importantly, showing actual harm does not require showing that she would have defeated DHS's allegations or obtained relief from removal. Instead, the prejudice standard has been interpreted to mean that the migrant must show a plausible or reasonably likely claim for relief.[60]

Combined, these three requirements to defend against illegal reentry charges form a difficult gauntlet to navigate. Despite the difficulty, migrants regularly do so successfully, though the particular route depends heavily on the case law of the relevant circuit. One basis available in some circuits is by showing that the immigration judge failed to advise them of their eligibility for discretionary relief, such as voluntary departure, relief under former § 212(c), or cancellation of removal.[61] One migrant, for example, successfully defended herself against an illegal reentry charge based on a removal decision by an immigration official who erroneously concluded she had been convicted of an aggravated felony that barred her from discretionary relief options.[62] Several circuits, however, take the opposite position with regard to discretionary relief such as these possibilities, concluding that an immigration judge's failure to inform a respondent of eligibility for relief does not render a removal order fundamentally unfair because migrants lack a liberty interest in discretionary relief, a

---

58. United States v. Torres, 383 F.3d 92, 103 (3d Cir. 2004).

59. United States v. Rojas-Pedroza, 716 F.3d 1253, 1263 (9th Cir. 2013) (quoting *Ubaldo-Figueroa*, 364 F.3d at 1048).

60. United States v. Luna, 436 F.3d 312, 321 (1st Cir. 2006); *Ubaldo-Figueroa*, 364 F.3d at 1050.

61. *See, e.g.*, United States v. Ortiz-Lopez, 385 F.3d 1202, 1204 (9th Cir. 2004) (voluntary departure); Copeland, 376 F.3d at 71 (§ 212(c) relief); Ubaldo-Figueroa, 364 F.3d at 1050 (§ 212(c) relief).

62. United States v. Garcia-Santana, 743 F.3d 666, 679–80 (9th Cir. 2014).

typical Fifth Amendment Due Process Clause requirement.[63] As the Third Circuit explained, discretionary relief provides a "mere hope" of remaining in the United States, and that is simply not enough to rise to the level of a due process liberty interest.[64] Courts even disagree about instances in which the immigration judge incorrectly informed a migrant that she was not eligible for certain relief options.[65]

Aside from defending against illegal reentry by pointing to the possibility of relief, migrants have had some success challenging illegal reentry prosecutions based on removal orders entered in absentia but lacking proper notice to the migrant.[66] Because notice is a core feature of procedural due process, this ground avoids the problem that discretionary relief encounters in many circuits (see previous paragraph).[67] Still, in absentia orders are statutorily authorized, issued regularly, and require only basic notice easily met through a Notice to Appear (NTA) mailed to a migrant or her attorney.[68] A variety of courts have held that the government provided sufficient notice if it did nothing more than send an NTA through ordinary first-class mail to the migrant's last known address even though the migrant no longer lived there.[69]

The right to counsel presents a similar scenario, especially as it plays out in bare bones proceedings frequently used by DHS. Though the Sixth

---

63. *See* United States v. De Horta Garcia, 519 F.3d 658, 661 (7th Cir. 2008); United States v. Torres, 383 F.3d 92, 105–06 (3d Cir. 2004); United States v. Aguirre-Tello, 353 F.3d 1199, 1204–05 (10th Cir. 2004); United States v. Wilson, 316 F.3d 506, 510 (4th Cir. 2003), *abrogated on other grounds by* Lopez v. Gonzales, 127 S. Ct. 625 (2006); United States v. Lopez-Ortiz, 313 F.3d 225, 231 (5th Cir. 2002).

64. United States v. Torres, 383 F.3d 92, 105–06 (3d Cir. 2004).

65. *Contrast* United States v. Pallares-Galan, 359 F.3d 1088, 1096 (9th Cir. 2004) (incorrectly telling migrant he was not eligible for 212(c) relief could result in successful collateral attack), *with Lopez-Ortiz*, 313 F.3d at 231 (informing migrant that he was ineligible for § 212(c) relief, a conclusion the Supreme Court would later clarify was incorrect, could not support a finding of fundamental unfairness).

66. *See, e.g.,* United States v. El Shami, 434 F.3d 659, 664–65 (4th Cir. 2005); Andia v. Ashcroft, 359 F.3d 1181, 1185 (9th Cir. 2003).

67. *See* United States v. Torres, 383 F.3d 92, 104 (3d Cir. 2004).

68. *See* INA § 240(b)(5); INA § 239(a)(1).

69. United States v. Perez-Valdera, 899 F. Supp. 181, 184–85 (S.D.N.Y. 1995) (interpreting a prior version of the INA's notice requirement and concluding that first-class mail satisfied it); United States v. Estrada-Trochez, 66 F.3d 733, 736 (5th Cir. 1995) (upholding notice sent to last-known address where migrant no longer lived); United States v. Hinojosa-Perez, 206 F.3d 832, 836–37 (9th Cir. 2000) (same).

Amendment right to counsel does not apply to removal proceedings, courts of appeals are steadfast that the Fifth Amendment Due Process Clause provides a right to hire counsel (only one federal circuit has ever held that it might, in some circumstances, require appointed counsel[70]). A migrant may be able to defend against illegal reentry charges if she can show that she was not meaningfully informed of the right to obtain counsel. The Ninth Circuit, for example, concluded that a migrant was removed in violation of due process requirements even though he signed a stipulated removal form that stated that he waived his right to counsel. According to the court, the "key question is whether the waiver is 'knowing and voluntary,'" and nothing in the stipulated removal process—which did not involve appearing before an immigration judge—assured the court that the migrant had knowingly and voluntarily waived his right to counsel.[71] The court concluded that the procedure used in that case was procedurally defective, but there is reason to believe that the Ninth Circuit might be convinced to take an even firmer stand against stipulated removal orders. Commenting on this case, Ninth Circuit Judge Kim McLane Wardlaw wrote, "The rise in the use of streamlined deportation proceedings creates the potential for widespread violations whenever speed of deportations is emphasized at the expense of procedural protections. To date, no case has decided that waivers in stipulated removal proceedings are a per se deprivation of a respondent's right to counsel, but such a case may be on the horizon."[72]

Successfully pursuing a collateral attack on an underlying removal order has the obvious benefit to a migrant of avoiding an illegal reentry conviction. By eliminating the underlying removal, it prevents a criminal prosecution for entering the United States without authorization after having been removed. It has the additional benefit of invalidating the original removal. While the fact of actual removal from the United States cannot be undone, a successful collateral attack eliminates the legal effect of that removal. The migrant is returned to whatever immigration status

---

70. Aguilera-Enriquez v. INS F. 2d 565, 568–69 (6th Cir. 1975).
71. United States v. Ramos, 623 F.3d 672, 682 (9th Cir. 2010).
72. Kim McLane Wardlaw, *The Latino Immigration Experience*, 31 Chicana/o-Latina/o L. Rev. 13, 43 (2012).

she held prior to entry of the initial removal order. Subsequent removals that depended on the initial removal order (e.g., reinstatements of the original removal) are also nullified.[73]

Sentencing Guidelines Concerns

Despite the availability of defenses, many migrants are convicted of illegal entry and illegal reentry every year. More than 92,000 people were convicted of one or the other offense in 2013 alone.[74] Courts and attorneys therefore regularly encounter decisions about the appropriate penalty to mete out for a violation. Though the INA provides statutory sentencing ranges for both, it leaves a great deal of discretion to judges.[75] Section 2L.1.2 of the U.S. Sentencing Guidelines (USSG) fills much of this gap for both offenses. Individuals convicted for the first time for either offense can be sentenced, at a minimum, to between zero and six months imprisonment.[76] Potential sentences begin to diverge quickly when a migrant is convicted after having been previously removed or having remained in the United States despite a removal order. Subsection (b) provides a dizzying variety of enhancements that apply to people who meet the specified criteria. A previously deported individual convicted of an aggravated felony, for example, can receive an eight-level increase, a bump that translates into an additional twenty-one months imprisonment if no other criminal history exists.

Navigating the Guidelines requires careful analysis. Attorneys must consider both axes of the USSG's sentencing table (found in chapter 5 of the Guidelines): the base offense level, which USSG § 2.L.1.2(a) provides as 8, and the migrant's criminal history points (listed in chapter 4, part A of the Guidelines). On top of this, they must consider enhancements listed in the Guidelines themselves (for example, the eight-level increase for an aggravated felony conviction mentioned in the previous paragraph). To accurately gauge the applicable sentencing range, therefore, attorneys

---

73. *See* United States v. Arias-Ordonez, 597 F.3d 972, 979, 982 (9th Cir. 2010).

74. Transactional Records Access Clearinghouse, *Despite Rise in Felony Charges, Most Immigration Convictions Remain Misdemeanors*, http://trac.syr.edu/immigration/reports/356/ (June 26, 2014).

75. *See* INA §§ 275(a), 276(a)-(b).

76. U.S. Sentencing Guidelines Manual § 2L1.2(a); ch. 5, pt. A (2013).

must gather comprehensive information about a migrant's criminal history. They must then use that information and the information provided at § 2.L.1.2 to map their client onto the sentencing table.

While this is a complicated assessment, it is not insurmountable. Many of the terms used in the Guidelines have specific definitions that leave room for interpretation. The Guidelines explicitly borrow the INA's definition of an aggravated felony.[77] That phrase, of course, is anything but straightforward. Consequently, reams of paper have been used to decipher whether a conviction constitutes an aggravated felony for the purpose of determining whether the aggravated felony sentencing enhancement applies. This, at least, involves a single—albeit convoluted—definition. In other instances, however, the Sentencing Guidelines use terms of art that are familiar to attorneys versed in criminal or immigration law but do so in a slightly different way. An earlier conviction for a "crime of violence," for example, can result in a sixteen-level offense increase, but that phrase has a different meaning for sentencing purposes than it does under the federal penal code or the INA. Under criminal and immigration law, "crime of violence" includes, among other offenses, any felony that "by its nature, involves a substantial risk that physical force against the person or property of another may be used."[78] The definition used for sentencing purposes, in contrast, lacks this language.[79] Even if an immigration judge deemed a particular conviction to be a crime of violence, therefore, does not mean that the migrant is necessarily subject to the crime of violence sentencing enhancement available in illegal entry and illegal reentry cases. The bottom line is that attorneys need to be wary of assuming that sentencing calculations are straightforward. They are anything but. What is clear, though, is that fitting inside or outside many of the categories that can result in enhancements is of obvious significance to defendants whose potential sentence can change drastically depending on where they fall.

Aside from trying to avoid the enhancements discussed above, defense attorneys should also be aware of the availability of a downward

---

77. *Id.* at § 2L1.2 cmt. (3)((A).

78. INA § 101(a)(43)(F) (referencing 18 U.S.C. § 16(b)).

79. U.S. Sentencing Guidelines Manual § 2L1.2 cmt. (1)(B)(iii).

departure for cultural ties to the United States. As of November 1, 2010, judges can depart downward from a guidelines range if a defendant's illegal entry or reentry conviction is linked to long-time residence in the United States.[80]

Just as they must do regarding a client's guilt, defense attorneys must be attuned to the risks that the Sentencing Guidelines present. A voluntary departure order, for example, normally avoids many of the adverse consequences associated with removal proceedings, but that may not be true of sentencing enhancements. Relying on language from decisions of two other circuits, the Fifth Circuit has held that a migrant who left the United States of his own volition under a voluntary departure order was nonetheless deported for purposes of an enhancement.[81]

> **Practice Pointer**
>
> The illegal entry and illegal reentry statutes contain possible sentence ranges. Identifying these is fairly straightforward. The Sentencing Guidelines, however, will largely drive the sentence that a defendant actually receives and these are often anything but clear. Attorneys must carefully consider enhancements and downward departures provided by the Guidelines before advising defendants about the all-important sentence they are likely to receive. This requires a careful assessment of a defendant's likely base offense level and criminal history points. Importantly, the ultimate sentence rests in the hands of the court, which has a remarkable amount of latitude through which to exercise its discretion. Attorneys, consequently, should never lead a defendant to believe that they can predict the actual sentence meted out.

Other Crimes

Illegal entry and illegal reentry are undeniably the most commonly prosecuted federal immigration crimes. They are not, however, the only two crimes in the INA. Throughout the late 1980s and 1990s Congress added or expanded the range of immigration activity criminalized by federal law. Because these offenses are prosecuted relatively infrequently, this book will do little more than flag the basic contours of several of these offenses.

---

80. *Id.* at § 2L1.2 cmt. (8).
81. United States v. Murillo-Acosta, 751 F.3d 682, 683 (5th Cir. 2014) (citing dicta from First and Second Circuit decisions).

A host of crimes are related to migrant registration requirements. Most migrants are required to register with the federal government and submit to fingerprinting.[82] Willful failure to do so is punishable by up to six months imprisonment.[83] Similarly, knowingly including false statements on the registration form can bring as much as six months imprisonment.[84] Once registered, migrants are required to carry with them at all times registration documents issued by the federal government. Failure to comply risks a misdemeanor conviction punishable by up to thirty days imprisonment, though it does not apply to individuals who never actually registered.[85] Migrants are then required to keep the federal government up-to-date on their address and not doing so can carry as much as thirty days of jail time.[86] Not surprisingly, counterfeiting a registration document is also criminalized, though much more severely—as much as five years imprisonment is possible.[87]

Much better known than the registration crimes is the criminal prohibition against smuggling a migrant into the United States. The INA punishes anyone who encourages a migrant to come to the United States without authorization, helps a migrant enter the United States outside a port of entry, helps such a migrant move throughout the country, or helps such a person to evade detection once here.[88] In effect, this series of provisions criminalize facilitating the clandestine entry into the United States that has existed for generations. While these provisions certainly target individuals who smuggle migrants into the United States for financial compensation, they also include individuals who do so without requiring payment—for example, political activists who participated in the 1980s "sanctuary movement" by helping Central American migrants enter the United States and avoid immigration officials.[89] Though these

---

82. INA § 262(a).
83. INA § 266(a).
84. INA § 266(c).
85. INA § 264(e); United States v. Mendez-Lopez, 528 F. Supp. 972, 973 (N.D. Okla. 1981).
86. INA § 266(b).
87. INA § 266(d).
88. INA § 274(a)(1)(A)(i)-(iv).
89. United States v. Aguilar, 883 F.2d 662, 667 (9th Cir. 1989).

provisions sweep broadly, they do not include merely providing shelter to an unauthorized migrant if done without the intent of helping the migrant evade immigration officials.[90] Conviction for one of these crimes can result in a wide range of punishments, most significantly life imprisonment if someone died during commission of the crime.[91]

Detention and Bail

As with other crimes, detention is one of the most poignant features of the criminal process that occurs when a migrant is charged with an immigration crime. When it comes to predisposition detention—that is, detention before a court concludes the case—immigration crimes lead the way. People charged with an immigration crime are more likely to be detained while criminal proceedings are pending than defendants charged with any other type of federal crime. While 87.5 percent of immigration crime defendants in 2010 were detained at any time prior to disposition, 86.1 percent of those charged with a violent crime and 85.6 percent of weapons crime defendants, the two next highest categories, saw the inside of a jail or prison during this stage of the criminal process.[92] Taking a broader view of the entire federal criminal law enforcement system's predisposition detention practice in 2010, immigration crime defendants made up 45 percent of all people detained prior to case disposition.[93] Immigration crime defendants, therefore, are not only the most likely group to spend time in jail awaiting their case outcomes; they also occupy an enormous space in the federal government's criminal detention system. Given immigration crime defendants' high likelihood of being detained pending criminal proceedings, getting out of jail is an unsurprisingly important concern for many migrants.

The Bail Reform Act of 1984 (BRA) sets out the parameters of release from federal confinement pending criminal proceedings, sentencing, or

---

90. United States v. Vargas-Cordon, 733 F.3d 366, 382 (2nd Cir. 2013); *see* DelRio-Mocci v. Connolly Properties, Inc., 672 F.3d 241, 246 (3d Cir. 2012).

91. INA § 274(a)(1)(B)(iv).

92. MARK MOTIVANS, FEDERAL JUSTICE STATISTICS 16 tbl.9 (Dec. 2013).

93. *Id.* at 16.

appeal.[94] Despite being an integral part of the criminal justice process, the Supreme Court held in its 1987 decision *United States v. Salerno* that pretrial detention governed by the BRA is not a form of punishment.[95] Instead, it is a form of civil regulatory detention just like detention pending removal proceedings.[96] The *Salerno* Court, in fact, cited two immigration detention cases for support.[97] Its civil designation means that pretrial detention is governed by a lower burden of proof than required to prove guilt: instead of beyond a reasonable doubt, courts use the common preponderance of the evidence standard for flight risk assessments and a clear and convincing evidence standard for dangerousness assessments.[98]

Though the BRA presumes that most detained defendants are entitled to release, it provides two critical justifications that the government can seek to show to overcome the presumption of liberty.[99] Detention, the statute provides, is required if "the judicial officer finds that no condition or combination of conditions will reasonably assure the appearance of the person as required and the safety of any other person and the community."[100] Importantly, individuals previously convicted of a crime of violence, as well as others,[101] are subject to a rebuttable presumption that no set of conditions can reasonably assure public safety.[102]

To protect detainees' due process rights, the BRA requires multiple procedural protections that the *Salerno* Court described as "extensive safeguards" that help immunize it from constitutional challenge.[103] Defendants charged with an offense and awaiting criminal proceedings to

94. Bail Reform Act of 1984, Pub. L. 98-473, Title II, §§ 201-210, 98 Stat. 1837 (codified at 18 U.S.C. §§ 3141–3156).

95. 481 U.S. 739, 747 (1987).

96. *Id.* at 747–48.

97. *Id.* at 748 (1987) (citing Carlson v. Landon, 342 U.S. 524, 537–42 (1952) and Wong Wing v. United States, 163 U.S. 228 (1896)).

98. United States v. Xulam, 84 F.3d 441, 442 (D.C. Cir. 1996); United States v. Orta, 760 F.2d 887, 891 (8th Cir. 1985).

99. 18 U.S.C. § 3142(a); *see* United States v. Sabhnani, 493 F.3d 63, 75 (2nd Cir. 2007) (regarding burden on government).

100. 18 U.S.C. § 3142(e)(1).

101. 18 U.S.C. § 3142(e)(2)(A); 18 U.S.C. § 3156(a)(4) (defining "crime of violence" under the BRA to include verbatim the same definition used for immigration law purposes but including a few minor expansions).

102. 18 U.S.C. § 3142(e)(2).

103. United States v. Salerno, 481 U.S. 739, 752 (1987); *see* Fed. R. Crim. P. 46.

follow their course are entitled to a prompt hearing in which a magistrate decides whether they ought to receive bail or remain detained.[104] This hearing "shall be held immediately upon the person's first appearance before the judicial officer" or within three or five days (excluding weekends and holidays) if the detainee or government, respectively, requests a continuance,[105] but failure to do so does not require release from detention.[106] Though the BRA does not explain what "first appearance" means, there is wide agreement that this is a hearing prescribed by Federal Rule of Criminal Procedure 5, which usually takes place within 48 hours of arrest.[107] At a bail hearing, a detained defendant is entitled to counsel, to present and cross-examine witnesses, testify on her own behalf, and present evidence. Rules of evidence do not apply, thus hearsay and other types of evidence that would normally be excluded from criminal proceedings are admissible.[108] Importantly, any evidence admitted during the detention hearing must address the two justifications for detention: dangerousness or flight risk. A defendant may be released on her own recognizance, an unsecured bond, or a combination of conditions.[109] The statute sets out a list of four factors that judges are to consider when deciding whether some set of conditions can reasonably assure the defendant's presence as well as public safety: the 1) nature and circumstances in which the charged offense allegedly occurred; 2) weight of the evidence against the defendant; 3) defendant's history and characteristics, including criminal history, family ties, and length of residence in the community; and 4) seriousness of any danger release would pose to the public.[110]

Though the statute does not include immigration status, courts often consider it through the third statutory factor, the defendant's history and characteristics, as a means of gauging whether a defendant is likely to

104. *Salerno*, 481 U.S. at 748; 18 U.S.C. § 3142(a).
105. 18 U.S.C. § 3142(f).
106. United States v. Montalvo-Murillo, 495 U.S. 711, 716–17 (1990).
107. United States v. Al-Azzawy, 768 F.2d 1141, 1144 (9th Cir. 1985), *abrogated on other grounds by, Montalvo-Murillo*, 495 U.S. 711; County of Riverside v. McLaughlin, 500 U.S. 44, 56 (1991).
108. 18 U.S.C. § 3142(f).
109. 18 U.S.C. § 3142(b)-(c).
110. 18 U.S.C. § 3142(g).

flee.[111] In one case, the Ninth Circuit, for example, discussed reputations as respected businessmen that two defendants had in foreign countries in assessing their character and a lack of personal or professional ties to the United States in assessing their connection to the United States.[112] In another case, the court considered that a defendant had obtained permanent residence in the United States, had many relatives in the region of the United States where he had spent almost a decade, and had fled his country of citizenship.[113] A federal district court in Florida also noted that a defendant's immigration law history—presumably a reference to past removals—"weighs heavily" on its flight-risk assessment.[114]

Special attention needs to be given to migrants who the government alleges are not lawful permanent residents. In an interesting twist to the standard detention and bail process that the BRA provides, Congress created a special procedure for certain migrants. The statute requires that a judge presiding over a detention hearing who learns that a detained migrant is not a lawful permanent resident then determine whether "the person may flee or pose a danger to any other person or the community," very much as is required under the usual detention hearing procedure.[115] If the judge concludes that a detained migrant poses such a risk, then the judge is required to order the migrant's detention for up to ten days (excluding weekends and holidays) and order the prosecutor to notify DHS of the migrant's presence.[116] The provision's purpose is quite clearly to afford immigration officials the opportunity to initiate removal proceedings and place the migrant into civil immigration detention. If DHS fails to take the migrant into its custody, the standard BRA provisions discussed above govern continued detention and bail pending criminal proceedings.[117] To avoid being subjected to this special detention process, a detained defendant bears the burden of proving that she is a United States

---

111. *See* United States v. Tapia, 924 F. Supp. 2d 1093, 1097 (D.S.D. 2013).
112. United States v. Townsend, 897 F.2d 989, 995–96 (9th Cir. 1990).
113. United States v. Motamedi, 767 F.2d 1403, 1407–08 (9th Cir. 1985).
114. United States v. Adomako, 150 F. Supp. 2d 1302, 1307 (M.D. Fla. 2001).
115. 18 U.S.C. § 3142(d)(2).
116. 18 U.S.C. § 3142(d)(1)(B).
117. 18 U.S.C. § 3142(d); *see* United States v. Chavez-Rivas, 536 F. Supp. 2d 962, 964 (E.D. Wis. 2008); *Adomako*, 150 F. Supp. 2d at 1307.

citizen or lawful permanent resident.[118] This is a peculiar requirement since traditionally the government bears the burden of proving that a person found in the United States is not a United States citizen.

Aside from the relevance of immigration status to flight risk or the special provision for nonlawful permanent residents, a contentious issue regarding detained migrants that has arisen with increasing frequency in recent years concerns the use of immigration detainers (for an in-depth discussion of detainers, including the legality of issuing and enforcing them, see chapter 10). Detainers are little more than requests by ICE to a local or state law enforcement agency to continue holding the named individual while ICE decides whether to take custody of the individual itself for the purpose of initiating removal proceedings. A detainer does not automatically result in transfer of the named individual to ICE custody. Instead, the detainer request attempts to prolong detention by local or state officials by up to 48 hours (excluding weekends and holidays) after the criminal proceeding, including any sentence that resulted from conviction, has ended. Indeed, in many instances DHS will issue a detainer but will not take the named individual into its custody. When this happens, the criminal justice system runs its course while civil immigration proceedings are on hold.

Federal courts grappling with whether or not to release a detained migrant, therefore, have been forced to decide how much weight to give detainers. To date, no federal court of appeals has conclusively announced the proper weight to place on an immigration detainer presented during a pretrial detention determination pursuant to the BRA. The federal district courts that have considered the issue, however, conclude that detainers can be considered, but are either minimally relevant or not relevant at all. Quite simply, the presence of an immigration detainer does not preclude normal operation of the BRA's provisions.[119] Judges are still required to assess a defendant's risk of absconding or endangering others. As part of that assessment, they may consider the existence of a detainer,[120] but they cannot conclude that the possibility that a migrant

---

118. 18 U.S.C. § 3142(d).
119. United States v. Trujillo-Alvarez, 900 F. Supp. 2d 1167, 1177 (D. Or. 2012).
120. *Id.* at 1173.

will be detained by ICE pending removal proceedings will result in her failure to appear for criminal proceedings. The risk that a defendant may fail to appear for criminal proceedings that the BRA guards against "is limited to the risk that the defendant may flee or abscond, that is, that he would fail to appear by virtue of his own volition, actions and will. If the government—through ICE or any other authority—prevents his appearance, he has not 'failed' to appear."[121] Without additional proof suggesting the possibility of fleeing, a detainer does not justify detention under the BRA.[122]

Cases involving a detainer's relevance to pretrial detention lead to the unmistakable conclusion that judges are exasperated by the federal government's attempts to have district courts order detention where there is insufficient evidence to show that the detainee poses a safety risk or is likely to abscond. A Minnesota district court's characterization of the tension in which prosecutors placed it illustrates this point. According to the court,

> The problem here is not that defendant will absent himself from the jurisdiction, but that two Article II agencies will not coordinate their respective efforts. The Executive, in the person of the Attorney General, wishes to prosecute defendant. The same Executive, in the person of the Secretary of Homeland Security for ICE, may want to deport him. It is not appropriate for an Article III judge to resolve Executive Branch turf battles. The Constitution empowers this Court to apply the will of Congress upon a criminal defendant on a personal and individualized basis. This Court ought not run interference for the prosecuting arm of the government.[123]

In effect, courts agree that the BRA's basic structure governs detention decisions largely without regard to ICE's decision to issue an immigration detainer. Detention hearings are meant to gauge the least restrictive

---

121. United States v. Villanueva-Martinez, 707 F. Supp. 2d 855, 858 (N.D. Iowa 2010).
122. United States v. Tapia, 924 F. Supp. 2d 1093, 1097 (D.S.D. 2013).
123. United States v. Barrera-Omana, 638 F. Supp. 2d 1108, 1111–12 (D. Minn. 2009).

means by which the court can reasonably ensure that a criminal defendant will appear from criminal proceedings and avoid endangering others. They are not meant to facilitate the government's attempt to remove an individual.

As is so often the case, the practical reality that migrants face is different and perhaps more important than courts' formal position. If released from pretrial custody, migrants against whom ICE has issued a detainer are likely to be taken into ICE's custody. At that point, ICE is very likely to initiate removal proceedings. Along with removal proceedings comes the lack of appointed counsel and ICE's power to transfer its detainees among its vast network of detention centers spread throughout the country. All of this may ultimately prevent criminal proceedings from moving forward, but it will do nothing to help the migrant remain in the United States if that is what she desires. For this reason, migrants sometimes do not request bail.

That said, there is some unresolved tension between immigration detainers and the BRA's provisions that suggests that federal courts should prohibit ICE from taking a migrant into custody outside the special provisions for nonlawful permanent residents. The BRA clearly states that if ICE fails to take custody of a nonlawful permanent resident who poses a risk of fleeing or endangering others, the normal BRA provisions apply "notwithstanding the applicability of other provisions of law governing release pending trial or deportation or exclusion proceedings."[124] The statute and regulation authorizing the use of immigration detainers are both provisions of law governing release pending removal proceedings, thus they would seem to clearly fall within this clause that the BRA renders subservient to the BRA's normal provisions. Congress appears to have made a deliberate choice to privilege the BRA over civil detention or release provisions contained in the INA. Were courts to allow ICE to take custody of a migrant after expiration of the ten days provided for this purpose by 18 U.S.C. § 3142(d), that provision would be meaningless. What would be the effect of a ten-day cap if ICE could get another 48 hours (not counting weekends or holidays) simply by issuing an immigration detainer?

---

124. 18 U.S.C. § 3142(d).

There is a similarly intuitive basis for concluding that ICE should not be allowed to detain migrants who have been released pending criminal prosecution except if ICE is actively attempting to remove the migrant. Detention has an undeniably detrimental impact on a person's ability to defend herself from criminal prosecution. This is only compounded by the fact that ICE can move detainees throughout the United States and that it has a remarkable track record of making communications between detainees and attorneys extremely difficult. Unless done expressly for the purpose of pursuing removal, shifting a migrant's custody from the United States Marshals Service, which houses pretrial detainees, to ICE, which is in charge of civil immigration detainees, makes no sense given that both are units of the Justice Department. Allowing ICE to detain a migrant who is in criminal proceedings but against whom it has not initiated removal proceedings allows ICE to trump Congress's directive that it is up to a federal judge to decide whether a migrant deserves to be detained pending criminal prosecution.

Post-Conviction Concerns

An overwhelming number of people charged with an immigration crime are ultimately convicted. According to statistics maintained by the federal courts, 96.6 percent of people charged with an immigration crime in a federal district court in the twelve months preceding March 31, 2013, were convicted, most after pleading guilty. Because the vast majority of immigration crime defendants in district court were charged with illegal reentry (21,039 illegal reentry defendants of a total of 25,380 total immigration crime defendants), it is worthwhile to consider those conviction rates separately. Among illegal reentry defendants that year, 97.4 percent were convicted, all but forty-four of whom pleaded guilty.[125] Importantly, these statistics do not include illegal entry prosecutions because almost none are prosecuted in district courts. Instead, federal magistrate judges deal with almost all illegal entry cases—97 percent in fiscal year 2010.[126] Unfortunately there are no data publicly available about conviction rates

125. ADMINISTRATIVE OFFICE OF THE U.S. COURTS, FEDERAL JUDICIAL CASELOAD STATISTICS: MARCH 31, 2013 [hereinafter 2013 FEDERAL COURT STATISTICS], tbl.D-4 (2013).
126. MOTIVANS, *supra* note 8, at 19.

for the illegal entry cases handled by magistrate judges. The few illegal entry prosecutions that take place in district court suggest that conviction rates are very high. In the year ending in March 31, 2013, 569 people were charged with illegal entry in a federal district court and 545 were convicted (535 by guilty plea).[127] This is a conviction rate of 95.8 percent.

Since all but a handful of people charged with illegal entry or illegal reentry can expect to be convicted, the post-conviction process is highly relevant to migrants and attorneys. Most can expect to see some jail time immediately after conviction. In fiscal year 2010, for example, 81 percent of people convicted of an immigration crime were sentenced to prison, 14 percent received a suspended sentence, 4 percent received nothing more than probation, and fewer than 1 percent received a fine only.[128] Actual prison terms differ for illegal entry and illegal reentry, but they tend to hover between one and two years. Again in 2010, the median prison sentence for illegal entry offenders was eighteen months, a drop from the twenty-four months median sentence in 2002, whereas the median illegal reentry prison term in 2010 was fifteen months, also a drop from twenty-eight months in 2002.[129] Even these sentences vary drastically depending where the migrant was convicted. In Arizona, immigration offenders convicted in 2010 tended to receive twenty-four months imprisonment while in neighboring New Mexico they received two months.[130]

Having been convicted of an immigration crime, removal is an obvious concern. The INA prohibits most offenders from being removed while serving a prison term no matter the crime and no matter whether the migrant is in state or federal custody.[131] As if to complicate things, Congress included exceptions for some but not all nonviolent offenses.[132] Congress, it seems, wanted to be sure that the most serious offenders served their criminal sentence before facing the possibility of removal. To complicate things further, the exceptions differ depending on whether a migrant is in state or federal custody. Migrants convicted of

---

127. 2013 FEDERAL COURT STATISTICS, *supra* note 125, at tbl.D-4.
128. MOTIVANS, *supra* note 8, at 29.
129. *Id.* at 30 tbl.10.
130. *Id.*
131. INA § 241(a)(4)(A).
132. INA § 241(a)(4)(B).

illicit trafficking in a controlled substance, for example, cannot be removed while serving a federal prison sentence, but they can be removed while serving a state prison sentence.[133]

Migrants convicted of any crime in a federal district court may also be subject to removal through the criminal sentencing process. Since 1994, Congress has authorized federal prosecutors to seek a judicial order of removal as part of the sentencing process for any convicted migrant who is deportable on the basis of criminal activity listed in INA § 237(a)(2)(A).[134] To do so, a prosecutor must follow a multipart process detailed by the statute. First, prior to trial or entry of a guilty plea, the prosecutor must inform the court and defendant that it plans to seek removal as part of the sentence.[135] With DHS's agreement and at least thirty days before sentencing, the prosecutor must then explain to the court the factual basis for the government's allegation that the defendant is not a United States citizen and why it claims the migrant is deportable under INA § 237(a)(2)(A), the provision that includes the crimes involving moral turpitude, aggravated felony, and a few other crime-based grounds of deportation.[136] Interestingly, a judicial order of removal cannot be issued if the basis for the migrant's deportation is a conviction for a controlled substance offense. The defendant is entitled to a reasonable opportunity to examine the evidence, cross-examine any witnesses the government calls, and offer evidence of her own.[137] She is also entitled to make a claim for relief. If she establishes her prima facie eligibility for relief, DHS is required to provide the court with its recommendation and the court decides whether to grant relief or not.[138]

While the judicial removal provision appears to facilitate removal, in some instances it can have the opposite effect. A deportable migrant who is eligible for relief can use the judicial removal statute to seek the government's support in securing relief from removal. Because INA § 238(c)(2)

---

133. *Id.*
134. INA § 238(c). The INA contains two sections labeled § 238(c). The provision discussed here is the second of the two.
135. INA § 238(c)(2)(A).
136. INA § 238(c)(2)(B).
137. INA § 238(c)(2)(D)(i).
138. INA § 238(c)(2)(C).

(C) requires DHS to give the sentencing court its recommendation about whether relief ought to be granted, a defendant can include a request for a favorable recommendation about relief in its plea negotiations checklist. It may be in the government's interest to agree to a favorable recommendation in exchange for a quick plea or other cooperation by the defendant.

In an interesting twist, a single line in the federal statute authorizing supervised release of convicted individuals appears to allow a more bare-bones alternative to judicial removal under INA § 238(c)(4). That provision, 18 U.S.C. § 3583(d), provides in whole, "If an alien defendant is subject to deportation, the court may provide, as a condition of supervised release, that he be deported and remain outside the United States, and may order that he be delivered to a duly authorized immigration official for such deportation." This provision precedes § 238(c)(4)'s judicial removal statute added in 1994 by many years (indeed an earlier version was enacted in 1931) and lacks the detailed procedural requirements of the newer statute.[139] Numerous courts of appeals have held that the older § 3583(d) simply allows sentencing courts to order, as a condition of supervised release, that a migrant be turned over to immigration officials for the civil removal process to run its course.[140] Anything else, these courts suggest, would tread on the complex procedures found in the INA that Congress created to govern removal.

A similar clause appears in the federal probation statute. That provision purports to grant sentencing courts the discretionary power to order deportation "as a condition of probation, if, after notice and hearing pursuant to such section, the Attorney General demonstrates by clear and convincing evidence that the alien is deportable."[141] Following the reasoning that courts of appeals have used regarding supervised release, the Tenth Circuit concluded that allowing courts to order deportation as a condition

---

139. Act of March 2, 1931, ch. 371, 46 Stat. 1469.

140. *See, e.g.*, United States v. Romeo, 122 F.3d 941, 943–44 (11th Cir. 1997); United States v. Quaye, 57 F.3d 447, 449–51 (5th Cir. 1995); United States v. Sanchez, 923 F.2d 236, 237 (1st Cir. 1991).

141. 18 U.S.C. § 3563(b)(21).

of probation would be "inconsistent" with the INA's statutory removal scheme.[142]

Whatever happens in the criminal sentencing process, once immigration offenders complete their sentences they then face the prospect of removal through the civil immigration system. This is true even for migrants against whom the government sought a judicial removal order that the court refused to issue.[143] For migrants convicted of illegal entry and illegal reentry, the likelihood of detention and removal is high given that they have a criminal record and a court has already concluded that they lack authorization to be in the United States. The INA does not require detention pending removal proceedings of individuals whose sole offense is an immigration crime, but DHS does consider them to be "criminal aliens" just like every other migrant convicted of a crime. Furthermore, lacking authorization to be in the United States, they will be removed unless they qualify for some type of relief.

Further Reading

Lena Graber and Amy Schnitzer, *The Bail Reform Act and Release from Criminal and Immigration Custody for Federal Criminal Defendants* (2013), http://www.nationalimmigrationproject.org/legalresources/practice_advisories/pa_Federal_Bail_Advisory.pdf.

Doug Keller, *Re-thinking Illegal Entry and Re-entry*, 44 LOY. U. CHI. L.J. 65 (2012).

U.S. Sentencing Commission, *Office of General Counsel, Immigration Primer* (2013), *available at* http://www.ussc.gov/sites/default/files/pdf/training/primers/Primer_Immigration.pdf.

---

142. United States v. Jalilian, 896 F.2d 447, 448 (10th Cir. 1990); *see* United States v. Abushaar, 761 F.2d 954, 960–61 (3d Cir. 1985); United States v. Castillo-Burgos, 501 F.2d 217, 219–20 (9th Cir. 1974), *abrogated on other grounds by*, United States v. Rubio-Villareal, 967 F.2d 294 (9th Cir. 1992).

143. INA § 238(c)(4).

CHAPTER 7

State Immigration Crimes

Since the late nineteenth century, conventional wisdom has held that the federal government dictates immigration law. Congress and the president, the view holds, enact laws, and the various law enforcement divisions within the Executive Branch enforce them. As the previous chapter illustrated, there is certainly a great amount of truth to this standard understanding of contemporary crimmigration law. But this is not the end of the story. In the years before immigration law became recognized as the exclusive province of the federal government, states and cities regularly criminalized certain immigration activity. In 1787, for example, Georgia enacted a statute requiring that felons transported from another state be arrested, removed, and ordered to never return lest they risk death. A few years later, Massachusetts "criminalized the knowing landing of persons who had been convicted in another state or country of infamous crime."[1]

---

1. Gerald Neuman, *The Lost Century of American Immigration Law (1776-1876)*, 93 COLUM. L. REV. 1833, 1842–43 (1993).

Most other states in existence at the country's founding and in the decades that followed enacted similar statutes. Eventually this trend tapered off, and by the late nineteenth century state immigration lawmaking seemed effectively prohibited by the federal government's entrance into immigration law and the Supreme Court's acknowledgement that this area of law was properly left to Congress and the president.

Roughly a century later, this understanding began to change. In the final decades of the twentieth century and more so in the early decades of the twenty-first century, states returned to their interest in using criminal law and procedure as a means to target migrants. Arizona may have gained enormous notoriety for its attempts to criminalize various aspects of migrants' lives, but it has not been alone. Several other states have used their traditional powers to criminalize unwanted activity related to immigration. Between 2005 and 2009 alone, states and localities enacted 118 laws regarding the use of criminal law enforcement tools to target immigration. Researchers Huyen Pham and Pham Hoang Van, the pair who tallied this list, concluded that only thirty could be characterized as having a positive impact on migrants (e.g., allowing use of consular identification cards to obtain state services); the rest had a negative impact.[2] Regardless of the impact, these efforts have given states an important role in crimmigration law's creation and evolution.

This chapter discusses many of the ways through which states and their subdivisions—cities and counties—have used their criminal justice systems to make life more difficult for migrants. With fifty states and the District of Columbia all having separate criminal justice systems, this is necessarily a survey of disparate tactics. Still, a number of trends appear. In some instances, states have created new crimes aimed explicitly at migrants or at activity done exclusively or predominantly by migrants. At other times they have expanded state courts' power to order migrants detained pending criminal proceedings. And in other instances they have attempted to use their own law enforcement and judicial processes to increase the penalty of violating federal immigration law. Each

---

2. Huyen Pham & Pham Hoang Van, *Measuring the Climate for Immigrants: A State-By-State Analysis, in* STRANGE NEIGHBORS: THE ROLE OF STATES IN IMMIGRATION POL-ICY 21, 30 tbl.1.1 (Carissa Byrne Hessick & Gabriel J. Chin eds. 2014).

of these trends will be discussed in turn. First, though, we have to address a preliminary question: What authority do states have to criminalize immigration-related activity?

The Legality of State Crimmigration Laws

It has been quite clear since the late nineteenth century that immigration law lies in the federal government's hands. When California enacted a statute requiring shipmasters to pay a bond for certain migrants arriving on their vessels, the Supreme Court struck it down. "The passage of laws which concern the admission of citizens and subjects of foreign nations to our shores," the Court wrote in 1875, "belongs to Congress, and not the states. It has the power to regulate commerce with foreign nations. . . . If it be otherwise, a single state can at her pleasure embroil us in disastrous quarrels with other nations."[3] Inartfully, the Court implicitly referenced the Constitution's Foreign Affairs Clause and the Commerce Clause as potential sources of this newly recognized federal prerogative. Roughly a decade-and-a-half later, the Court began to solidify the source of the federal government's power to control immigration law that today remains the leading justification: sovereignty. "It is an accepted maxim of international law," the Court announced in *Nishimura Ekiu v. United States*, "that every sovereign nation has the power, inherent in sovereignty and essential to self-preservation, to forbid the entrance of foreigners . . . or to admit them only in such cases and upon such conditions as it may see fit to prescribe."[4] Sovereignty, transferred from the British Crown to the federal government at the moment of independence, allows—perhaps obligates—the federal government to dictate who may enter the United States and who must be kept out. To carry out this responsibility, Congress is authorized to enact statutes regulating immigration that the president is charged with enforcing.

The federal government's power to regulate immigration is more limited than the Supreme Court's sweeping language in these nineteenth-century opinions suggests. Congress and the president surely may enact

---

3. Chy Lung v. Freeman, 92 U.S. 275, 280 (1875).
4. 142 U.S. 651, 659 (1892).

statutes regulating which migrants are to be allowed to cross the imaginary boundaries into the United States that constitute our borders. As the INA attests, they have done so with vigor. That power, however, is not all that matters to migrants. Once in the United States migrants carry on their lives largely without encountering immigration officials or immigration law. Instead, migrants' ordinary activities, like the daily lives of United States citizens, largely involve interactions with state and local government officials, to the extent that they interact with officials of any government unit. Migrants drive vehicles subject to state laws enforced largely by local police. Their children generally attend schools operated by municipal school districts. And when they are prosecuted for a crime, they are usually required to appear in state courts. Each of these activities and many more small-time incidents of interacting with government officials as part of ordinary life are left to the discretion of the states. It is true, as the Supreme Court explained in 1875, that "by our Constitution, [the states] can hold no exterior relations with other nations,"[5] but it is equally true that, according to the Tenth Amendment, "[t]he powers not delegated to the United States by the Constitution . . . are reserved to the states respectively, or to the people."

This divided authority—federalism in the parlance of law—means that the states can enact legislation that significantly impacts migrants' lives without treading on the federal government's power to regulate cross-border movement. Legal scholar Hiroshi Motomura has described this distinction as the difference between direct and indirect regulation of migrants.[6] The federal government is permitted to directly regulate immigration as it does through the INA, but the states are capable of doing so indirectly by legislating in areas traditionally within their control. There are few areas of law more traditionally a part of states' legislative portfolios than criminal law and procedure. States enforced common law crimes (e.g., murder) since the earliest days of British colonization in what is now the United States and have enacted their own statutory crimes and procedures applicable to criminal proceedings (e.g., the right to counsel) since not long after. With independence and the adoption of

---

5. *Chy Lung*, 92 U.S. at 279.
6. Hiroshi Motomura, Immigration Outside the Law 58 (2014).

state constitutions, the states quickly began to embed various crimes and procedures, many of which remain with us today, into their foundational documents. State courts, meanwhile, have constantly been called upon to determine the exact contours of these substantive crimes and procedural requirements. Today, every state has a detailed penal code identifying substantive crimes and procedures, plus a well-developed body of judicial opinions refining those offenses and procedural requirements.

The federal-state division of labor regarding immigration regulation is usually fairly clear. The federal government and only the federal government can decide the criteria for admission into the United States. The same goes for decisions about who to remove. Meanwhile, for their part, the states can criminalize a wide variety of activity or adopt an array of procedural requirements. If it wanted, for example, Colorado could criminalize sending text messages while driving or guarantee that every person arrested was assigned an attorney.

The difficulty arises when states tread on federal power in one of two ways. First, states might attempt to weaken procedural protections guaranteed by federal law. For example, a state is prohibited from refusing to appoint counsel for a criminal defendant in a way that differs from what the Sixth Amendment requires. Nor could a state legislature enact a statute requiring police officers to arrest people solely for the purpose of checking immigration status because the Fourth Amendment requires probable cause that a person has committed a crime before that type of seizure is permissible. A statute that lowers the legal threshold that must be crossed for the government to be able to intrude into a person's affairs would be susceptible to a constitutional challenge. Second, states sometimes enact legislation that conflicts with federal law. For example, a state might criminalize the act of being physically present in the state without authorization to be physically present in the United States. This would conflict with Congress's deliberate decision to criminalize illegal entry and illegal reentry, but not unlawful presence alone.

Most legal challenges to state or local immigration laws in recent years have focused on the second problem, known as preemption. As a result, understanding crimmigration law requires understanding preemption's legal basis and effect on state and local efforts to regulate immigration.

Preemption

At its most basic, the doctrine of preemption is rather straightforward: Does a state or local law conflict with a federal law? Applied to immigration laws enacted by states, counties, or cities, preemption, as Hiroshi Motomura phrased it, asks: "Does state or local involvement in enforcement conflict with federal immigration law?"[7] Intuitively it is not hard to see why some form of conflict resolution mechanism has to exist in a system of separate sovereigns like the United States. There are bound to be many instances in which one government prohibits conduct that another allows. Sometimes one government will prohibit what another requires. How do we decide which law governs? In the United States, the second paragraph of Article VI of the Constitution gives us an answer when the conflict erupts between state and federal laws: "This Constitution, and the laws of the United States which shall be made in pursuance thereof . . . shall be the supreme law of the land; and the judges in every state shall be bound thereby, anything in the Constitution or laws of any State to the contrary notwithstanding." Often referred to as the Supremacy Clause, these words make it clear that state and local laws must give way to the federal Constitution and statutes.

The difficult task follows. When a party challenges a state or local law on the basis that it is preempted by federal law, courts must determine whether there is in fact a conflict between the two. Reams of ink have been spilled on the proper way to determine whether a conflict exists, but the Supreme Court has settled on three possibilities: express preemption, implied conflict preemption, and implied field preemption.

First, express preemption exists when Congress explicitly states in a statute that other laws in a particular area are preempted. An INA section on unlawful employment of migrants, for example, provides, "The provisions of this section preempt any State or local law imposing civil or criminal sanctions (other than through licensing and similar laws) upon those who employ, or recruit or refer for a fee for employment, unauthorized aliens."[8] In adopting this language, the Supreme Court has held, Congress expressly preempted subfederal attempts to impose civil

---

7. *Id.* at 128.
8. INA § 274A(h)(2).

or criminal sanctions on those who employ unauthorized migrants except through licensing statutes.[9]

The second form of preemption, implied conflict preemption, actually takes two forms: impossibility and obstacle. Impossibility implied conflict preemption exists when it would be impossible for someone to comply with both a state or local law and a federal law. A Wisconsin statute that prohibited maple syrup from being labeled in a certain way that was required by a federal statute was preempted, the Supreme Court held, because it was impossible for maple syrup producers to comply with both.[10] Obstacle implied conflict preemption exists when a state or local law impedes an important objective of a federal law. For example, the National Labor Relations Act (NLRA) encourages workers to file unfair labor practice charges against employers with the National Labor Relations Board (NLRB) as opposed to pursuing other tactics such as strikes. A Florida statute that denied unemployment benefits to anyone who filed an unfair labor practice charge with the NLRB, the Supreme Court held, was preempted because it interfered with Congress's objective of encouraging parties to resolve labor disputes through NLRB proceedings rather than strikes or other means.[11]

Third, implied field preemption occurs when Congress regulates so heavily in an area that it evidences an intent that federal law be the sole regulatory scheme in this area or where Congress has legislated in an area "in which the federal interest is so dominant that the federal system will be assumed to preclude enforcement of state laws on the same subject."[12] An example of implied field preemption came from Pennsylvania when the legislature enacted a statute that required migrants to register with the state every year. The Supreme Court concluded that the Pennsylvania statute was field preempted because Congress had adopted a "broad and comprehensive" federal statutory scheme regulating migrants' entry and presence in the United States, including a requirement that they register with the federal government.[13]

---

9. Chamber of Commerce v. Whiting, 131 S. Ct. 1968, 1977 (2011).
10. McDermott v. State of Wisconsin, 228 U.S. 115, 126–27 (1913).
11. Nash v. Florida Industrial Commission, 389 U.S. 235, 239 (1967).
12. Rice v. Santa Fe Elevator Corp., 331 U.S. 218, 230 (1947).
13. Hines v. Davidowitz, 312 U.S. 52, 59–60, 69 (1941).

Practice Pointer

The Supreme Court recognizes three forms of preemption:

- Express preemption occurs when a federal statute explicitly states that subfederal laws are preempted.
- Implied conflict preemption
  - Impossibility implied conflict preemption occurs when it would be impossible for a person to comply with federal and subfederal requirements.
  - Obstacle implied conflict preemption occurs when a subfederal law impedes an important objective of federal law.
- Implied field preemption occurs when federal regulation in an area is so heavy that it occupies the field or when the federal interest is so dominant that federal law is assumed to preclude enforcement of subfederal laws.

States' power to push the boundaries of crimmigration law came to a head when the Supreme Court took up the federal government's challenge to a wide-ranging Arizona statute intended to push out unauthorized migrants—"attrition through enforcement," the statute's opening lines explained.[14] Formally titled the Support Our Law Enforcement and Safe Neighborhoods Act, the contested statute is more commonly referred to as S.B. 1070 (short for Senate Bill 1070, its denomination in the Arizona Senate). Though civil rights groups challenged the statute on a variety of bases, the federal government took the extraordinary step of bringing its own lawsuit against Arizona in which it claimed that federal laws preempted four sections of the state statute. The federal government claimed that the following sections were preempted:

- § 2(B) which requires that police officers check the immigration status, where practicable, of all people stopped, detained, or arrested "where reasonable suspicion exists that the person is an alien and is unlawfully present" and "requires officers to verify—with the federal government—the immigration status of all arrestees before they are released, regardless of whether or not reasonable suspicion exists that the arrestee is an undocumented immigrant";

---

14. 2010 Ariz. Legis. Serv. ch. 113, § 1 (West).

- § 3 which "essentially makes it a state crime for unauthorized immigrants to violate federal registration laws";
- § 5(C) which makes it a state crime for an undocumented person to apply for, solicit, or perform work in Arizona;
- § 6 which permits warrantless arrests if probable cause exists that a suspect "has committed any public offense that makes the person removable from the United States."[15]

In *Arizona v. United States*, the Supreme Court held that three of the four challenged provisions—§§ 3, 5(C), and 6—were preempted. Section 3, the Court held, concerns migrant registration, an area in which Congress has "occupied the field."[16] Section 5(C), the Court went on, is impliedly preempted because, by imposing criminal penalties where Congress chose not to, it poses an obstacle to federal laws prohibiting employment of unauthorized migrants.[17] Similarly, § 6, the Court added, "creates an obstacle to the full purposes and objectives of Congress" by authorizing state officers greater authority to arrest possibly removable individuals than does the INA.[18]

The Court allowed only one provision, § 2(B), to stand. Often described derisively as the "show-me-your-papers" provision, § 2(B) was perhaps the most contentious of all S.B. 1070 sections. By requiring police officers to investigate the immigration status of a person otherwise stopped, detained, or arrested, § 2(B) dramatically augments the immigration consequences of encountering any part of the criminal justice system. Expanding state and local police officers' role in flagging potentially removable individuals to the federal government, however, is not necessarily unconstitutional. The Court made much of the fact that a number of provisions of federal law envision state and local cooperation with federal immigration officials. INA § 287(g)(10)(A), the Court noted, allows state officers to communicate with federal immigration officials about

---

15. For explanations of the challenged sections, see United States v. Arizona, 641 F.3d 339, 347, 355, 357, 360 (9th Cir. 2011), *aff'd and rev'd in part and remanded by*, Arizona v. United States, 132 S. Ct. 2492 (2012).

16. *Arizona*, 132 S. Ct. at 2502.

17. *Id.*

18. *Id.* at 2507.

anyone's immigration status. Likewise, 8 U.S.C. § 1373(c) "obligate[s] ICE to respond to any request made by state officials for verification of a person's citizenship or immigration status."[19] To the five justices who joined the majority opinion, these and other federal laws were sufficient proof that "[c]onsultation between federal and state officials is an important feature of the immigration system."[20] S.B. 1070's § 2(B) does nothing to disrupt this consultation. If anything, it merely increases the amount of consultation that would occur by requiring all Arizona police officers to ask DHS to verify the immigration status of people who meet the criteria specified in § 2(B). DHS can then do as it wishes, including nothing, with whatever information it obtains from the Arizona officers.

Though the Court concluded that Congress permitted routine follow-up checks as part of the normal policing practices of state officers, the Court warned that § 2(B) could venture into unconstitutionality if applied too broadly. An ordinary stop or arrest that is prolonged for no reason except to check a person's immigration status "would raise constitutional concerns," the Court noted before citing to two Fourth Amendment cases.[21] It might also disrupt federal laws regarding removal, thereby raising the prospect of being preempted.[22] The Court then took pains to provide multiple ways that Arizona state courts could limit § 2(B)'s breadth so as to avoid these potential constitutional infirmities. State courts could interpret § 2(B) to prohibit officers from prolonging an otherwise lawful stop solely to ask DHS about the stopped person's immigration status. Courts could adopt much the same reading regarding otherwise lawfully arrested individuals: § 2(B) does not allow prolonged detention.[23] Building off the Court's analysis, legal scholar Christopher N. Lasch suggests that ICE's heavy reliance on immigration detainers violates the Fourth Amendment because it prolongs detention solely to verify immigration

19. *Id.* at 2508.
20. *Id.*
21. *Id.* at 2509 (citing Arizona v. Johnson, 555 U.S. 323 (2009), and Illinois v. Caballes, 543 U.S. 405 (2005)).
22. *Arizona*, 132 S. Ct. at 2509.
23. *Id.*

status, a position that several courts have recently adopted (see chapter 10 for a detailed discussion of immigration detainers).[24]

The Court's decision in *Arizona* quickly reverberated through the court system as other states' statutes were challenged on preemption grounds. Louisiana's Supreme Court, for example, held that a state statute criminalizing operating a vehicle without authorization to be present in the United Statute was preempted. The statute, the court held, "operates in the field of alien registration and is, therefore, preempted by federal law under the Supremacy Clause of the U.S. Constitution," relying explicitly on the *Arizona* reasoning.[25] Similarly, the Fifth Circuit held that a variety of criminal ordinances related to housing adopted by the Dallas suburb of Farmers Branch were preempted.[26] More closely related to Arizona's S.B. 1070, the Fourth Circuit held that state police officers are constitutionally precluded from detaining or arresting individuals for no reason except on suspicion of having violated a civil immigration law. "[A]llowing local law enforcement officers to arrest individuals for civil immigration violations," the court determined, "would infringe on the substantial discretion Congress entrusted to the Attorney General in making removability decisions, which often require the weighing of complex diplomatic, political, and economic considerations."[27] *Arizona* also led to the demise of South Carolina legislation modeled on S.B. 1070. The Supremacy Clause, the Fourth Circuit held in that case, preempted South Carolina's attempts to criminalize "(1) a person unlawfully present in the United States to conceal, harbor, or shelter herself from detection, or allow herself to be transported within the state; (2) a third party to participate in concealing, sheltering, or transporting a person unlawfully present in the United States; (3) an alien 18 years or older to fail to carry an alien registration card; and (4) an individual to display or possess a false identification card for the purpose of proving lawful presence."[28] Legislation enacted in Georgia, known

---

24. *See* Christopher N. Lasch, *Federal Immigration Detainers After* Arizona v. United States, 46 LOY. L.A. L. REV. 629 (2013); Christopher N. Lasch, *Preempting Immigration Detainer Enforcement Under* Arizona v. United States, 3 WAKE FOREST J.L. & POL'Y 281 (2013).
25. State v. Sarrabea, 126 So. 3d 453, 455 (La. 2013).
26. Villas at Parkside Partners v. City of Farmers Branch, Tex., 726 F.3d 524, 529 (5th Cir. 2013).
27. Santos v. Frederick County Bd. of Com'rs, 725 F.3d 451, 464–65 (4th Cir. 2013).
28. United States v. South Carolina, 720 F.3d 518, 522 (4th Cir. 2013).

as House Bill 87, inspired by S.B. 1070 but broader, met a similar fate. Statutes criminalizing transporting or harboring unauthorized migrants, the Eleventh Circuit concluded, were preempted because they intruded upon an area of law in which Congress has comprehensively regulated, and they posed an obstacle to realization of that federal statutory scheme.[29]

Surviving State Crimes

Despite the *Arizona* decision's significant impact on state laws targeting immigration and migrants' conduct, numerous states have adopted statutes that remain in effect. Arizona again leads the country in scope and creativity. The state legislature criminalized aggravated identity theft and trafficking in identity documents, two crimes targeting the use of identification information not belonging to the accused.[30] Though not to be ignored, neither is as extraordinary as the state's human smuggling offense enacted in 2005.[31] As written, the statute criminalizes "intentionally engag[ing] in the smuggling of human beings for profit or commercial purpose."[32] This language undeniably targets people who receive payment for helping migrants sneak into the United States. Placed into the hands of enterprising prosecutors, however, this text was quickly deployed innovatively and expansively. Instead of limiting charges to the people helping unauthorized migrants enter the country, law enforcement agencies and prosecutors in Maricopa County, where Phoenix is located, elected to target the smuggled migrants too. The county attorney and sheriff created special units within their offices to target what has come to be known as "self-smuggling."

The arrest and prosecution of one of the self-smuggling offense's early targets, Juan Barragan-Sierra, illustrates the statute's novelty. An unauthorized migrant trying to reach Washington, Barragan-Sierra paid someone to help him cross the border and make his way through southern Arizona. Soon after crossing near Yuma, however, the plan went awry

---

29. Georgia Latino Alliance for Human Rights v. Governor of Georgia, 691 F.3d 1250, 1263–67 (11th Cir. 2012).

30. Ariz. Rev. Stat. Ann. §§ 13-2009, 13-2010.

31. S. 1372, 47th Leg., 1st Reg. Sess. (Ariz. 2005) (codified as amended at Ariz. Rev. Stat. Ann. § 13-2319 (2010)).

32. Ariz. Rev. Stat. Ann. § 13-2319 (2010).

when sheriff's deputies noticed that the pickup truck in which Barragan-Sierra was being transported had a broken brake light. A chase ensued in which the vehicles reached speeds in excess of 100 miles per hour. Deputies eventually forced the driver to pull over at which point he and a couple of passengers fled into a cornfield. Rather than chase the driver, the deputies decided that he and the others who fled could not be caught. Instead, the officers arrested Barragan-Sierra and four others who had been riding in the pickup bed. A jury convicted Barragan-Sierra of smuggling himself into the United States and the judge sentenced him to two years of unsupervised probation.[33]

Arizona's notoriety stands apart from other states, but it is not alone in using its own legislative powers over law enforcement to regulate immigration. According to one tally, thirty-seven states enacted a total of 145 laws that, in one way or another, used law enforcement tactics to regulate immigration between 2008 and 2013.[34] This includes the statutes preempted in Arizona and elsewhere described in the previous section, but it also includes statutes enacted in states from Alabama to Washington. Alabama, for example, created a single "State Law Enforcement Agency" with oversight of immigration enforcement efforts among other duties.[35] Other states have used their legislative processes to criminally punish human smuggling, as Colorado, Oklahoma, Florida, and Missouri did,[36] or the purchase or possession of firearms by unauthorized migrants, as South Carolina did.[37] California, Oregon, and Wyoming criminalize using fraudulent citizenship or immigration documents, or genuine

---

33. State v. Barragan-Sierra, 196 P.3d 879, 882-83 (Ariz. Ct. App. 2008).

34. National Conference of State Legislatures, *Immigration Enactments Database* (last accessed July 29, 2014), http://www.ncsl.org/research/immigration/immigration-laws-database.aspx.

35. ALA. CODE §§ 41-27-1, 41-27-2(d).

36. COLO. REV. STAT. § 18-13-128; 21 OK. STAT. ANN § 446(A)-(B); FLA. STAT. ANN. § 787.07; MO. STAT. ANN. § 577.675. Colorado's human smuggling statute is currently under review by the Colorado Supreme Court. People v. Fuentes-Espinoza, 2013 WL 174439 (Colo. Ct. App. Jan. 17, 2013), *cert. granted*, 2014 WL 1190061 (Colo. Mar. 24, 2014). A similar statute in Utah, Utah Code Ann. § 76-10-2901(2), was deemed preempted. Utah Coalition of La Raza v. Herbert, 2014 WL 2765195, *15 (D. Utah June 18, 2014) (unpublished).

37. S.C. CODE ANN. § 16-23-530(A), (C).

documents belonging to someone else.[38] The diversity of approaches that states have taken toward immigration suggests that they have taken seriously Justice Louis Brandeis's famous description of the states as laboratories of experimentation.[39]

While some state regulation operates independently of the federal government entirely, much of it depends on federal cooperation. Any state statute that applies solely or uniquely to migrants requires that someone verify a suspect or defendant's immigration status. State-level attempts to ascertain a person's immigration status with the certainty necessary to attach criminal punishment face preemption problems. To avoid this problem, Congress has directed ICE to assist states and localities "to verify or ascertain the citizenship or immigration status of any individual within the jurisdiction of the agency for any purpose authorized by law, by providing the requested verification or status information."[40] This congressional mandate has important constitutional and practical consequences. On a constitutional level, the Supreme Court pointed to this statutory section as evidence that "Congress has obligated ICE to respond to any request made by state officials for verification of a person's citizenship or immigration status."[41] This suggests, the Court went on, that Congress did not mean to preempt state statutes like Arizona's law requiring police officers to ask ICE about the immigration status of people who the police encounter during their normal duties.[42] On a practical level, ICE operates the Law Enforcement Support Center (LESC) to accomplish this obligation. Located in Vermont, the LESC operates around-the-clock every day of the year and fields calls from law enforcement officials around the country. As ICE explains the LESC's role, "The center is a single national point of contact that provides timely immigration status, identity information, and real-time assistance to local, state, and federal law enforcement agencies on aliens suspected, arrested, or convicted of criminal

---

38. CAL. PENAL CODE ANN. § 114; OREGON REV. STAT. §§ 165.800(2), (4)(b)(D); OREGON REV. STAT. § 161.603(3); WY. STAT. ANN. § 6-3-615(a).
39. New State Ice Co. v. Liebmann, 285 U.S. 262, 311 (1932) (Brandeis, J., dissenting).
40. 8 U.S.C. § 1373(c).
41. Arizona v. United States, 132 S. Ct. 2492, 2508 (2012).
42. Id.

activity." Though it received relatively few calls in the mid-1990s, the LESC fielded more than 1.4 million requests in fiscal year 2013.[43]

Pretrial Detention and Bail

As with any other crime, individuals suspected of violating a state or local immigration-related offense face the possibility of jail time both while criminal proceedings are ongoing and upon conviction. With so many jurisdictions involved, it is impossible to know just how many people are jailed on suspicion of or due to a conviction for an immigration-related state or local crime. Given the increasing number of state and local crimes touching on immigration and the greater amount of funding devoted to enforcing such laws, it is likely that more and more people are arrested for allegedly committing a state or local immigration crime. What little evidence does exist of arrests for state immigration offenses supports this conclusion. In a 2011 legal analysis of Arizona's human smuggling offense that remains the most thorough to date, legal scholar Ingrid V. Eagly found that "hundreds of migrants were arrested in Maricopa County for smuggling themselves" within just a few months of the law's adoption.[44]

As with the creation of substantive criminal offenses, Arizona has taken an important role in the recent evolution of state laws pertaining to migrant detention and bail. Jail and prison officials throughout the state are required to determine every arrestee's citizenship status.[45] Judges are required to determine a defendant's immigration status when deciding to grant bail,[46] and they are authorized to enhance a sentence if the defendant is present in the United States without authorization.[47] Law enforcement agencies have the power to detain for up to seven days any witness who, because of her immigration status, might not be available

43. U.S. Dep't of Homeland Security, Immigration & Customs Enforcement, Law Enforcement Support Center (last visited July 29, 2014), http://www.ice.gov/lesc/.

44. Ingrid V. Eagly, *Local Immigration Prosecution: A Study of Arizona Before SB 1070*, 58 UCLA L. Rev. 1749, 1762 (2011).

45. ARIZ. REV. STAT. ANN. § 13-3906.

46. ARIZ. REV. STAT. ANN. § 13-3967(B)(11).

47. ARIZ. REV. STAT. ANN. § 13-701(D)(21).

to testify at a human smuggling trial.[48] Most importantly, since 2006 the state constitution has prohibited judges from granting bail to anyone charged with a "serious felony offense[] . . . if the person charged has entered or remained in the United States illegally and if the proof is evident or the presumption great as to the present charge."[49] A "serious felony offense" includes almost all state felonies.[50] Human smuggling, including the self-smuggling variety, is a felony that falls within the serious felony offense categorization.[51] The confluence of the state constitution's no-bail provision with human smuggling's statutory recognition as a felony meant that, as legal scholar Ingrid Eagly put it, for several years "[u]ndocumented immigrants charged with smuggling themselves could now be detained without any possibility of bond."[52] Given its sweeping reach, it is not surprising that Arizona's efforts raised complicated legal questions and sustained litigation. Indeed, the Ninth Circuit issued two decisions regarding Arizona's no-bail constitutional provisions. Initially, the state law survived a constitutional challenge when reviewed by a three-judge panel of the Ninth Circuit. The Ninth Circuit panel concluded that the no-bail law does not violate the Fourteenth Amendment's substantive due process protections because it is not intended to punish and deter immigration offenses, and because it is reasonably related to the legitimate governmental objective of limiting the flight risk of defendants accused of a felony.[53] Similarly, the law provides sufficient procedural protections to meet the federal Constitution's procedural due process guarantees, does not violate the Eight Amendment's prohibition against excessive bail, is not implemented in such a way as to require appointed counsel at the defendant's initial appearance before a magistrate, and is not preempted.[54] The Ninth Circuit then reheard the case en banc and came to the opposite

---

48. Ariz. Rev. Stat. Ann. § 13-4085(A), (E).

49. Ariz. Const. art. II, sec. 22(A)(4), *held unconstitutional by* Lopez-Valenzuela v. Arpaio, 2014 WL 5151625 (9th Cir. Oct. 15, 2014).

50. Ariz. Rev. Stat. Ann. § 13-3961(A)(b).

51. Ariz. Rev. Stat. Ann. § 13-2319(B)-(C).

52. Ingrid V. Eagly, *Local Immigration Prosecution: A Study of Arizona Before SB 1070*, 58 UCLA L. Rev. 1749, 1763 (2011).

53. Lopez-Valenzuela v. County of Maricopa, 719 F.3d 1054, 1060–61 (9th Cir. 2013), *rev'd* 770 F.3d 772 (9th Cir. 2014) (en banc).

54. *Id.* 1066-70. (9th Cir. 2013), *rev'd* 770 F.3d 772 (9th Cir. 2014) (en banc).

conclusion: Arizona's no-bail clause is unconstitutional. The law violates the substantive due process principles of the Fourteenth Amendment, the court held, by, first, impermissibly infringing on arrestees' liberty interest and, second, imposing punishment prior to trial. The Fourteenth Amendment requires that any infringement on liberty be narrowly tailored to serve a compelling state interest. While the court acknowledged Arizona's interest in ensuring that unauthorized migrants show up to court dates and do not endanger the public, the law violates the Fourteenth Amendment because it imposes a broad prohibition against granting bail to a large group of migrants without any evidence that unauthorized migrants released on bail are more likely than others to abscond or endanger the public.[55] Second, the state failed to show that unauthorized migrants actually pose an unmanageable risk of flight through the standard bail procedures, thus the state's attempt to solve this unproven problem is necessarily excessive.[56]

Arizona may be the most prominent state to have limited bail possibilities for migrants, but it is not alone. In Utah, unauthorized migrants are subject to a rebuttable presumption that they are flight risks.[57] Missouri has had a similar no-bail provision since 2008.[58] That statute goes one step further than Arizona or Utah by presuming that anyone who the judge "reasonably believes . . . is an alien unlawfully present in the United States" can ever be released under any conditions that will reasonably assure her presence in court.[59] Thus far no one has challenged the constitutionality of Missouri's no-bail provision.

Other state law provisions raise Fourth Amendment concerns. Except when a person consents to being seized by a police officer, the Fourth Amendment requires that officers have reasonable suspicion that a person has or is engaged in criminal activity in order to temporarily detain a person. Often called a *Terry* stop in acknowledgement of *Terry v. Ohio*, the Supreme Court decision that recognized the constitutionality of this type

---

55. Lopez-Valenzuela v. Arpaio, 770 F.3d 772, 782–89 (9th Cir. 2014) (en banc).
56. *Id.* at 789.
57. UTAH CODE ANN. § 17-22-9.5(4).
58. 2008 Mo. Legis. Serv. H.B. 2366.
59. MO. STAT. ANN. § 544.470(2).

of police activity, such stops are supposed to be limited in nature. Their purpose is to allow police officers the flexibility needed to "approach a person for purposes of investigating possibly criminal behavior."[60] Reasonable suspicion, however, is insufficient for an arrest. For that, police officers must have probable cause that the arrestee has or is engaged in criminal activity.[61]

It is doubtful that information about a migrant's immigration status alone can meet Fourth Amendment requirements to justify a seizure or arrest. Neither suspicion nor knowledge that a person has committed a civil immigration law violation provides the reasonable suspicion or probable cause that the Fourth Amendment requires to justify detaining or arresting the person.[62] The reason is that the information necessary to justify a Fourth Amendment seizure—whether detention or arrest—must relate to commission of a crime. Violating a civil provision of the INA sheds little light on whether a migrant has also violated a criminal provision of the statute. A person who is unlawfully present may have entered the United States clandestinely, overstayed a visa, or been convicted of a removable offense. Though all those constitute bases for removal, only one, clandestine entry, forms an element of immigration crimes (illegal entry and illegal reentry). Knowing nothing more about a migrant than that she has violated a civil immigration law does little to clarify whether she engaged in activity that might also constitute a crime or not. The Supreme Court cast a dark constitutional cloud on this type of argument when it addressed section 6 of Arizona's S.B. 1070, which allowed officers to arrest anyone whom the officer has probable cause to believe has committed a removable offense. The Court explained, "As a general rule, it is not a crime for a removable alien to remain present in the United States. If the police stop someone based on nothing more than possible removability, the usual predicate for an arrest is absent."[63] Building off this analysis, the Fourth Circuit concluded, "Because civil immigration violations do not constitute crimes, suspicion or knowledge that an individual

---

60. Terry v. Ohio, 392 U.S. 1, 22–23 (1968).
61. Devenpeck v. Alford, 543 U.S. 146, 152 (2006).
62. Santos v. Frederick County Bd. of Com'rs, 725 F.3d 451, 464–65 (4th Cir. 2013).
63. Arizona v. United States, 132 S. Ct. 2492, 2505 (2012).

has committed a civil immigration violation, by itself, does not give a law enforcement officer probable cause to believe that the individual is engaged in criminal activity."[64]

Understanding Convictions

Once prosecuted, the key question becomes whether a migrant is convicted of a crime. A perennial headache for crimmigration law practitioners and migrants stems from the fact that not all convictions are equal. Prosecutors, defense attorneys, and judges are very familiar with the nuances of criminal procedure. Crimmigration practitioners, however, must add to that knowledge an understanding of how criminal procedure rules interact with immigration law. There are few experiences more frustrating than learning that a favorable outcome from the narrow perspective of criminal law has horrendous immigration law consequences. That is exactly what happens on a regular basis due to discrepancies in how the states define a conviction and what constitutes a conviction for immigration law purposes.

The definition of "conviction" used for immigration law is both clear and broad (for more on "conviction" as used in the INA, see chapter 2). Any adjudication of guilt by a judge or jury, admission to sufficient facts to justify a guilty finding, or guilty or nolo contendere plea is sufficient so long as the court imposes "some form of punishment, penalty, or restraint" on the offender.[65]

In contrast, state laws frequently define "conviction" to exclude adjudications that fit the federal definition. A "deferred judgment" in Colorado, for example, does not constitute a conviction under state law.[66] Neither does a guilty plea expunged after successful completion of judicial diversion in Tennessee.[67] State criminal practitioners and judges in these states would be correct to inform criminal defendants that such dispositions would be quite favorable if the defendant is concerned only with the outcome of the criminal case. For migrants concerned with remaining in

---

64. *Santos*, 725 F.3d at 465.
65. INA § 101(a)(48)(A).
66. Kazadi v. People, 291 P.3d 16, 22 (Colo. 2012).
67. Rodriguez v. State, 437 S.W.3d 450, 456 (Tenn. 2014).

the country, however, neither would lead to a positive conclusion of the defendant's legal predicament since both satisfy the INA's definition of conviction. A migrant, in other words, can be "convicted" for purposes of immigration law but not for purposes of state criminal law.

Practice Pointer

Lawful permanent resident Yanick Kazadi pleaded guilty to two drug offenses, possession with intent to distribute marijuana and possession of not more than one ounce of marijuana. With the prosecutor's agreement, the sentencing court granted Kazadi deferred judgment for two years. According to the deferred judgment's terms, if, upon completion of those two years, Kazadi had stayed out of further trouble, the court would allow him to withdraw his guilty plea. Thinking about nothing other than the criminal prosecution, this is a great outcome for someone facing conviction of multiple drug crimes. The complication for Kazadi arises from his lack of United States citizenship.

In Colorado, where Kazadi was convicted, deferred adjudication essentially holds the criminal proceeding in abeyance. As the Colorado Supreme Court explained the deferred adjudication mechanism, no conviction or sentence is entered. Instead, "a deferred judgment is a continuance of the defendant's case in lieu of the imposition of sentence, where a sentence may be issued if the defendant fails to abide by prescribed conditions." *Kazadi v. People*, 291 P.3d 16, 22-23 (Colo. 2012). As a result, Kazadi could not seek to vacate a conviction to try to remedy an alleged ineffective assistance of counsel problem.

While Kazadi could try to withdraw his plea, the dissent sums up the predicament that Kazadi and other migrants face: "The irreversible effects of some collateral consequences may have already occurred—such as the mandatory deportation to Congo that Kazadi faces here—and may therefore render the benefit of a successfully completed deferred judgment of little or no value to the defendant." *Id.* at 24 (Bender, C.J., dissenting). If Kazadi wants to continue living in the United States, therefore, his favorable criminal case outcome was a terrible immigration case outcome.

Understanding Sentences

All convictions, of course, carry with them some punishment. That punishment is not only the sentence that offenders must serve but also an important factor in determining whether particular bases of removal apply (see following section). The INA provides a remarkable amount of detail about what Congress had in mind when it referenced particular sentences throughout the statute. The phrase "term of imprisonment" or word "sentence," INA § 101(a)(48)(B) explains, "include[s] the period of incarceration or confinement ordered by a court of law regardless of any suspension of the imposition or execution of that imprisonment or sentence in whole or part." In other words, unless a statutory section says otherwise, what matters for immigration law purposes is the actual sentence meted out rather than the amount of time a migrant actually spent in a cell. Suspending a sentence, a common means of ameliorating the impact of a sentence used by criminal courts across the country, does not affect the sentence computed for immigration law purposes.

Immigration-Safe Pleas and Sentences

Upon conviction, the key question facing defendants is what punishment they will receive. Obviously migrants can be imprisoned and fined just like any other defendant without regard to whether they were convicted of an immigration-related offense. In some instances, the length of the sentence imposed or actually experienced matters immensely. For defense attorneys, the goal should be to search for an immigration-safe plea and sentence whenever a client is concerned about remaining in the United States.

Though prosecutors and judges clearly lack the same obligation to defendants that defense attorneys have, it may nonetheless be in their interest—and the interest of the criminal justice system as a whole—to encourage immigration-safe pleading. All but a small number of convictions result from pleas. Acknowledging this reality in 2012, the Supreme Court quoted two legal scholars who wrote, "To a large extent . . . horse trading [between prosecutor and defense counsel] determines who goes to jail and for how long. That is what plea bargaining is. It is not some adjunct to the criminal justice system; it *is* the criminal justice system."[68] Widespread plea-bargaining allows prosecutors to conserve resources—time, energy, and money—necessary to build a case.[69] Applied specifically to the crimmigration context, the Supreme Court noted in *Padilla v. Kentucky* that a single criminal episode could frequently give rise to

---

68. Missouri v. Frye, 132 S. Ct. 1399, 1407 (2012) (quoting Robert E. Scott & William J. Stuntz, *Plea Bargaining As Contract*, 101 YALE L.J. 1909, 1912 (1992)).
69. *Frye*, 132 S. Ct. at 1407.

multiple charges some of which might result in removal and others which would not. "[T]he threat of deportation," the Court surmised, "may provide the defendant with a powerful incentive to plead guilty to an offense that does not mandate that penalty in exchange for a dismissal of a charge that does."[70]

Immigration-safe sentences can take a variety of forms. One of the most common is to avoid a sentence that is sufficiently long to trigger the bases of removal that require a minimum sentence or term of imprisonment. An important example concerns the so-called petty offense exception to the crime involving moral turpitude basis of inadmissibility, INA § 212(a)(2)(A)(i)(I). A migrant who is subject to this provision can avoid removal if she was sentenced to a term of imprisonment of six months or less and the maximum penalty possible for the crime was no more than one-year imprisonment.[71] Avoiding a sentence of six months or less, therefore, would preserve eligibility for the petty offense exception.

Other bases of removal simply require a particular term of imprisonment to apply. Two of the most common aggravated felony categories turn on whether a term of imprisonment of at least one year was ordered: the crime of violence, INA § 101(a)(43)(F), and theft or burglary, INA § 101(a)(43)(G), categories.[72] Three less commonly invoked aggravated felony categories include a similar one-year term of imprisonment requirement: passport offenses, INA § 101(a)(43)(P); commercial bribery and counterfeiting, INA § 101(a)(43)(R); and obstruction of justice or perjury, INA § 101(a)(43)(S). A couple of others require longer terms of imprisonment: failure to appear for sentencing requires that the underlying offense be punishable by at least five years of imprisonment, INA § 101(a)(43) (Q), and failure to appear for a court hearing involving a felony requires at least two years imprisonment for the underlying felony, INA § 101(a) (43)(T). Regardless of the substantive elements of a crime, migrants can

---

70. Padilla v. Kentucky, 559 U.S. 356, 373 (2010).

71. INA § 212(a)(2)(A)(ii)(II).

72. *See* Matter of Ramos, 23 I&N Dec. 336, 338–39 (BIA 2002) (explaining that the statutory text, "for which the term of imprisonment [is] at least," contained in every provision discussed in this paragraph, requires that "an alien receives a term of imprisonment of at least" the specified amount).

avoid falling into these categories by steering clear of a sentence of the specified length.

Still other bases of removal apply only if a sentence of a specified duration could have been issued. The petty offense exception, for example, imposes such a requirement. The corresponding basis of deportation for having been convicted of a crime involving moral turpitude includes a similar limitation. That provision only applies if the offense is punishable by a sentence of one year or longer.[73] Certain racketeering and gambling offenses are considered aggravated felonies if "a sentence of one year imprisonment or more may be imposed."[74] Using one year as a cut-off point poses an important dilemma because most misdemeanors are punishable by as much as one year. It is not at all uncommon, therefore, for migrants to be convicted of minor crimes that can result in a sentence of exactly one year but receive very little or no jail time. This might be considered a favorable outcome if not for the fact that such sentences place migrants at risk of removal. To remedy what many see as an unjust result, legislators in California, Illinois, Nevada, and Washington altered their penal codes to cap the maximum possible penalty for some misdemeanors at 364 days—exactly one day less than necessary to trigger the crime involving moral turpitude ground of deportation—a world of difference under immigration law but a trivial difference when it comes to the impact of a criminal punishment.[75]

Immigration-Safe Records of Conviction

Two other immigration-safe options exist divorced from negotiating the length of the migrant's sentence. Instead, they involve careful consideration of the contents of the record of conviction during plea negotiations. The first option turns on the intersection of a procedural and substantive issue. The INA places the burden of proof on DHS to show that a

---

73. INA § 237(a)(2)(A)(i)(II).

74. INA § 101(a)(43)(J).

75. CAL. PENAL CODE § 18.5 (applying to misdemeanors); 720 IL. COMP. STAT. 5/2-11; NEV. REV. STAT. § 193.140 (applying to gross misdemeanors; misdemeanors are punishable by up to six months); WASH. REV. CODE § 9A.20.0212(2) (applying to gross misdemeanors; misdemeanors are punishable by up to ninety days).

migrant who has been admitted is deportable.[76] Lawful permanent residents and nonimmigrant visitors all fall into this category. In addition,
the controlled substances offense, INA § 237(a)(2)(B), is triggered only if
the drug involved in the crime is also regulated by the federal Controlled
Substances Act (CSA). Because most state penal codes do not overlap perfectly with the CSA—the states tend to criminalize more substances than
the federal government—immigration judges usually must confirm the
identity of the drug involved to ensure that a migrant convicted of a drug-
related crime was actually convicted of a controlled substance offense
(see chapter 2). When the drug type involved in the offense is one that is
also criminalized by the CSA, admitted migrants can make it more difficult for DHS to meet its burden by keeping information about the drug
type out of the record of conviction, including plea documents. In other
instances, however, migrants may want to be sure to include information
about the drug type and quantity in the record to take advantage of the
controlled substance offense exemption for a single offense involving possession of 30 grams or less of marijuana for one's own use.[77] A person
convicted of simple possession of a few joints of marijuana, for example,
could ensure that there is no question about her eligibility for this exemption by convincing the prosecutor to agree to include such information in
the plea documents or stipulating to it during the plea colloquy.

The second option entails equally careful consideration of the presen-
tence report (PSR). Defendants often fail to challenge the facts included
in a PSR. This is especially common when defendants have successfully
negotiated a plea that involves little or no jail time. In the rush to finalize
the criminal proceedings, defendants pay little heed to the PSR. Ignoring the PSR, however, can be perilous. The Supreme Court has made it
clear that immigration judges can consider the contents of a PSR when
using the "circumstance-specific" approach of statutory analysis (for more
on the circumstance-specific approach, see chapter 2). The circumstance-
specific approach is undeniably a significant deviation from the Supreme
Court's otherwise steadfast commitment to the categorical and modified

76. INA § 240(c)(3).
77. INA § 237(a)(2)(B)(i).

categorical approaches. It allows immigration judges to consider the facts underlying a conviction rather than the elements of the offense for which the migrant was convicted and nothing else. Because facts are included in the PSR if they are proven by a preponderance of the evidence instead of the higher beyond a reasonable doubt standard required for the elements of a conviction,[78] and because it is up to the defendant to challenge information included in the PSR,[79] it is much easier for the government to include adverse facts in the PSR than in the allegations required for a conviction. Add to this the fact that the PSR is written by court officials rather than the prosecutor, and it becomes much easier for unflattering allegations to make their way into the record.

Consider Ricardo Hinojosa's criminal case as an illustration of the risk inherent in PSRs. Hinojosa pleaded guilty to possession with intent to distribute 211 kilograms of marijuana. The PSR claimed that he participated in other crimes involving a total of 2,860 kilograms of marijuana. This was no meaningless increase. The difference between involvement with 211 kilograms and 2,860 kilograms meant that Hinojosa's offense of conviction, which involves a mandatory minimum sentence of five years, resulted in a recommended sentencing range of 151 to 188 months (roughly twelve-and-a-half to fifteen-and-a-half years). Inclusion of these additional incidents more than doubled the amount of jail time that Hinojosa thought he would see when he pleaded.[80] Though the Supreme Court adopted the circumstance-specific approach in the context of the fraud or deceit type of aggravated felony and has yet to deviate from that limited application,[81] it would be unwise to assume that the BIA and lower courts will universally stick to this limitation. Indeed, the BIA has already extended this deviation from the Supreme Court's otherwise steadfast commitment to the categorical and modified categorical approaches in one instance: the 30 grams of marijuana exemption to the controlled substance offense.[82]

78. United States v. Bieganowski, 313 F.3d 264, 294 (5th Cir. 2002).
79. United States v. Alaniz, 726 F.3d 586, 619 (5th Cir. 2013).
80. See United States v. Hinojosa, 749 F.3d 407 (5th Cir. 2014).
81. Nijhawan v. Holder, 557 U.S. 29, 34 (2009) (addressing INA § 101(a)(43)(M)(i)).
82. Matter of Davey, 26 I&N Dec. 37 (BIA 2012) (discussing INA § 237(a)(2)(B)(i)).

Alternative Adjudications

Migrants can also take advantage of dispositions that provide an alternative to the traditional criminal process of an adjudication of guilt followed by confinement. Every state offers some alternative adjudication process with most offering multiple options. Though states use different names, the most common are pretrial diversion (sometimes referred to as deferred prosecution), deferred adjudication (or deferred judgment), and community supervision (often referred to as supervised release). The first two can benefit migrants if they avoid a finding of guilt or imposition of a sentence. The final option can be useful to migrants wishing to avoid a prison sentence. Every state structures their alternative adjudication options somewhat differently so this section can only describe them in general terms. The key task for advocates is to become familiar with the nuances of whatever options their jurisdiction offers.

Moving through the criminal process chronologically, pretrial diversion comes first. This alternative stops the criminal prosecution before the defendant enters a plea of guilty or nolo contendere. In return,

> [t]he State agrees to dismiss the case if the defendant performs certain conditions within a specified period of time. Both the State and the defendant request that the trial court continue the present trial setting to a certain date in the future to give the defendant time to comply with the agreed conditions. The agreement is then presented to the trial court for its approval. If the trial court does not approve the agreement, the case proceeds to trial as scheduled on the docket. If the trial court approves the agreement, it grants the joint request for continuance and resets the trial to a certain date in the future. On that date, the defendant must appear before the trial court. If the defendant has complied with the conditions of the agreement, the trial court grants the State's motion to dismiss the pending criminal charges. If the defendant has not complied with the conditions of the agreement, the case proceeds to trial as scheduled.[83]

---

83. Fisher v. State, 832 S.W.2d 641, 643–44 (Tex. Ct. App. 1992).

Defendants benefit by avoiding "the burden and stigma of a criminal conviction."[84] The state, meanwhile, benefits by saving the resources that would otherwise be required to prosecute the case. If the defendant meets the program's conditions, the state further benefits by avoiding the cost of punishment as well as the cost of eventually reintegrating a convict into the community. This analysis is largely applicable to cases involving migrant defendants, except that the stakes are even higher. Avoiding entering a guilty or nolo contendere plea puts a migrant outside the INA's definition of a conviction because it requires, among other things, exactly this type of admission of culpability.[85]

Importantly, many of the statutes governing pretrial diversion programs are very loosely worded. They often do not explicitly reference pleas. Texas's statute, for example, simply authorizes the state department of corrections to operate pretrial intervention programs without saying anything about the program's requirements, while another statute authorizes the amount of fees that program participants can be charged.[86] As a result, counties can and occasionally do change their program requirements to include a plea component.[87] When this happens, pretrial diversion ceases to benefit migrant defendants.

Problem 7.1

Fidel Grullón, a migrant who overstayed his nonimmigrant visa, was charged in Florida with possession of a controlled substance (cocaine). With the prosecutor's agreement and the court's consent, he participated in Florida's pretrial intervention program. The statute governing the program provides that it is available "for persons charged with a crime, before or after any information has been filed or an indictment has been returned in the circuit court." Fla. Stat. Ann. § 948.08(1).

(continued)

84. State v. Rice, 350 A.2d 95, 100 (N.J. Super. 1975).
85. INA § 101(a)(48).
86. Tex. Gov. Code § 76.011(a); Tex. Code of Crim. P. § 102.012.
87. Greg Abbott, Attorney General of Texas, *Opinion No. GA-0986, to David Slayton, Administrative Director, Office of Court Administration*, (Feb. 5, 2013), https://www.oag.state.tx.us/opinions/opinions/50abbott/op/2013/pdf/ga0986.pdf; César Cuauhtémoc García Hernández & Carlos Moctezuma García, *Change to Pretrial Diversion Policy Could Lead to Deportation*, Voice for the Defense Online (July 2, 2011), http://voiceforthedefenseonline.com/story/change-pretrial-diversion-policy-could-lead-deportation.

The statute further states, "Resumption of pending criminal proceedings shall be undertaken at any time if the program administrator or state attorney finds that the offender is not fulfilling his or her obligations under this plan or if the public interest so requires." *Id.* at (4). There was never any question that Grullón met the program conditions so his case was dismissed at the end of the appointed period. DHS initiated removal proceedings claiming that Grullón was convicted of a controlled substance offense. Is DHS correct?

No. For purposes of immigration law, Grullón was not convicted. There is no indication that he pleaded guilty or nolo contendere, as required by the INA's definition of a conviction, INA § 101(a)(48). Moreover, the Florida pretrial diversion statute explicitly applies to criminal cases even before an information or indictment has been filed or returned. "Clearly then," the BIA wrote in the case from which this example is drawn, "entry into the program precedes a pleading by the accused or a finding of guilt by the court." Matter of Grullon, 20 I&N Dec. 12, 14 (BIA 1989).

Like pretrial diversion, deferred adjudication stops the criminal process in its tracks. The major difference between these two alternative adjudication options leads to a critical difference for migrants. Deferred adjudication processes require entry of a guilty or nolo contendere plea. After that, deferred adjudication resembles pretrial diversion. The Colorado Supreme Court described its own "deferred judgment" process in a way that reflects the standard process for these alternative adjudications:

It authorizes a trial court to defer judgment and sentencing when accepting a guilty plea and continue the case for a period up to four years from the date of the plea. As a condition of continuing the case, the trial court is empowered to implement probation-like supervision conditions that the defendant must adhere to. If the defendant completes the term of the deferred sentence without violating a condition, his guilty plea is withdrawn and his case must be dismissed with prejudice. If the defendant violates any of the stipulated conditions, however, the court has authority to revoke the deferral and enter judgment and sentence upon his guilty plea.[88]

---

88. Kazadi v. People, 291 P.3d 16, 20 (Colo. 2012) (internal citations omitted).

Deferred adjudication statutes typically require no further adjudication of guilt if a defendant fails to comply with the program's terms. The court simply enters a sentence. Moreover, like the Colorado version, these statutes usually allow the court to impose some type of supervision short of imprisonment.

Both parties benefit from deferred adjudication essentially identically to pretrial diversion programs. Defendants usually avoid a conviction, as state criminal law defines that term,[89] and always avoid imprisonment if they comply with the program requirements. For its part, the state saves resources.

Typical deferred adjudication procedures like Colorado's, however, do not provide migrants with the significant immigration law benefits that pretrial diversion brings. Again, the reason turns on criminal law's intersection with the INA's definition of "conviction." By requiring entry of a guilty or nolo contendere plea, deferred adjudication statutes satisfy the INA's plea requirement.[90] If the court also orders the defendant to submit to supervision of any kind, the deferred adjudication procedure is likely to meet the INA's second requirement for a conviction: "some form of punishment, penalty, or restraint."[91] Reviewing Congress's 1996 amendments to the INA in which it adopted the existing definition of "conviction," the BIA concluded, "it is clear that Congress intends that an alien be considered convicted, based on an initial finding or admission of guilt coupled with the imposition of some punishment, even in a state where further proceedings relating to the alien's actual guilt or innocence may be required upon his violation of probation in order for him to be considered convicted under the state law."[92]

There remains more doubt about fines or fees ordered as part of a deferred adjudication process. Though the BIA and federal courts have not decided this issue, the likelihood is that the Board at least will conclude that such monetary costs are sufficient to constitute a conviction as defined by the INA. The BIA has taken a broad view of what constitutes

---

89. *See, e.g., id.* at 22.
90. INA § 101(a)(48)(A)(i).
91. INA § 101(a)(48)(A)(ii).
92. Matter of Roldan, 22 I&N Dec. 512, 518 (BIA 1999).

"some form of punishment, penalty, or restraint," including court costs actually imposed.[93] There is some basis to distinguish court costs and other nonincarceratory sanctions suspended rather than imposed since the INA requires that the judge actually impose the punishment, penalty, or restraint on the migrant's liberty. A suspended fine represents nothing more than the threat of a fine, and a threat cannot be said to lead to a loss of wealth or liberty.[94]

The final alternative occurs after the criminal process follows its traditional route through the guilt stage. Instead of imposing a term of confinement, courts are often empowered to mete out an alternative to incarceration. There are many forms of community supervision, ranging from formalized probation to occasional reporting to court personnel. Legislatures have adopted mandatory minimum prison sentences for many offenses, and for these community supervision options are unavailable in lieu of incarceration. For other offenses, however, defendants tend to prefer the least restrictive supervisory requirements that the court will agree to. No matter how favorable, migrants should be aware that any type of supervision is likely to meet the INA's definition of "some form of punishment, penalty, or restraint," thereby constituting a conviction for purposes of immigration law. Despite that, community service supervision remains an attractive option for a subset of migrants: those facing conviction for a small number of aggravated felony grounds of removal that require actual imposition of a term of imprisonment (including crimes of violence and theft offenses). Because community supervision is not equivalent to imprisonment, it can help avoid removal under the crime of violence or theft bases.

Measuring Sentences

Since the length of imprisonment is an essential element of several bases of removal, it is important to be cognizant of how sentences are measured. Computing a sentence is straightforward enough when a migrant received a single defined punishment. Attorneys are well aware that does not always happen. Often defendants are convicted of multiple offenses and a

---

93. Matter of Cabrera, 24 I&N Dec. 459, 462 (BIA 2008).
94. See Retuta v. Holder, 591 F.3d 1181, 1188 (9th Cir. 2010).

court issues multiple sentences with the additional instruction that they are to run concurrently. According to the BIA, for immigration law purposes, concurrent sentences are not to be added together to identify the term of imprisonment. Rather, the longest concurrent sentence dictates the term of imprisonment.[95] In other instances defendants are sentenced to a particular range rather than a specific number of months or years (for example, a minimum of four years and a maximum of five years) with the actual release date decided by a parole board or similar body. Called indeterminate sentencing, this was a common practice throughout the United States until the early 1990s when it lost favor among politicians who wanted to be viewed as tough on crime. Considering a case involving multiple indeterminate sentences, the BIA announced that the sentence is considered to be the maximum sentence possible (for example, five years where the minimum sentence was four years and the maximum sentence was five years).[96]

Removal as Part of Sentence

Courts occasionally incorporate removal provisions into sentencing. The results are a mixed bag. Several state appellate courts, for example, conclude that a state court cannot order removal as part of the sentence.[97] They reason, as a Georgia intermediate appellate court did, that the INA entrusts removal authority exclusively to the federal government's immigration officials and any attempt by a state court to require that a person leave the country as a condition of a sentence exceeds the state's power.[98] In effect, these cases hold that federal law preempts state law when it comes to deciding who is allowed to remain in the United States. Despite

---

95. Matter of Aldabesheh, 22 I&N Dec. 983, 988 (BIA 1999) (discussing Matter of Fernandez, 14 I&N Dec. 24, 25 (BIA 1972)).

96. Matter of D--, 20 I&N Dec. 827, 829 (BIA 1994); see LaFarga v. INS, 170 F.3d 1213, 1215-16 (9th Cir. 1999); Nguyen v. INS, 53 F.3d 310, 311 (10th Cir. 1995).

97. See, e.g., State v. Silvera, 309 P.3d 1277, 1283 (Alaska Ct. App. 2013); Gutierrez v. State, 380 S.W.3d 167, 173 (Tex. Crim. App. 2012); People v. Antonio-Antimo, 29 P.3d 298, 303 (Colo. 2000); Sanchez v. State, 508 S.E.2d 185, 187 (Ga. Ct. App. 1998); State v. Pando, 921 P.2d 1285, 1286-87 (N.M. Ct. App. 1996); Rojas v. State, 450 A.2d 490, 442-43 (Md. Ct. Spec. App. 1982); Torros v. State, 415 So.2d 908, 908 (Fla. Dist. Ct. App. 1982) (per curiam).

98. Sanchez, 508 S.E.2d at 187 (discussing United States v. Romeo, 122 F.3d 941 (11th Cir. 1997), and United States v. Abushaar, 761 F.2d 954 (3d Cir. 1985)).

this consistent line of cases, some state courts continue to include removal as part of a defendant's sentence without being challenged.[99]

Even without the ability to require removal as part of a criminal sentence, the states can wield enormous power to entice migrants to accept removal as part of the criminal process. The states can simply release a convicted and imprisoned migrant early if DHS agrees to initiate removal proceedings. Washington, for example, makes this option available for imprisoned individuals against whom there is already a removal order.[100] Neither Washington nor another state could force DHS to accept custody of a migrant fitting this criterion. Likewise, they could not require DHS to initiate removal proceedings. But there is certainly no constitutional or statutory provision that prevents the states from asking for DHS's cooperation. Furthermore, 8 U.S.C. § 1373—which allows state agencies to ask DHS to verify any individual's immigration status and obligates DHS to respond—suggests that Congress wanted to encourage this type of communication.

Further Reading

Ingrid V. Eagly, *Local Immigration Prosecution: A Study of Arizona Before SB 1070*, 58 UCLA L. Rev. 1749 (2011).

Gerald Neuman, *The Lost Century of American Immigration Law (1776–1876)*, 93 Colum. L. Rev. 1833 (1993).

Strange Neighbors: The Role of States in Immigration Policy (Carissa Byrne Hessick & Gabriel J. Chin eds. 2014).

---

99. *See, e.g.,* State v. Barragan-Sierra, 196 P.3d 879, 883 (Ariz. Ct. App. 2008).
100. Wash. Rev. Code 9.94A.685(1).

ENFORCING CRIMMIGRATION LAW

This book's first two parts have taken an in-depth look at important developments in the substantive law of crimmigration. Focusing first on the civil immigration law regime, then on the federal and state criminal justice systems, the chapters included in those parts have mapped crimmigration law as it appears in statutory codes and judicial decisions.

Part 3 addresses how crimmigration law appears on the ground. Chapter 8 opens by examining the Unites States' borders. Since the 1980s, one topic has taken center stage in legal and political discussions about cross-border movement that has influenced most legal developments affecting crimmigration law on the border: drugs. The vast overlap of drug law enforcement authorizations and immigration law enforcement powers has created two aberrant but constitutionally permissible policing norms along the border that this chapter addresses: suspicionless searches and the use of race-based criteria to acquire the suspicion necessary for law enforcement officers to stop someone in compliance with the Fourth

Amendment. Though these legal issues apply to all of the nation's borders, all are especially salient along the border with México.

Chapter 9 follows by turning a penetrating eye to the nation's sprawling civil immigration detention system. The hundreds of facilities that DHS uses to detain migrants pending removal proceedings or while they await actual removal are located in major metropolitan areas and rural towns. This chapter goes into detention centers to reveal living conditions inside the troubled immigration detention estate while addressing the remarkable role that detention has come to play in enforcing civil immigration law.

Chapter 10 closes Part 3 by turning special attention to states' involvement in enforcing crimmigration law. Despite the enormous civil detention system and historically unprecedented funding available to federal immigration law enforcement agencies, they remain a fraction of the size of state and local law enforcement bodies. Recognizing this, the federal government has come to rely quite heavily on state and local police officials to identify potentially removable individuals. This chapter addresses the difficult legal questions that many of these innovative policy initiatives—including the Secure Communities program, 287(g) agreements, and immigration detainers—present. The states have not become simple tools at the federal government's disposal. As chapter 7 illustrated, many have devised creative uses of their traditional police powers to target migrants. This chapter pays special attention to the Fourth Amendment implications those enforcement efforts raise.

CHAPTER 8

Border Policing

The United States' borders are vast and course through intimidating territory. From the cold of northeastern Maine to the deserts of southern Arizona, they include large segments barely dotted by communities of any size. They also include the millions of people who live in Detroit, El Paso, the Río Grande Valley of South Texas, and San Diego. Though often forgotten, the border also runs up and down the nation's two coasts. Charleston, New York, and San Francisco are as much border communities as any city sitting across the Río Grande River from México. Indeed, port cities on the East and West Coast have played an enormously significant role in the history of immigration to the United States. New York and San Francisco alone welcomed most generations of migrants from before the country's founding until the middle of the twentieth century. Since then other communities have taken their turn as major entry points: Miami in the 1960s and again in the late 1970s and early 1980s, South Texas in the 1980s, Arizona in the 2000s, among others.

Despite migration flows moving throughout the country across the years, so often when policymakers and commentators think of the border they think only of the boundary with México. That is factually incorrect and historically naïve, but it has nonetheless had a profound impact on legal developments concerning migration. This chapter addresses the law's role in authorizing, shaping, and sometimes limiting policing on the border, especially in the Southwest.

To be clear, when I refer to border policing I am talking about unique powers granted to law enforcement officials on or near the United States' borders to investigate violations of civil or criminal law. In effect, border policing is about the Fourth Amendment's far more deferential posture toward law enforcement officials working along the border. These powers are not limited to any substantive area of law. They include potential violations of civil or criminal immigration law, as well as powers to investigate other areas of law. What unites the topics discussed in this chapter is that they rely on the unique features of the border as justification for departing from Fourth Amendment principles that are the norm in the rest of the country. The Fourth Amendment allows government intrusions into private activity without suspicion or, in part, on the basis of a person's race, the courts have repeatedly held, because there is something uniquely difficult and uniquely dangerous about the border.

The Exceptional Border

Cross-border movement of people and goods long precedes the existence of geopolitical boundaries separating nations. As the United States' international boundaries concretized into their modern forms, cross-border traffic continued largely unabated. Binational communities prospered and struggled with the times. The number of people migrating fluctuated as wars and natural disasters peaked and waned. Through these cycles, however, the border largely failed to operate as a barrier. Neither the state governments prior to the late 1800s nor the federal government after that devoted many resources to regulating who or what crossed the border. Indeed, Congress did not establish a dedicated border law enforcement agency, the Border Patrol, until 1924.[1] Its initial round of hires numbered

---

1. KELLY LYTLE HERNÁNDEZ, MIGRA! A HISTORY OF THE U.S. BORDER PATROL 17 (2010).

all of 104 agents.[2] Many years later the number of agents had not grown
too much. The agency counted on roughly 300 agents through 1940, and
it did not employ more than 2,000 agents until 1979.[3] The Border Patrol's
fortunes suddenly changed in the closing decades of the twentieth century. By 1992 it employed more than 4,000 agents. Within a few years the
number began to rise dramatically: almost 6,000 agents in 1996; 8,000 in
1998; 10,000 in 2002; and 20,000 in 2009.[4]

What changed? Two things. First, Congress amended the INA in 1965
to abolish the century-old national origins quotas that had limited the number of migrants who could be granted permission to enter the United States
based on their racial classification. President Harry Truman had vetoed
the racial quota regime in 1952 calling it "a slur on the patriotism . . . of
our citizenry," but Congress overrode him.[5] Thirteen years later Congress
finally got around to repealing the quota system and replacing it with the
family- and employment-based selection system that is largely still in place.
People are allowed to come to the United States based on their family rela-
tionships and skills. Having eliminated the explicitly racist quota system,
the 1965 Act was hailed as promoting a liberal vision of formal equality.
Everyone was thought to have an equal opportunity to come to the United
States. The catch was that the 1965 Act and its 1976 amendments capped
the number of people who could come from any given country. This would
not necessarily have become problematic had the chosen cap—excluding
parents, spouses, and unmarried minor children of United States citizens,
20,000 migrants per year per country—not been well below the number
of people already coming from countries with longstanding relations with
the United States, especially México. More than 200,000 Mexicans were
regularly coming to the United States in the 1960s, roughly ten times the
number permitted under the new immigration law regime.[6]

2. *Id.* at 37–38.
3. JOSEPH NEVINS, OPERATION GATEKEEPER AND BEYOND: THE WAR ON "ILLEGALS"
AND THE REMAKING OF THE U.S.-MEXICO BOUNDARY 227 appx. F (2nd ed. 2010).
4. *Id.*
5. MAE N. NGAI, IMPOSSIBLE SUBJECTS: ILLEGAL ALIENS AND THE MAKING OF
MODERN AMERICA 239 (2004).
6. *Id.* at 261.

Rather than stop Mexicans from coming to the United States, the cap merely changed the legality of their longstanding activity. In other words, the cap, as the historian Mae Ngai wrote, simply "recast Mexican migration as 'illegal'."[7] Available statistics bear out this claim. "Net unauthorized migration—that is, the difference between the number of unauthorized individuals who entered the country and those who left—jumped from zero before the 1965 Act was enacted to approximately 300,000 per year by the close of the 1980s."[8] Now viewed as lawbreakers—as people who had simply chosen to skirt the legal options for coming to the United States—unauthorized migrants came to be viewed as moral scofflaws.[9] Immigration authorities lost no time targeting these offenders with strongarmed enforcement. In 1976, the federal government deported 781,000 Mexicans plus another 100,000 people from the rest of the world.[10]

Tough immigration law enforcement did not dramatically curtail immigration to the United States. In fact, three large groups of migrants flocked to the United States during the late 1970s and 1980s. Roughly 125,000 Cubans reached the United States in 1979 and 1980 after the Cuban government announced that it would not stop anyone from leaving through the island's port in Mariel.[11] Around this time another 15,000 or so Haitians arrived, mostly on rickety vessels that miraculously survived the journey across the Caribbean.[12] Neither of these flows compared in size to the hundreds of thousands of Central Americans who made their way across México to reach the United States by land seeking refuge from the civil wars ravaging that region. Though Cubans were treated measurably more favorably than Haitian or Central American migrants, all presented political problems and administrative headaches to government officials who had to decide how to respond to so many people literally walking or rowing their way into the United States without the

---

7. *Id.*

8. César Cuauhtémoc García Hernández, *Creating Crimmigration*, 2013 BYU L. Rev. 1457, 1491.

9. *Id.* at 1492.

10. NGAI, *supra* note 5, at 261.

11. NEVINS, *supra* note 3, at 82–83.

12. Jonathan Simon, *Refugees in a Carceral Age: The Rebirth of Immigration Prisons in the United States,* 10 PUB. CULTURE 577, 579 (1998).

government's knowledge or permission. As President Ronald Reagan claimed in 1984, "our borders are out of control."[13]

The second development leading to an expanded emphasis on border law enforcement was the onset of the war on drugs. Candidates Richard Nixon and George Wallace had harped about rampant crime during their 1968 presidential campaigns, but it would take another decade before crime control became a salient feature of federal policymaking. Ronald Reagan managed to harness the fear that soon began to revolve around discussions of crime-plagued communities into a key component of his successful presidential run and in 1982 he officially announced what has come to be known as the "war on drugs."[14] Reagan's presidency would come to be synonymous with a litany of anti-drug initiatives.

At the same time, "drugs that had previously been routed through the Caribbean began making their way into the United States across the Mexican border."[15] Almost before it began, the drug war had a new front: the southwest border. Policymakers and political pundits began talking of unauthorized migrants and drug traffickers in the same breath. The language of war that was gaining popularity in the drug context was repurposed to discuss immigration as unauthorized migrants were said to be invading the country.

And because all of this activity was happening along the southwest, the border with México came to be seen as a weak link in the nation's defense. Border security, the Reagan Administration concluded, was a national security concern.[16] His successor, George H. W. Bush, claimed that the border represented "the front lines of the war on drugs," a comment he made while signing the Immigration Act of 1990.[17] As explained in this book's Introduction, the Immigration Act of 1990 and many other

---

13. *1984-Ronald Reagan on Amnesty*, Youtube.com, https://www.youtube.com/watch?v=JfHKIq5z80U (last visited Aug. 5, 2014).

14. MICHELLE ALEXANDER, THE NEW JIM CROW: MASS INCARCERATION IN THE AGE OF COLORBLINDNESS 49 (2010).

15. García Hernández, *supra* note 8, at 1506.

16. TIMOTHY J. DUNN, THE MILITARIZATION OF THE U.S.-MEXICO BORDER, 1978-1992: LOW-INTENSITY CONFLICT DOCTRINE COMES HOME 42 (1996).

17. George H.W. Bush, *Presidential Statement on Signing the Immigration Act of 1990* (Nov. 29, 1990), http://www.presidency.ucsb.edu/ws/?pid=19117.

bills enacted from the middle of the 1980s through the present day have intertwined efforts to curtail drug activity with efforts to toughen immigration law. Immigration officials increasingly took on a more active role in drug enforcement, including the 1991 decision designating the Border Patrol as the federal agency with primary responsibility for drug interdiction between ports of entry.[18] Along with more responsibility came more funding. Meanwhile, criminal justice agencies were tasked with greater involvement in immigration law enforcement.

This ramp up in authority and responsibility led to a heightened law enforcement presence along the southwest border. In 1989, Lloyd Bentsen, at the time a United States Senator representing Texas, complained to the Attorney General that "INS policy will turn South Texas into a massive detention camp."[19] Such an intense law enforcement presence—perhaps inevitably—eventually led to claims of government overreach. For example, political scientist and border resident Tony Payan claimed "the war on drugs, the war on immigration, and the war for Homeland Security, are now a daily fixture of the lives of the border people."[20]

As is their role, the courts entered the fray to demarcate the permissible contours of law enforcement power along the border. The remainder of this chapter devotes its attention to the ways that courts have interpreted the Fourth Amendment—the key constitutional provision concerning law enforcement—in light of the border's new normal.

Fourth Amendment Norms

The Fourth Amendment prohibits "unreasonable searches and seizures" and guarantees that "no warrants shall issue, but upon probable cause." It is a hallmark of the Fourth Amendment that government agents cannot intrude into a person's private affairs without some indicia of suspicion that the individual is engaging in wrongdoing. The Fourth Amendment

18. Southwest Border Enforcement Affected by Mission Expansion and Budget, Testimony Before the Subcomm. on Int'l L., Immig. & Refugees, H. Comm. of Judiciary, 102d Cong. 1 (1991) (statement of Harold A. Valentine, Assoc. Director, Administration of Justice Issues).

19. ROBERT S. KAHN, OTHER PEOPLE'S BLOOD: U.S. IMMIGRATION PRISONS IN THE REAGAN DECADE 207 (1996).

20. TONY PAYAN, THE THREE U.S.-MEXICO BORDER WARS: DRUGS, IMMIGRATION, AND HOMELAND SECURITY xiii (2006).

itself explicitly imposes the well-known probable cause requirement before police officers can search or arrest. In *Terry v. Ohio*, the Supreme
Court famously announced that police may engage in a temporary seizure
that does not rise to the level of an arrest with nothing more than reasonable suspicion of wrongdoing.[21] While engaging in that *"Terry* stop"
or "investigatory stop," officers are empowered to perform a patdown
search of the seized individual in an effort to learn whether the individual
is carrying a weapon.[22] To allow police officers to stop anyone "on the
chance" of finding evidence of illegal activity, Chief Justice Taft famously
wrote in a Prohibition-era case involving a stop of a vehicle on a public
road, "would be intolerable and unreasonable."[23]

Suspicionless Searches

Border searches depart from traditional Fourth Amendment doctrine by authorizing government agents to search and seize private individuals without
any suspicion of wrongdoing. The most straightforward border policing exceptions occur directly at ports-of-entry. Here the federal government pos-
sesses extraordinary power and prospective entrants few entitlements. As the
Supreme Court explained in 1925, "Travelers may be so stopped in crossing
an international boundary because of national self-protection reasonably requiring one entering the country to identify himself as entitled to come in,
and his belongings as effects which may be lawfully brought in."[24] Despite
the "plenary authority to conduct routine searches and seizures at the border,
without probable cause or a warrant" that "Congress has granted the Executive" since the nation's founding, port-of-entry encounters sit on a spectrum
of constitutionally permissible governmental activity.[25]

Congress has long authorized searches of vehicles entering the United
States and their passengers. Though the current statute goes back to 1930,
it traces its roots to a statute enacted in 1790 by the first Congress.[26]

---

21. 392 U.S. 1, 21 (1968).
22. *Id.* at 24.
23. Carroll v. United States, 267 U.S. 132, 153–54 (1925).
24. *Id.* at 154.
25. United States v. Montoya de Hernandez, 473 U.S. 531, 537 (1985).
26. Act of June 17, 1930, ch. 497, § 581, 46 Stat. 747 (codified at 19 U.S.C. § 1581(a));
see Act of Aug. 4, 1790, ch. 35, § 31, 1 Stat. 164–5.

Today's version authorizes customs officials—members of DHS's Customs and Border Protection unit—at ports-of-entry to "examine, inspect, and search the vessel or vehicle and every part thereof and any person, trunk, package, or cargo on board, and to this end may hail and stop such vessel or vehicle, and use all necessary force to compel compliance."[27] A separate provision extends much the same power to ICE agents. INA § 287(a)(3) authorizes immigration officials to board any vehicle "within a reasonable distance from any external boundary of the United States. . . for the purpose of patrolling the border to prevent the illegal entry of aliens into the United States."[28] DHS defines a "reasonable distance" as "within 100 air miles from any external boundary of the United States."[29]

No suspicion of wrongdoing is required. On the contrary, the Supreme Court has made it quite clear that vehicles can be stopped, seized, and inspected as a matter of course. In the leading case on this issue, *United States v. Flores-Montano,* the Court upheld an hour-long seizure during which the gas tank on the defendant's car was removed from the vehicle and disassembled.[30] The officers made no claim that they suspected Flores-Montano of any wrongdoing, and the Court concluded that none was needed. The government's interest in controlling the movement of people and goods "is at its zenith at the international border," the Court wrote, thus "[t]ime and again, we have stated that 'searches made at the border, pursuant to the longstanding right of the sovereign to protect itself by stopping and examining persons and property crossing into this country, are reasonable simply by virtue of the fact that they occur at the border.'"[31] In a different case, the Court made its view crystal clear when it explained that "[r]outine searches of the persons and effects of entrants are not subject to any requirement of reasonable suspicion, probable cause, or warrant."[32] Given its treatment of vehicles and people, it should come as no surprise that the Court extended this reasoning to arriving

---

27. 19 U.S.C. § 1581(a); 19 C.F.R. §§ 162.6–162.7; *see* 19 U.S.C. § 482(a).
28. INA § 287(a)(3).
29. 8 C.F.R. § 287.1(a)(1).
30. 541 U.S. 149, 151 (2004).
31. *Id.* at 152–53.
32. United States v. Montoya de Hernandez, 473 U.S. 531, 538 (1985).

international mail.[33] The Fourth Amendment, it seems, has no bearing on ordinary encounters with federal law enforcement officers at the border.

The government's power begins to wane a bit when a person—rather than a vehicle—is subjected to intrusive examination during a prolonged seizure. Rosa Elvira Montoya de Hernández was detained at the Los Angeles International Airport for sixteen hours after arriving on a flight from Bogota, Colombia. During this time she was held incommunicado. Despite a patdown and strip search finding no evidence of illegal activity, she was given the option of submitting to an x-ray of her abdomen or electing to wait until she had a bowel movement that officers would inspect for contraband. She was eventually subjected to a court-ordered rectal examination that revealed eighty-eight balloons in her rectum containing cocaine.[34] The Court upheld the resulting convictions. Part of its analysis is simple enough given *Flores-Montano*. Anyone seeking to enter the United States is subject to examination and inspection by federal officials even if the officials have no basis upon which to suspect wrongdoing.[35]

But is everyone subject to such prolonged and intrusive detention as Montoya de Hernández experienced? Clearly no. Her experience was constitutionally permissible because "customs agents, considering all the facts surrounding the traveler and her trip, reasonably suspect[ed] that the traveler [wa]s smuggling contraband in her alimentary canal."[36] In other words, federal law enforcement officers can perform a lengthy seizure and intrusive search of a person seeking to enter the United States at a port-of-entry if they have reasonable suspicion, based on specific articulable facts, that the person is engaged in criminal activity, evidence of which is to be found in the place searched, including the person's body.

Notably the Court takes the position that there is no legal distinction between a land, air, or sea port-of-entry. Flores-Montano had his gas tank searched at a secondary inspection area at some undisclosed distance from the imaginary line dividing two countries.[37] In all likelihood this was no more than a few hundred yards from the borderline so there is an intuitive

---

33. United States v. Ramsey, 431 U.S. 606, 616 (1977).
34. Montoya de Hernandez, 473 U.S. at 534–36.
35. *Id*. at 538.
36. *Id*. at 541.
37. United States v. Flores-Montano, 541 U.S. 149, 152 (2004).

appeal to the Court's description of this area as "the international border." Montoya de Hernandez, however, was searched at the Los Angeles International Airport, 138 miles from San Ysidro, the California town just to the north of Tijuana, México. Still, for purposes of the Court's border search jurisprudence, the Los Angeles International Airport is an international border.[38] Any other official port-of-entry receives the same status. Similarly, the search of arriving international mail that led the Court to clarify that mail is no different from vehicles or people took place at a New York City post office. The search did not occur at an international airport. Still, the Court flatly explained, "There is no dispute that this is the 'border' for purposes of border searches."[39] Though the Court provides no further explanation, this conclusion is unsurprising given that the post office is the first location within the territorial United States that the mail was handled. For purposes of border search doctrine, this is the border or, at least, its functional equivalent. As the Court explained in another case, "searches of this kind may in certain circumstances take place not only at the border itself, but at its functional equivalents as well."[40]

Practice Pointer

The Constitution applies differently to immigration criminal policing than to most other types of law enforcement activity. In general, the Fourth Amendment gives government officials much greater leeway in this context. It permits

- suspicionless searches at ports-of-entry and their functional equivalents
- suspicionless searches at fixed Border Patrol checkpoints almost 100 miles from the border
- during a roving patrol stop, Border Patrol officers can consider a person's race to determine whether reasonable suspicion exists that she is violating immigration law.

Similarly, en masse hearings of federal criminal prosecutions are allowed despite Federal Rules of Criminal Procedure Rule 11's requirement that the judge, prior to accepting a plea, address every defendant personally, a requirement that is rooted in the Fifth Amendment Due Process Clause.

---

38. *Montoya de Hernandez*, 473 U.S. at 537.
39. United States v. Ramsey, 431 U.S. 606, 608 n.2 & 616 (1977).
40. Almeida-Sanchez v. United States, 413 U.S. 266, 273 (1973).

Race on the Border

Race has a sordid presence in the history of policing in the United States. For much of that time, the courts were willing enablers of official racism that not infrequently manifested itself in the most vicious exercises of brutality imaginable. This volume, of course, is not the place in which to recount that history. It is enough to note an important lesson resulting from that history: race is an unwanted and illegal factor of most policing decisions.[41] As the Tenth Circuit explained, "Racially selective law enforcement violates this nation's constitutional values at the most fundamental level."[42] Except when it comes to border policing.

Like with its suspicionless search cases at international borders and their functional equivalents, the Supreme Court's cases about stops at some distance from the international boundary make it clear that, in the justices' view, the border region is exceptional. Law enforcement officials, therefore, need extraordinary flexibility if they are to successfully fight lawlessness. Unauthorized migrants, the Court explained in *United States v. Brignoni-Ponce*, move through the border region in such high numbers and with such stealth that immigration law enforcement authorities are simply outpowered.[43] "[E]ven a vastly reinforced Border Patrol," the Court claimed, "would find it impossible to prevent illegal border crossings," nonetheless identifying and apprehending migrants who enter with the federal government's permission only to violate some provision of civil immigration law later.[44] The "public interest demands effective measures to prevent the illegal entry of aliens at the Mexican border," the Court went on, and it is nothing more than a "minimal intrusion" to allow immigration officials to stop a vehicle if they have reasonable suspicion that unauthorized migrants are inside.[45] "The officer may question the driver and passengers about their citizenship and immigration status, and he may ask them to explain suspicious circumstances, but any further detention or search must be based on consent or probable cause," the Court held.[46]

41. *See* Whren v. United States, 517 U.S. 806, 813 (1996).
42. Marshall v. Columbia Lea Regional Hosp., 345 F.3d 1157, 1167 (10th Cir. 2003).
43. 422 U.S. 873, 879–80 (1975).
44. *Id.* at 879.
45. *Id.* at 878, 881.
46. *Id.* at 881–82.

In assessing reasonable suspicion, officers can consider a wide range of factors. Proximity to the border, characteristics of the area, whether the road on which the vehicle is encountered is often used to transport unauthorized migrants, the driver's behavior, number of passengers, even the size and style of the vehicle are permissible considerations.[47]

Had the Court's analysis ended there it could be characterized as an ordinary Fourth Amendment case. The Court's additional reasoning, however, moves it beyond the bounds of typical Fourth Amendment doctrine and into the realm of exceptional border search and seizure cases. The unique circumstances present near the border, the Court suggested, demand unique calculations of reasonable suspicion. "The Government also points out that trained officers can recognize the characteristic appearance of persons who live in Mexico, relying on such factors as the mode of dress and haircut," the Court announced.[48] Standing alone, Mexican appearance is not sufficient to establish reasonable suspicion, because, the Court acknowledged, many people who appear to be Mexican are United States citizens or authorized migrants. Nonetheless, "[t]he likelihood that any given person of Mexican ancestry is an alien is high enough to make Mexican appearance a relevant factor."[49]

A year later, the Court returned to its race-based border policing doctrine in *United States v. Martinez-Fuerte*.[50] Unlike *Brignoni-Ponce*, which involved a roving stop by Border Patrol officers, *Martinez-Fuerte* involved a number of cases in which people were stopped at fixed Border Patrol checkpoints while traveling on public highways well away from the border. One checkpoint was approximately sixty-six miles from the border and another roughly ninety miles away. In a common practice familiar to border travelers even today, every vehicle approaching the checkpoint was required to stop while passengers were asked about their immigration status.[51] As with stops at ports-of-entry, no suspicion of wrongdoing is necessary.[52] After this initial seizure and inquiry most vehicles are allowed

47. *Id.* at 886.
48. *Id.*
49. *Id.* at 886–87.
50. 428 U.S. 543 (1976).
51. *Id.* at 546.
52. *Id.* at 557.

to proceed without additional delay, but a small number are ordered to a secondary inspection area where they are subjected to more in-depth questioning. Here again the Court concluded that no suspicion of wrong-doing is required.[53] But as with *Brignoni-Ponce*, the Court went one step further. Because no individualized suspicion of wrongdoing is required, the Court explained that it could "perceive no constitutional violation" "even if it be assumed that such referrals are made largely on the basis of apparent Mexican ancestry."[54] Racial profiling, these cases evidence, is a constitutionally permissible law enforcement practice.

Despite openly accepting race-based policing, *Brignoni-Ponce* and *Martinez-Fuerte* have yet to be overturned. Both cases are frequently cited for support. Defendants in immigration crime prosecutions regularly rely on *Brignoni-Ponce*, claiming that immigration officials relied solely on race to stop a moving vehicle, clearly violating the Court's admonishment that Mexican appearance alone is insufficient to establish reasonable suspicion. For their part, however, government attorneys often try to steer clear of this factor and courts frequently make no mention of race when assessing whether an officer had reasonable suspicion to pull over a vehicle.

Perhaps because they raise such fraught topics, the lower courts have struggled to apply the holdings of *Brignoni-Ponce* and *Martinez-Fuerte* in the four decades since the opinions were issued. The Sixth Circuit, for example, limited *Martinez-Fuerte*'s reach to locations near the Mexican border in a case involving a stop in Ohio not far from the Canadian border.[55] The Fifth Circuit, meanwhile, cautioned that the border search doctrine does not empower law enforcement officials to engage in an otherwise impermissible seizure. Border Patrol agents, for example, cannot use the leeway that *Brignoni-Ponce* and *Martinez-Fuerte* grant them in their efforts to curtail unauthorized migration to look for illegal drugs.[56] In contrast, the Tenth Circuit relied on *Martinez-Fuerte* to conclude that

---

53. *Id.* at 562.

54. *Id.* at 563.

55. Farm Labor Organizing Comm. v. Ohio State Highway Patrol, 308 F.3d 523, 541 n.7 (6th Cir. 2002).

56. United States v. Portillo-Aguirre, 311 F.3d 647, 655–56 (5th Cir. 2002); United States v. Machuca-Barrera, 261 F.3d 425, 431 (5th Cir. 2001).

Border Patrol officers could engage in a "cursory visual inspection of the vehicle" and ask "a few brief questions concerning such things as vehicle ownership, cargo, destination, and travel plans . . . if reasonably related to the agent's duty to prevent the unauthorized entry of individuals into this country and to prevent the smuggling of contraband."[57]

The Ninth Circuit has taken the harshest approach toward the use of race in immigration policing along the border. In *United States v. Montero-Camargo*, the appellate court departed from *Brignoni-Ponce*'s logic on the basis that the Supreme Court "relied heavily on now-outdated demographic information."[58] In particular, the Ninth Circuit explained that the statistical data about the Mexican population along the Southwest upon which the Supreme Court placed a great deal of emphasis is vastly different from the comparable data in 2000, the year in which the Ninth Circuit's decision was issued. Moreover, the Ninth Circuit noted that race and ethnicity are increasingly disfavored means of government decisionmaking, citing recent Supreme Court decisions limiting affirmative action policies.[59] For those reasons, the *Montero-Camargo* court concluded, "Hispanic appearance is, in general, of such little probative value that it may not be considered as a relevant factor where particularized or individualized suspicion is required," that is, in the context of an investigatory *Terry* stop.[60] Even then, however, the Ninth Circuit undercut *Montero-Camargo* in a later case, *United States v. Manzo-Jurado*, where it announced that "[a]n individual's inability to speak English may support an officer's reasonable suspicion that the individual is in this country illegally."[61]

Courts are similarly unsure how far into the nation's interior to extend the border search doctrine. There is no geographic bright line—a border, so to speak—that confines the border search doctrine. Aside from airports serving international flights, it is unclear to what extent immigration officials can rely on border search cases when engaging in law enforcement operations at a great distance from the border.[62] A DHS regulation

57. United States v. Rascon-Ortiz, 994 F.2d 749, 752 (10th Cir. 1993).
58. 208 F.3d 1122, 1132 (9th Cir. 2000).
59. *Id.* at 1134–35.
60. *Id.* at 1135.
61. 457 F.3d 928, 936-37 (9th Cir. 2006).
62. *See* United States v. Rico-Soto, 690 F.3d 376, 378 n.1 (5th Cir. 2012).

claims this power extends 100 miles from the nearest external boundary.[63]
Courts tend to grant immigration officials this much leeway, but have
shown some skepticism about the border search doctrine's applicability
at much greater distances from the border.[64] Still, courts have upheld use
of the border search doctrine to stops as far as 200 or 300 miles from the
nearest border with a foreign country.[65] For decades this was largely an
irrelevant concern since immigration stops far removed from the border
were rare; immigration officials instead focused almost all their efforts
on the border region. Recently, however, the border search exception's
applicability in the country's interior has become an increasingly relevant
question since ICE has expanded the practices long used in border communities to communities far from any international boundary.

Ironically, convincing a court that immigration officials violated the
Fourth Amendment by relying on the border search doctrine inappropri-
ately is not guaranteed to lead to success for migrant criminal defendants.
In *INS v. Lopez-Mendoza*, the case in which the Supreme Court held that
the exclusionary rule typically does not apply in civil immigration proceedings, the Court also stated, "The 'body' or identity of a defendant or
respondent in a criminal or civil proceeding is never itself suppressible as
a fruit of an unlawful arrest, even if it is conceded that an unlawful arrest,
search, or interrogation occurred."[66] This is highly problematic for migrants because it means that they can be prosecuted civilly or criminally
even if police officers arrested them in violation of the Constitution. Examples of this are not uncommon. Mario Roque-Villanueva, for example,
was prosecuted for illegal reentry even though the Border Patrol officer
who stopped him may have had no reasonable suspicion or probable cause
to do so.[67] Similarly, José Hernández-Mandujano was also indicted for
illegal reentry after an illegal stop led to questioning in which Border Patrol officers learned about Hernández-Mandujano's immigration status.

63. 8 C.F.R. § 287.1(a)(2).
64. *See, e.g.*, United States v. Hernandez-Mandujano, 721 F.3d 345, 349 (5th Cir.
2013) (450 miles from the nearest border crossing).
65. *See, e.g.*, United States v. Orozco, 191 F.3d 578, 581 (5th Cir. 1999); United States
v. Lamas, 608 F.2d 547, 548 (5th Cir. 1979).
66. 468 U.S. 1032, 1039 (1984).
67. United States v. Roque-Villanueva, 175 F.3d 345, 346 (5th Cir. 1999).

Despite determining that the officers had no legal basis upon which to stop Hernández-Mandujano, the Fifth Circuit, following *Lopez-Mendoza*, concluded that neither Hernández-Mandujano's identity nor his immigration file could be suppressed.[68]

Whether or not this is what *Lopez-Mendoza* actually requires is up for debate. The Fourth Circuit put it best when it wrote that "[t]he meaning of the *Lopez–Mendoza* 'identity statement' has bedeviled and divided our sister circuits."[69] Some circuits take the position that *Lopez-Mendoza* precludes suppression of a migrant's identity and evidence of immigration status.[70] Others, in contrast, read the Supreme Court's statement as nothing more than an unilluminating comment that an illegal arrest does not deprive a court of jurisdiction over the arrested person; these courts allow for the possibility of suppression.[71] So far the Supreme Court has failed to explain which position is correct.

Enforcing Federal Immigration Crimes

Though immigration crimes, in particular illegal entry and illegal reentry, have been part of federal law for many decades, the federal government has shown unprecedented interest in prosecuting these offenses in recent years. Almost 92,000 people were prosecuted for an immigration offense in the 2012 fiscal year, an experience that 97,384 people went through the following year.[72] The bulk of these were for illegal entry or illegal reentry. Indeed, illegal entry prosecutions alone comprised 55 percent of all immigration prosecutions in 2013 and illegal reentry cases made up another

68. United States v. Hernandez-Mandujano, 721 F.3d 345, 351 (5th Cir. 2013).

69. United States v. Oscar-Torres, 507 F.3d 224, 228 (4th Cir. 2007).

70. *See, e.g.,*, United States v. Farias-Gonzalez, 556 F.3d 1181, 1185-86 (11th Cir. 2009); United States v. Garcia-Garcia, 633 F.3d 608, 616 (7th Cir. 2011); United States v. Del Toro Gudino, 376 F.3d 997, 1001 (9th Cir. 2004); United States v. Bowley, 435 F.3d 426, 430–31 (3d Cir. 2006); United States v. Navarro-Diaz, 420 F.3d 581, 588 (6th Cir. 2005); United States v. Roque-Villanueva, 175 F.3d 345, 346 (5th Cir. 1999).

71. *See, e.g.,* Pretzantzin v. Holder, 736 F.3d 641, 647–48 (2d Cir. 2013); United States v. Oscar-Torres, 507 F.3d 224, 230 (4th Cir. 2007); United States v. Olivares-Rangel, 458 F.3d 1104, 1106 (10th Cir. 2006); United States v. Guevara-Martinez, 262 F.3d 751, 754–55 (8th Cir. 2001).

72. Transactional Records Access Clearinghouse, *At Nearly 100,000, Immigration Prosecutions Reach All-Time High in FY 2013* (Nov. 25, 2013), http://trac.syr.edu/immigration/reports/336/.

38 percent.[73] The remaining 7 percent was divided among the large group of immigration-related activity that is criminalized through offenses such as those described in chapter 6. Since 2009, immigration defendants have competed with drug defendants for the most heavily prosecuted type of federal crime.[74] This trend is most pronounced in a handful of federal court districts along the Southwest border. In fiscal year 2012, for example, 71 percent of prosecutions heard in the Southern District of California were illegal entry or illegal reentry cases. Likewise, 66 percent of cases in the Southern District of Texas that year, an enormous jurisdiction stretching from Houston several hundred miles south to the Río Grande Valley along the border, focused on one of these two offenses.[75] A federal magistrate judge in South Texas "who estimates he has presided over 17,000 [illegal entry] cases, described his role as 'a factory putting out a mold.'"[76]

The high number of prosecutions is historically anomalous. In 1961, for example, the INS forwarded 5,005 cases for criminal prosecution and U.S. Attorneys actually brought charges in 2,459.[77] As recently as 2007, during the waning years of President George W. Bush's administration and in the aftermath of enormous immigrants' rights marches in 2006, roughly 12,000 people were prosecuted for illegal entry and another 18,000 for illegal reentry. Going back to the start of the Clinton Administration puts contemporary prosecutions in even starker relief. In 1993, a negligible number of people were prosecuted for illegal entry, while about 2,000 were prosecuted for illegal reentry.[78]

To accomplish this impressive, machine-like growth in the number of federal immigration criminal prosecutions, federal prosecutors rely principally on two innovative prosecutorial initiatives: Operation Streamline and fast-track plea agreements.

---

73. *Id.*

74. MARK MOTIVANS, FEDERAL JUSTICE STATISTICS, 2010, at 17 fig.9 (2013).

75. HUMAN RTS. WATCH, TURNING MIGRANTS INTO CRIMINALS: THE HARMFUL IMPACT OF U.S. BORDER PROSECUTIONS 21 fig.3 (2013).

76. *Id.* at 35 (quoting a 2012 interview with Magistrate Judge Felix Recio in Brownsville, Texas).

77. IMMIGRATION & NATURALIZATION SERVICE, ANNUAL REPORT OF THE IMMIGRATION AND NATURALIZATION SERVICE 10 (1961).

78. TRAC, *supra* note 72.

Operation Streamline

The most significant prosecutorial initiative affecting crimmigration law is Operation Streamline. This initiative has changed how federal criminal courts operate and raised the stakes of unauthorized entry into the United States. Rather than rely solely on the civil immigration law regime to identify, apprehend, process, and remove individuals who lack authorization to be in the United States, Operation Streamline inserts federal prosecutors and criminal courts into the process. Before turning to the civil immigration system to actually order a migrant removed and carry out the removal order, Operation Streamline mandates that ICE and CBP refer migrants who are allegedly unauthorized to U.S. Attorneys Offices for criminal prosecution. Federal prosecutors then charge migrants with illegal entry or illegal reentry. In the face of possible jail time, most migrants quickly plead guilty. Before Operation Streamline, most individuals in similar situations were simply processed through the civil removal system.

Launched in December 2005 in rural Del Rio, Texas, Operation Streamline has since expanded to CBP districts throughout the Southwest. The program's goal is to criminally prosecute 100 percent of apprehended migrants. Though that goal has been frustrated by resource constraints, federal prosecutors have nonetheless brought criminal charges against an impressive number of people who in the past would have been removed through the civil immigration court system. In Tucson, for example, magistrate judges hear seventy Operation Streamline cases every business day, a caseload that the Ninth Circuit's Judicial Council described as "crushing" and "taking a severe toll on staff."[79] Data from other jurisdictions in which Operation Streamline exists present a similar picture. Not surprisingly, by the end of the 2012 fiscal year, 208,939 people had been prosecuted through Operation Streamline.[80] Importantly, the program's "zero tolerance" approach means that anyone caught in the United States without authorization faces the possibility of jail time and the stigma of a criminal conviction.

---

79. In re Approval of Jud. Emer. Decl. in Dist. of Ariz., 639 F.3d 970, 975, 979 (9th Cir. Jud. Council 2011).

80. Marc R. Rosenblum, Border Security: Immigration Enforcement Between Ports of Entry 8 (2013).

To move this many people through the federal court system, Operation Streamline adopted a key procedural innovation that departs from traditional criminal proceedings. Instead of having every defendant receive the judge's undivided attention, prosecutors present cases en masse. As many as 50 to 100 defendants appeared in court simultaneously during the first several years of the program's existence.[81] More recently, the maximum number of migrants who can be brought before a judge at the same time has been capped at forty, but reports suggest that this cap is exceeded regularly.[82]

Regardless of the exact number, judges in these en masse hearings address defendants jointly. After explaining to defendants collectively the various rights applicable to criminal proceedings, the presiding judge in an Operation Streamline hearing asks them whether they agree to waive those rights. Defendants then respond with a "[g]eneral yes answer," as the Ninth Circuit put it.[83] In a slight twist, some judges now ask defendants to respond individually. In all these situations, however, judges struggle to ensure that defendants understand the proceeding and the effect of pleading guilty. As the chief judge of the U.S. District Court for the District of New Mexico explained in 2008, "Our magistrate judges try very hard to conduct their hearings in a way that is understandable to the defendants. But most of our defendants have a first or second grade education in their native countries. Some of them are not even able to read in their native languages. And so, we explain to them their constitutional rights in a legal system entirely foreign to them. . . . It is a difficult atmosphere in which to waive important constitutional rights, and to ask them if they understand their rights."[84]

Courts have begun to cast doubt on whether Operation Streamline defendants do in fact understand the rights they waive by pleading guilty. Federal Rule of Criminal Procedure 11(b) requires that a judge, prior to accepting a plea, address each defendant "personally" and ensure that the

81. DONALD KERWIN AND KRISTEN MCCABE, MIGRATION POLICY INSTITUTE, ARRESTED ON ENTRY: OPERATION STREAMLINE AND THE PROSECUTION OF IMMIGRATION CRIMES at 3 (April 29, 2010).

82. ROSENBLUM, *supra* note 80, at 8.

83. United States v. Diaz-Ramirez, 646 F.3d 653, 655 & n.2 (9th Cir. 2011).

84. ADMIN. OFFICE OF THE U.S. COURTS, REPORT ON THE IMPACT ON THE JUDICIARY OF LAW ENFORCEMENT ACTIVITIES ALONG THE SOUTHWEST BORDER 16 (2008).

plea was entered voluntarily. This mandate is rooted in the Fifth Amendment Due Process Clause's requirement that all pleas be knowing and intelligent. It is next to impossible, however, for a judge to determine whether a plea was entered voluntarily if all she hears is "an indistinct murmur or medley of yeses."[85] Despite this conclusion, courts had upheld convictions obtained through Operation Streamline because of migrants' inability to show the requisite prejudice.[86] That changed in 2013 when the Ninth Circuit concluded that Operation Streamline's en masse hearings not only violated FRCP 11(b), but that the government, the party that bore the burden of showing that the migrant would have pleaded guilty even without the Rule 11(b) violation, failed to show that the migrant would have pleaded guilty had the judge complied with Rule 11(b).[87]

Aside from Operation Streamline's impact on judges' ability to comply with procedural requirements, the initiative's quick pace also affects defense attorneys' ability to comply with the obligations they owe defendants. Though the Sixth Amendment right to counsel does not apply to migrants in removal proceedings, Operation Streamline concerns criminal proceedings, thus the Sixth Amendment applies fully. Criminal defense attorneys representing Operation Streamline defendants typically have little time to meet with clients and almost no time to investigate the circumstances of a client's apprehension.[88] Often they represent multiple defendants in the same hearing. In the words of a magistrate judge who frequently presides over Operation Streamline hearings, defense attorneys function as "'ushers on the conveyor belt to prison'."[89] Indeed, migrants sometimes are shuffled through the courtroom so quickly that they appear to be standing on a conveyor belt.

The fact remains, however, that the Sixth Amendment obligates criminal defense attorneys to investigate the law and facts relevant to a client's

---

85. United States v. Roblero-Solis, 588 F.3d 692, 700 (9th Cir. 2009).

86. *See Diaz-Ramirez*, 646 F.3d at 655, 658; United States v. Escamilla-Rojas, 640 F.3d 1055, 1058, 1063 (9th Cir. 2011).

87. United States v. Arqueta-Ramos, 730 F.3d 1133, 1141-42 (9th Cir. 2013).

88. DONALD KERWIN AND KRISTEN McCABE, MIGRATION POLICY INSTITUTE, ARRESTED ON ENTRY: OPERATION STREAMLINE AND THE PROSECUTION OF IMMIGRATION CRIMES 3 (April 29, 2010).

89. HUMAN RTS. WATCH, *supra* note 75, at 38 (quoting 2013 interview with Magistrate Judge Bernardo Velasco).

legal predicament.[90] Defense attorneys, the Supreme Court announced in
Strickland v. Washington, "ha[ve] a duty to make reasonable investigations or to make a reasonable decision that makes particular investigations
unnecessary."[91] Courts have yet to address whether defense attorneys can
comply with Operation Streamline's fast-paced expectations while also
meeting Sixth Amendment duties. It is important for defense attorneys to
remember, however, that Operation Streamline is merely a policy initiative through which large numbers of illegal entry and illegal reentry cases
are brought. In any of these cases, the possibility exists that a viable defense is available. Though some possible defenses are factually and legally
rather straightforward and can be quickly considered and dismissed—
e.g., the possibility that CBP agents erroneously concluded that a migrant
found near the border had crossed without authorization—other possible
defenses, especially derivative citizenship claims, are factually and legally
complicated. No matter how complex, it is always the defense attorney's
duty to make reasonable inquiries of a defendant to determine whether
a viable defense exists, and in most instances that takes time—time that
Operation Streamline puts at a premium.

Fast-Track Plea Agreements

Another policy initiative that helps quicken the pace of federal immigration
criminal prosecutions is a process of fast-track pleading. Begun by federal
prosecutors in southern California in the 1990s, fast-track pleading became available on March 1, 2012, in all jurisdictions where illegal reentry
cases are prosecuted.[92] Based on a uniform Justice Department policy that
went into effect on that date, all such agreements involve a crimmigration-
specific twist on a routine prosecutorial practice. Prosecutors agree to request a downward departure from the sentencing range prescribed by the
U.S. Sentencing Guidelines if an illegal reentry defendant makes a host
of concessions: agrees to the factual allegations made by the government,

---

90. Strickland v. Washington, 466 U.S. 668, 690–91 (1984); *see* Cullen v. Pinholster,
131 S. Ct. 1388, 1406–07 (2011).
91. 466 U.S. at 691.
92. Memorandum from James M. Cole, Deputy Attorney General, to All United
States Attorneys, *Department Policy on Early Disposition or "Fast-Track" Programs* 4
(Jan. 31, 2012) http://www.justice.gov/dag/fast-track-program.pdf.

including regarding any prior conviction or removal; foregoes any motions available under Federal Rule of Criminal Procedure 12(b)(3), including motions to suppress; waives appeal; waives post-conviction challenges, except those based on ineffective assistance of counsel; and waives requests for a sentencing variance.[93] Importantly, a defendant must agree within thirty days of being taken into custody on the criminal charges.[94]

For defendants, the incentive to accept a fast-track plea is measureable. In most cases, the government agrees to seek a four-level downward departure from the Sentencing Guidelines base offense level (eight). For migrants with no prior criminal history, a four-level downward departure results in the same sentencing range (zero to six months), but for individuals with almost any criminal history the applicable sentencing range decreases in varying but significant amounts.

Fast-track pleading both responded to and facilitates processing large numbers of immigration criminal cases. The program began after the federal government increased the amount of resources devoted to targeting immigration law violators in southern California. Alan D. Bersin, the U.S. Attorney for the Southern District of California at the time and later to become Commissioner of CBP, subsequently explained that his office developed the fast-track plea process to deal with an influx of cases resulting from the Border Patrol obtaining a new computerized database that allowed officials to track every person apprehended entering the United States clandestinely.[95] By presenting illegal reentry defendants with the option of quickly pleading to illegal entry, Bersin's office was able to dramatically increase the number of immigration cases it prosecuted. Instead of the 250 illegal reentry cases prosecuted in 1994, the office prosecuted 1,334 in 1995.[96] In Bersin's words, "[t]he fast track system allowed this explosion in filings."[97]

Fast-track pleading's use in other jurisdictions has had a similar effect. An analysis of 2008 data indicates that fast-track cases across the country were disposed of in a median of less than 10 days, dramatically less time

---

93. *Id.* at 3–4.
94. *Id.* at 3.
95. Alan D. Bersin & Judith S. Feigin, *The Rule of Law at the Border: Reinventing Prosecution Policy in the Southern District of California*, 12 Geo. Immigr. L.J. 285, 300 (1998).
96. *Id.* at 301.
97. *Id.*

than the 250 days it took to process white-collar crimes, the next fastest category.[98] As Bersin noted, moving individual cases through the court system more quickly means that courts can handle more cases. Indeed, a 2013 study found that the number of immigration crimes prosecuted increased in almost every jurisdiction that used fast-track pleading between fiscal years 2006 and 2009.[99] Relatedly, a notable 38.1 percent of all immigration criminal cases disposed of during that time period in districts with fast-track programs in place were fast-tracked.[100]

Like Operation Streamline (discussed above), the high number of criminal immigration cases making their way through the federal courts under fast-track procedures raises important questions for defense attorneys. Under the current Justice Department policy, defendants are given up to thirty days from being taken into custody on federal criminal charges to decide whether they will accept a plea bargain that conforms to the fast-track requirement. Under the best of circumstances, thirty days is not very much time especially when the strongest defenses to illegal reentry and illegal entry prosecutions involve factually and legally complicated derivative citizenship claims.

The reality is, however, that criminal defense attorneys often do not operate under the best of circumstances. Two delays built into the appointment of counsel process mean that attorneys representing clients in fast-track proceedings frequently have less than thirty days to advise a defendant. First, the date on which DHS officials apprehend a migrant is not necessarily the date on which the migrant is taken into custody for federal criminal charges. On the contrary, migrants charged with an immigration crime are frequently apprehended by CBP or ICE agents on suspicion that the migrant has violated a civil provision of immigration law. Though this is undoubtedly a form of custody, it is not custody on federal criminal charges.[101] To illustrate this distinction between civil and criminal immigration custody, compare two cases. In one, Rocío Chávez was arrested on identity theft charges. A few hours later, immigration

---

98. Ingrid V. Eagly, *Prosecuting Immigration*, 104 Nw. U. L. Rev. 1281, 1324–25 (2010).

99. KiDeuk Kim, Organizational Efficiency and Early Disposition Programs in Federal Courts 34 (2013), https://www.ncjrs.gov/pdffiles1/nij/grants/244386.pdf.

100. *Id.* at 40 exhibit 6.

101. *See* United States v. Encarnacion, 239 F.3d 395, 399 (1st Cir. 2001).

officials learned that she lacked authorization to be present in the United States and initiated removal proceedings. The Eighth Circuit concluded that Chávez was arrested on criminal charges, thus criminal procedure protections, including the right to counsel, applied from the moment of arrest.[102] In another case, INS officers arrested Ernesto Encarnación as he tried to enter Puerto Rico on an international flight. After eight days of detention, federal prosecutors charged him with illegal reentry. The First Circuit concluded that Encarnación was originally taken into custody on a civil matter, and his criminal custody did not begin until a federal prosecutor obtained enough evidence to have probable cause that Encarción had illegally reentered the United States.[103] Though the First Circuit had no occasion to consider how Encarnación's predicament interacted with the fast-track initiative's thirty-day requirement, it is not difficult to see the logical conclusion: the thirty-day window available for fast-track pleading might not start running until several days after a migrant has been detained. The stress of detention, however, does not wait, thus defendants who are not accustomed to incarceration begin to feel the pressure of confinement before an attorney is assigned to the case.

Secondly, federal law regarding appointment of counsel in criminal proceedings does not require that a defendant receive counsel immediately upon being taken into criminal custody. Instead, appointment is required from the moment that a defendant initially appears in court, usually no later than 48 hours after arrest.[104] This time gap may strike the outsider observer as trivial, but it adds to the pressure that detained migrants frequently feel to move the legal process along as quickly as possible so as to be released. In the view of two senior federal public defenders, the result of fast-track's time pressures is that attorneys sometimes assistant clients to plead guilty "before we have adequate time to investigate their lives and circumstances . . . learning only later that they were U.S. citizens."[105] Despite the well-meaning assessment by these two

---

102.   United States v. Chavez, 705 F.3d 381, 383–84 (8th Cir. 2013).
103.   *Encarnacion*, 239 F.3d at 399.
104.   County of Riverside v. McLaughlin, 500 U.S. 44, 56 (1991); Fed. R. Crim. P. 44(a).
105.   Joint Statement of Thomas W. Hillier II, Fed. Pub. Defender, W. Dist. of Wash., & Davina Chen, Assistant Fed. Pub. Defender, Cent. Dist. of Cal., The Sentencing Reform Act of 1984: 25 Years Later: Public Hearings Before the U.S. Sentencing Comm. 28 (May 27, 2009).

attorneys, the Fifth Circuit's conclusion that a defense attorney's failure to identify a derivative citizenship claim constitutes ineffective assistance of counsel suggests that this type of representation might not pass constitutional standards of competency.[106]

Federal Investigations, State Prosecutions

One scenario that frequently arises along the border involves investigations by federal officials that ultimately lead to criminal prosecutions in state courts. Both ICE and CBP have sizeable presences along the border so it is not at all uncommon for them to encounter activity that violates state criminal laws during the course of their duties. Normally there is no question that federal officials can hand over a suspect to state officials for potential prosecution. Questions arise, however, when federal officials acted in violation of state law while investigating the crime. The U.S. Supreme Court is clear that evidence obtained in violation of state law can be admitted in a federal criminal prosecution.[107] This, however, has no bearing on whether that evidence can be used in state criminal proceedings. One state high court to have directly addressed this issue, the New Mexico Supreme Court, held that such evidence is excludable from a state criminal prosecution.[108]

Further Reading

César Cuauhtémoc García Hernández, *Creating Crimmigration*, 2013 BYU L. Rev. 1457.

César Cuauhtémoc García Hernández, *La Migra in the Mirror: Immigration Enforcement and Racial Profiling on the Texas Border*, 23 Notre Dame J.L. Ethics & Pub. Pol'y 167 (2009).

Kelly Lytle Hernández, Migra! A History of the U.S. Border Patrol (2010).

Kevin R. Johnson, *The Case Against Race Profiling in Immigration Enforcement*, 78 Wash. U. L.Q. 675 (2000).

Joseph Nevins, Operation Gatekeeper and Beyond: The War on "Illegals" and the Remaking of the U.S.-Mexico Boundary (2nd ed. 2010).

Memorandum from Attorney General John Ashcroft Setting Forth Justice Department's "Fast-Track" Policies (Sept. 22, 2003), *reprinted in* 16 Fed. Sent'g Rep. 134, 134–35 (Dec. 2003)

---

106. United States v. Juarez, 672 F.3d 381, 387 (5th Cir. 2012).
107. *See* Virginia v. Moore, 553 U.S. 164, 170–71 (2008).
108. State v. Cardenas-Alvarez, 25 P.3d 225, 232 (N.M. 2001).

CHAPTER 9

The Civil Immigration Detention System

Migrants facing removal are likely to spend at least some time detained. Chapter 4 addressed the legal bases for detention and tactics migrants can utilize to regain their liberty. This chapter returns to the nation's civil immigration detention system, but with a different purpose and from a different perspective: to explain what the detention system looks like, how it became the enormous network that it now is, and, most importantly, to give readers a glimpse into the conditions that detainees experience. There is nothing uplifting about immigration detention. As we will see, it involves separated families, detained children, sexual abuse, death, and more. To offer a small glimmer of hope, the chapter ends with a discussion of alternatives to detention.

Legal Authority and Structure

Detention has been part of immigration law enforcement since Congress began to exclude people possessing specified characteristics—in particular, Chinese and others of Asian ancestry—in the late nineteenth century.

239

Indeed, the United States' first federal statute authorizing immigration detention was enacted in 1891.[1] Immigration law enforcement responsibilities have shifted in the 125 years or so since then, but detention has always been an available power. Today, DHS is the principal executive branch department responsible for enforcing civil immigration laws. Accordingly, it is also responsible for detaining migrants who are in removal proceedings and are subject to detention for one of the reasons discussed in great detail in chapter 4: because Congress requires their detention through the INA's mandatory detention provision, § 236(c), because they have been deemed a flight risk or public safety threat, or who have been ordered removed. The INA quite simply provides that DHS "shall arrange for appropriate places of detention for aliens detained pending removal or a decision on removal."[2]

Detention System's Key Characteristics

Despite the federal government's longstanding power to detain migrants as part of the removal process, throughout much of the nation's history it avoided doing so in substantial numbers. Indeed, the INS had a policy of releasing individuals suspected of violating civil immigration laws from 1954 until the early 1980s.[3] Exceptions exist of course. Immigration detention began with a concern about Chinese migrants, so it is perhaps not surprising that the first instance of mass detention affected the Chinese. Angel Island in San Francisco Bay was synonymous with Chinese detention. On the opposite coast, Ellis Island, remembered as a migrant welcoming center, doubled as a detention center. These exceptions aside, most migrants suspected of having violated a civil provision of immigration law never saw the inside of a jail cell. In most situations, they were issued an order to appear for immigration court hearings at a future date and released into the interior or, for Mexicans, at the border.

   Civil immigration looks much differently today. The immigration detention estate began to grow in the 1980s and expanded dramatically in the years since 1996. By way of comparison, the INS had the capacity

---

1. Act of March 3, 1891, ch. 551, § 8, 26 Stat. 1084, 1085.
2. INA § 241(g)(1).
3. Mark Dow, American Gulag 7 (2004).

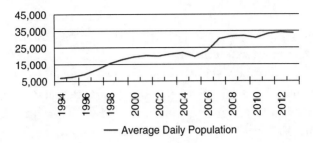

Figure 9.1   Civil Immigration Detention Average Daily
Population FY 1994–2013

to detain approximately 1,700 migrants on average per day in 1982 and
about 7,000 in 1990.[4] By the end of the century, the agency held just shy
of 20,000 each day. Ten years later, as figure 9.1 shows, the average daily
population had again grown by 10,000. At last count, the number was
still increasing consistently.[5]

Over the course of a given year, ICE now detains hundreds of thousands
of migrants. For the first time in the nation's history, more than 400,000
people were confined pending immigration proceedings in fiscal year
2011.[6] That was a record number, but only one in a consistent string of
records-setting years. ICE surpassed that mark the following year when it
detained 477,523 people.[7]

Much of this growth can be attributed to the increasingly punitive
views of immigration law violators that started in the 1980s and have
yet to abate. In the last three decades, as this book has shown, Congress
and multiple presidential administrations have intertwined criminal law
and immigration law so that tactics traditionally associated with one are
now prominent features of the other. In this case, criminal punishment's

4. TIMOTHY J. DUNN, THE MILITARIZATION OF THE U.S.-MEXICO BORDER, 1978-1992:
LOW-INTENSITY CONFLICT DOCTRINE COMES HOME 47, 72 (1996).

5. DHS, CONGRESSIONAL BUDGET JUSTIFICATION, FISCAL YEAR 2015 at 42 (FY
2013-14 data); ICE, *ICE Detainee Population Statistics By Fiscal Year*, http://www.ice.
gov/doclib/foia/reports/ero-facts-and-statistics.pdf (FY 2001-12 data); DONALD KERWIN
& SERENA YI-YING LIN, IMMIGRANT DETENTION: CAN ICE MEET ITS LEGAL IMPERATIVES
AND CASE MANAGEMENT RESPONSIBILITIES? 6 (2009).

6. JOHN F. SIMANSKI & LESLEY M. SAPP, DEP'T OF HOMELAND SEC., IMMIGRATION
ENFORCEMENT ACTIONS: 2011 ANNUAL REPORT 5 tbl.4 (2012).

7. *Id.* at 5.

long reliance on incarceration as a means of deterring—theoretically at least—and punishing undesirable conduct has become an accepted part of immigration law enforcement.

Aside from the many statutes that authorize or require detention discussed in chapter 4, the size of today's civil immigration detention estate can be attributed to a congressional directive known as the "bed mandate." Since at least 2010, Congress has tucked into annual appropriations legislation a requirement that DHS "shall maintain a level of not less than 34,000 detention beds."[8] DHS has generally interpreted this language as a requirement that it detain almost 34,000 migrants per day. Figure 9.1 leaves no doubt that ICE has met this directive. Despite DHS's interpretation of the budget language, a close reading of the statutory text suggests that the so-called bed mandate may be nothing more than that: a mandate to pay for 34,000 beds. Congress has never included language requiring detention of 34,000 people. Of course, Congress could include such language in a future appropriations bill, but DHS should not read more into the statutory text than the words require, especially when it comes to such an important decision as depriving people of their liberty.

Detaining so many people requires a similarly large number of facilities. In recent years, DHS has relied on a network of roughly 250 county jails, prisons, and stand-alone immigration detention centers to house civil immigration detainees. Though all migrants detained pending removal proceedings are legally in the custody of DHS, the department only operates a handful of facilities. About half of the 250 facilities are standard county jails in which DHS simply pays for a certain number of beds through contracts known as intergovernmental agency service agreements.[9] Most of the remaining facilities are ICE-owned "service

---

8. H.R. 3547, Consolidated Appropriations Act, 2014, Div. F, U.S. Immigration & Customs Enforcement; *see* H.R. 933, Consolidated and Further Continuing Appropriations Act, 2013, Div. D, U.S. Immigration & Customs Enforcement 150 (using identical language); Consolidated Appropriations Act, 2012, Pub. L. 112-74, 125 Stat. 786, 950, Div. D (same); Continuing Appropriations Act, 2011, Pub. L. 111-242, 124 Stat. 2607 (continuing appropriations enacted for the 2010 fiscal year); Dep't of Homeland Security Appropriations Act, 2010, Pub. L. 111-83, 123 Stat. 2142, 2149 (providing, "[t]hat funding made available under this heading shall maintain a level of not less than 33,400 detention beds).

9. HUMAN RIGHTS FIRST, JAILS AND JUMPSUITS: TRANSFORMING THE U.S. IMMIGRATION DETENTION SYSTEM—A TWO-YEAR REVIEW iii (2011).

processing centers" that are operated by private sector contractors and "contract detention facilities" owned and operated by private companies. ICE occasionally relies on federal prisons or medical centers to meet its detention obligation.[10] Most county jails house a small number of detainees, sometimes as few as one or two. The largest service processing centers, in contrast, can house 2,500 or more people.

To operate its detention system, ICE relies on a variety of entities. Sheriffs and municipal police departments run the hundreds of county and city jails with which ICE contracts. Local government officials often view ICE detention contracts as lucrative sources of revenue. Since DHS pays the entire cost of detaining migrants pending removal, civil immigration detention is seen as a way of injecting federal dollars into local economies. The former mayor of Oakdale, Louisiana, a small town that now houses one of the largest immigration detention centers in the country, explained that he lobbied the INS to build an immigration detention center in town because the facility "would lead to the 'economic rebirth' of Oakdale."[11] So long as ICE continues sending a constant number of detainees to a particular facility, local governments can profit from such arrangements. The problem local governments encounter, however, is that ICE routinely shifts its detainee population for a host of reasons. When this happens, local governments see their federal revenue stream diminish. Because counties come to rely on ICE revenue to fund jail operations, maintenance costs, or payments on government debts, fewer inmates means they struggle to meet their financial obligations. Reflecting on this experience in Glade County, Florida, a county commissioner lamented, "They [ICE] knew they either had to send us inmates or we would close down."[12]

---

10. Dora Schriro, Immigration Detention Overview and Recommendations 9–10 (2009).

11. Robert S. Kahn, Other People's Blood: U.S. Immigration Prisons in the Reagan Decade 151–52 (1996).

12. Charles Murphy, Glades County Sheriff to Close Jail Facility; Says Federal Government Cut Back on Arrests of Illegal Immigrants and Large Jail Facility is Losing Money; 100 Jobs Lost, Glades County Democrat (Glades County, Florida), April 9, 2014, http://florida.newszap.com/gladescounty/131120-113/glades-county-sheriff-to-close-jail-facilitysays-federal-government-cut-back-on-arrests-of-illegal-i.

Aside from local governments, ICE relies heavily on private prison corporations. Though private prisons companies are active in every segment of the United States' incarceration system—from local jails to federal prisons—Congress has expressly commanded DHS to consider leasing or purchasing an existing facility prior to constructing any new detention center.[13] This provision has the effect of enhancing the role that private prison companies play in immigration detention compared to other types of incarceration. Roughly 8 percent of all prisoners in the United States and 18 percent of all federal prisoners are held in private prisons. By contrast, between 40 and 50 percent of the civil immigration detention population is held in a privately owned or operated facility.[14] The two largest private prison corporations in the United States, the Corrections Corporation of America (CCA) and GEO Group, are heavily involved in civil immigration detention. Both regularly report multimillion-dollar contracts and billions of dollars in annual revenue from ICE.[15]

Characteristics of Detention Population

Inside this network of facilities, ICE confines a diverse group of people. Though adult males make up the majority of detainees, they are not alone. ICE also detains women and, on-and-off over the years depending on political pressures, children.[16] After numerous lawsuits, widespread objections by advocates, and rampant allegations of abuse, in 2009 ICE limited its practice of detaining family units by converting its family detention facility at the 500 bed T. Don Hutto Residential Center near Austin, Texas to a facility for women only. Though that closure substantially reduced ICE's family detention capacity, the agency continued

---

13. INA § 241(g).

14. E. ANN CARSON & WILLIAM J. SABOL, PRISONERS IN 2011, app. tbl.15, at 32 (Dec. 2012); CODY MASON, DOLLARS AND DETAINEES: THE GROWTH OF FOR-PROFIT DETENTION 5 (2012).

15. *See* César Cuauhtémoc García Hernández, *Invisible Spaces and Invisible Lives in Immigration Detention*, 57 HOWARD L.J. 869, 886–87 (2014).

16. DORIS MEISSNER ET AL., IMMIGRATION ENFORCEMENT IN THE UNITED STATES: THE RISE OF A FORMIDABLE MACHINERY 125–26 (2013); KERWIN & YI-YING LIN, *supra* note 5, at 11.

operating the eighty-five bed Berks Family Residential Facility in Lees-
port, Pennsylvania.[17] Housed in a former nursing home, the Berks facility
grants detainees broad freedom of movement within the center, provides
on-site educational services for children, and is equipped with many common furnishings of ordinary homes. As a result, advocates and the United
Nations High Commissioner for Refugees have described it as a model
civil immigration detention center.[18] Five years after ceasing to hold families at the Hutto facility, the government rapidly returned to its prior
practice during the summer of 2014 in response to a large increase in the
number of Central American children and families apprehended along
the border after having entered the United States without authorization.
ICE opened facilities in Artesia, New Mexico and Karnes, Texas that
could hold roughly 650 and 530 individuals, respectively, at a given time.
Perceiving a need for even more family detention beds, the agency quickly
contracted with the private prison contractor CCA to build a 2,400 bed
institution in remote Dilley, Texas, more than one hour southeast of San
Antonio. From only eighty-five beds at the beginning of June, therefore,
the government's family detention capacity grew to over 4,000 beds by
the end of the year.

Just as ICE detains people of all ages and genders, it also detains migrants regardless of their immigration status. Unauthorized migrants are
detained, but so too are longtime lawful permanent residents and asylum applicants. While some detainees have a criminal record (including
a record of committing immigration crimes), roughly half had never been
convicted of a crime.[19] Toward the end of 2014, DHS announced that it
would no longer prioritize detention of certain vulnerable individuals—the
elderly, pregnant or nursing women, or individuals with serious physical or
mental illnesses. It would instead target individuals subject to mandatory
detention or whose removal falls into one of the department's enforcement

---

17. THE NAKAMOTO GROUP, INC., BERKS FAMILY RESIDENTIAL CENTER: BI-ANNUAL
COMPLIANCE REVIEW REPORT 4 (2008), *available at* http://www.ice.gov/doclib/foia/dfra-
ice-dro/compliancereportberksfamilyresidentialcenter0714172008.pdf.

18. Tim Irwing, *In Rural Pennsylvania, A Model of Civil Immigration Detention*,
UNHCR NEWS (Jan. 6, 2011), *available at* http://www.unhcr.org/4d25c4fb6.html.

19. KERWIN & YI-YING LIN, *supra* note 5, at 20.

priorities.[20] No data were available at the time of this writing to indicate how or if this announcement had actually affected the civil immigration detention population.

Good data on the amount of time that migrants are detained is difficult to come by. Former ICE official Dora Schriro reported that migrants average thirty days in detention.[21] These averages can be misleading because they are lowered by the fact that many detainees spend very little time in custody. Individuals who agree to be removed are often released in a matter of days as soon as transportation to their country of citizenship becomes available. One analysis found that migrants who agree to voluntarily return to their country of citizenship spend an average of four days detained. In contrast, individuals who challenge their removal or seek relief from removal are most likely to face longer detention periods. Ironically, detainees who successfully challenge removal spent 113 days, on average, detained.[22] Because longtime lawful permanent residents are the most likely migrants to have plausible bases for contesting removal as well as the strongest ties to the United States, they are among the most likely to be detained longest. A report by independent researchers at the Migration Policy Institute, a well-respected, nonpartisan organization, supports the conclusion that challenging removal means spending more time detained. The researchers analyzed ICE's data about its detention population as of January 25, 2009, and found that, on average, migrants still awaiting a decision in a removal case had been detained 81 days. They also learned that migrants, on average, were detained 72 days following a removal order.[23]

Detention Conditions

With so many people detained in hundreds of facilities operated by almost as many different government entities, it is no wonder that everyone

---

20. Jeh Charles Johnson, Secretary, U.S. Dep't of Homeland Security, Memorandum for Thomas S. Winkowski, Acting Director, ICE, *Policies for the Apprehension, Detention and Removal of Undocumented Immigrants* (Nov. 20, 2014), available at http://www.dhs.gov/sites/default/files/publications/14_1120_memo_prosecutorial_discretion.pdf.

21. SCHRIRO, *supra* note 10, at 6.

22. Transactional Records Access Clearinghouse, *Legal Noncitizens Receive Longest ICE Detention* (June 3, 2013), http://trac.syr.edu/immigration/reports/321/.

23. KERWIN & YI-YING LIN, *supra* note 5, at 16–17.

from internal auditors to external immigrants' rights advocates have criti-cized living conditions in immigration detention facilities.

To begin with, no matter where they are located and what they are officially called, these facilities almost always have the look and feel of jails or prisons. It is of course to be expected that the county and city jails housing civil immigration detainees look and feel exactly like they penal environments they are intended to be. What is more surprising is that the stand-alone facilities that ICE uses share many characteristics with their penal counterparts. Typically, fences secure the facilities' perimeter and access is highly controlled by guards. Contact with outside visitors is lim-ited to designated hours and spaces within the facility. Visits with family members are often available only through plexiglass partitions or video-conferencing equipment. Detainees are not free to move about the facility at will. Some facilities place detainees in solitary confinement, at times for reasons so trivial as because a detainee chose to watch Spanish-language television programming.[24] Though such conditions are not usually associ-ated with civil detention, the fact of the matter is that, according to the former ICE official Schriro,

> Immigration Detention and Criminal Incarceration detainees tend to be seen by the public as comparable, and both confined popula-tions are typically managed in similar ways. Each group is ordinar-ily detained in secure facilities with hardened perimeters in remote locations at considerable distances from counsel and/or their com-munities. With only a few exceptions, the facilities that ICE uses to detain aliens were originally built, and currently operate, as jails and prisons to confine pre-trial and sentenced felons. Their design, construction, staffing plans, and population management strategies are based largely upon the principles of command and control. Like-wise, ICE adopted standards that are based upon corrections law and promulgated by correctional organizations to guide the opera-tion of jails and prisons.[25]

---

24. *See* García Hernández, *supra* note 15, at 892–93.
25. SCHRIRO, *supra* note 10, at 4.

Given this history, it should come as no surprise that all civil immigration detention centers tend to look and feel like jails or prisons.

That the nation's civil immigration detention system is modeled on facilities intended to punish and control is no excuse for its persistent failings. ICE is regularly criticized for providing shoddy health care to detainees. The department's Inspector General found that four out of five facilities it reviewed did not meet DHS's own policies in 2006.[26] Three years later Schriro expressed her concern about medical care.[27] Neither report seems to have been sufficient to remedy the problems since in 2011 the Inspector General found that ICE had outsourced mental health treatment so much that it "is not fully aware of all detainees with mental health conditions, or the level of care provided."[28] Numerous reports have also questioned ICE's ability to prevent sexual abuse. Because it is a supremely intimate type of violence, it is difficult to know how much sexual abuse occurs inside civil immigration detention centers just as it is anywhere else. Blame for that certainly cannot be placed at ICE's feet. Despite being notoriously underreported, ICE received almost 200 complaints of sexual abuse from 2007 to 2011.[29] The Government Accountability Office reviewed complaints received during a separate time period—October 2009 to March 2013—and found that at least fifteen could be substantiated. Shockingly, it also found that ICE staff failed to report as many as 40 percent of allegations despite an agency directive instructing them to do so.[30] Compounding ICE's communications failures, detainees who complain about sexual abuse are sometimes transferred to other facilities or removed from the United States sending an unmistakable signal that

26. U.S. Dep't of Homeland Sec., Office of Inspector Gen., Treatment of Immigration Detainees Housed at Immigration and Customs Enforcement Facilities 1, 3–5 (2006).

27. Medical Care and Treatment of Immigration Detainees and Deaths in DRO Custody, Hearing Before the H. Appropriations Comm. Subcomm. on Homeland Sec., 5 (Mar. 3, 2009) (statement of Dora Schriro, Special Advisor to Secretary Janet Napolitano on Detention and Removal Operations).

28. U.S. Dep't of Homeland Sec., Office of Inspector Gen., Mgmt. of Mental Health Cases in Immigration Det. 1, 1 (2011).

29. ACLU, Sexual Abuse in Immigration Detention Facilities, https://www.aclu.org/maps/sexual-abuse-immigration-detention-facilities.

30. U.S. Gov't Accountability Office, Immigration Detention: Additional Actions Could Strengthen DHS Efforts to Address Sexual Abuse 20, 60–62 (2013).

the agency is not particularly interested in hearing allegations or taking them seriously.[31] Persistent failure to adequately address this long-known problem suggests that ICE leadership lacks an interest in—certainly an ability to—stopping it.

Worse yet, admission into a detention facility has sometimes led to death. According to ICE, 141 people died while detained in the ten years between October 7, 2003, and December 2, 2013.[32] While it is tempting to believe that this is an accurate accounting, for many years ICE kept poor records of detainee deaths and even stalled journalists' attempts to piece together what was happening inside detention centers.[33]

Transfers

Detention center conditions are compounded by the fact that migrants are often transferred between facilities. After analyzing ICE data, the advocacy group Human Rights Watch reported almost 1.4 million transfers between 1999 and 2008.[34] For many years, almost every detained migrant could expect to be transferred at some point. The DHS Inspector General, for example, reported that during the 2007 fiscal year, "ICE detained more than 311,000 aliens . . . and transferred 261,910 detainees from one detention facility to another."[35] Some detainees were transferred more than once so it is not possible to do a one-to-one comparison of detainees to transfers. Still, it is evident that transfer was a palpable feature of detention.

DHS insists that transfers are sometimes necessary. A policy directive issued in 2012 by John Morton, at the time ICE's director, lists seven justifications for a detainee's transfer: 1) to provide appropriate medical or mental health care, 2) at a detainee's request, 3) for safety or security

---

31. NAT'L PRISON RAPE ELIMINATION COMM'N REPORT, NAT'L PRISON RAPE ELIMINATION REPORT 179–80, 186 (2009).

32. U.S. Dep't of Homeland Sec., Immigr. & Customs Enforcement, *List of Deaths in ICE Custody: October 2003-December 2, 2013*, http://www.ice.gov/doclib/foia/reports/detaineedeaths2003-present.pdf.

33. *See* Nina Bernstein, *Officials Obscured Truth of Migrant Deaths in Jail*, N.Y. TIMES, Jan. 9, 2010, at A1.

34. HUMAN RIGHTS WATCH, LOCKED UP FAR AWAY: THE TRANSFER OF IMMIGRANTS TO REMOTE DETENTION CENTERS IN THE UNITED STATES 29 (2009).

35. U.S. Dep't of Homeland Sec., Office of Inspector Gen., *Immigration and Customs Enforcement's Tracking and Transfers of Detainees* [hereinafter ICE Detainee Transfers], March 2009, at 2.

reasons, 4) to move the detainee closer to the immigration court where removal proceedings are ongoing, 5) to house the migrant in a facility that is better suited to his individual circumstances and risk factors, 6) because a facility closes or an emergency develops, and 7) to prevent or relieve overcrowding.[36] If one of these conditions is met, ICE officials are authorized to move a detainee to another facility. They are supposed to comply with § 7.4 of the 2011 Performance-Based National Detention Standards (see the following section), which, among other things, requires that ICE officials notify a detainee's attorney "as soon as practicable" but no later than 24 hours after a detainee's transfer.

Much of the criticism levied against ICE for its rampant transferring of detainees stems from the fact that transfers pose significant problems for detainees. ICE, for example, often failed to inform attorneys despite its policy.[37] At best this made consistent communications between attorneys and clients difficult. At worst, it made continued representation impossible. In addition, transfers often involve moving a detainee from a facility near a metropolitan area or near where she was apprehended to a facility located in a distant rural area. This often results in hardship for migrant's who suddenly find themselves far from family members. Individuals who were trying to obtain counsel, meanwhile, often end up in communities that have few or no immigration attorneys.

In response to some of the criticism, ICE has moved to reduce the number of transfers while also reducing the impact of those transfers that still occur. After increasing its detention capacity near Los Angeles and New York, ICE claimed that as of January 2012 almost no one was transferred out of the Los Angeles region and migrants detained in the New York area were 80 percent less likely to be transferred.[38] Likewise, in 2010 the agency launched an Online Detainee Locator System (available

---

36. U.S. Immigr. & Customs Enforcement, *Policy 11022.1: Detainee Transfers* 3 (Jan. 4, 2012), https://www.ice.gov/doclib/detention-reform/pdf/hd-detainee-transfers.pdf.

37. *See* Orantes-Hernandez v. Thornburgh, 919 F.2d 549, 566 (9th Cir. 1990); ICE Detainee Transfers, *supra* note 35, at 1, 8.

38. Performance-Based National Detention Standards (PBNDS) 2011: *Hearing Before the Subcomm. on Immigration Policy and Enforcement of the H. Comm. on the Judiciary, 112th Cong.* (2012) (statement of Kevin Landy, Assistant Director, U.S. Immigr. and Customs Enforcement Office of Detention Policy and Planning), http://www.dhs.gov/news/2012/03/27/written-testimony-us-immigration-and-customs-enforcement-house-judiciary.

at https://locator.ice.gov/odls/homePage.do) that allows anyone to locate the whereabouts of any adult detainee using the detainee's identification information ("A number" and country of birth, or name and country of birth).

Detention Standards

Despite notoriously troublesome conditions across its network of detention centers, ICE has attempted to limit the worst excesses by promulgating a body of national standards. Illustrating the challenge ICE faces, ICE does not use a single set of standards nationwide. Instead, there are currently three sets of national standards that apply to civil immigration detention facilities. When ICE was created in 2003, it inherited detention guidelines created in 2000. In 2008 it adopted a new set of guidelines. Most recently it issued revised standards in 2011. Titled "Performance-Based National Detention Standards 2011" (PBNDS 2011), ICE is slowly expanding these standards across the entire detention network. Because so many facilities are owned or operated by local governments or private prison corporations and operated under contracts with ICE that reference the earlier standards, many facilities continue to use standards that ICE now deems outdated.

As the future of civil immigration detention standards, the PBNDS 2011 sets the marker for best practices for detention conditions. The 463-page document is replete with all manner of specific directives falling under seven broad categories: safety, security, order, care, activities, justice, and administration and management. Subtopics address many of the worst problems that have plagued detention, including poor medical care and sexual abuse. It remains to be seen whether the PBNDS 2011 standards spell a lasting change in detention operations. What is clear already, though, is that they do not represent a break from the security-minded approach that has dominated civil immigration detention for decades. The PBNDS 2011 imagines a detention system in which detainees must be observed 24 hours a day and housed in secure environments with closed access.

Detainee Classification

Though immigration judges are authorized to determine whether a migrant is subject to mandatory detention or merits detention as a matter of discretion, the initial decision to detain someone is made by ICE officers. Historically a hodgepodge process characterized these decisions. The criteria used and how certain criteria were weighed often differed from field office to field office and even from officer to officer. Inevitably there was little uniformity and it often seemed that decisions to detain were motivated by officers' subjective perceptions rather than more defensible objective analyses.

In an effort to standardize the detention decisionmaking process across the country, ICE adopted an automated "Risk Classification Assessment" (RCA) system in 2013. The RCA has been incorporated into ICE's book-in process so that everyone apprehended by ICE is subjected to the same initial screening. According to ICE, the RCA "contains objective criteria to guide decisionmaking, regarding whether an alien should be detained or released, and if detained, the alien's appropriate custody classification level." Among those criteria are ICE's civil enforcement priorities.[39] ICE, in turn, has prioritized removal of migrants convicted of crime.[40] ICE has not made publicly available much more information about the RCA complicating any effort to adequately gauge its effectiveness. The Department of Homeland Security's Inspector General, however, did not paint a favorable picture. In a February 2015 report, it concluded that "RCA does not enhance the quality of [ICE] field office release decisions."[41]

Alternatives to Detention and Alternative Forms of Custody

While tens of thousands of migrants are detained every day, not everyone who comes into contact with ICE is detained. Some who are detained initially are later released because ICE or an immigration judge decides they are neither subject to mandatory detention nor do they merit detention.

39. U.S. Dep't of Homeland Sec., Immigr. & Customs Enforcement, *Detention Reform Accomplishments*, http://www.ice.gov/detention-reform/detention-reform.htm.

40. See Memorandum from Jeh Charles Johnson, Secretary, U.S. Dep't of Homeland Security, to Thomas S. Winkowski, *Policies for the Apprehension, Detention and Removal of Undocumented Immigrants* (Nov. 20, 2014), *available at* http://www.dhs.gov/sites/default/files/publications/14_1120_memo_prosecutorial_discretion.pdf.

41. U.S. DEP'T OF HOMELAND SEC., OFFICE OF INSPECTOR GENERAL, U.S. IMMIGRATION AND CUSTOMS ENFORCEMENT'S ALTERNATIVES TO DETENTION (REVISED) 11 (2015).

So long as removal proceedings are pending, ICE maintains an interest in having migrants appear for their hearings. ICE has a similar interest in maintaining regular contact with people who have been ordered removed, but for whom removal is not imminent.

Over the years immigration authorities have had many tools at their disposal that can limit the possibility that a nondetained migrant absconds. The most common historically were Orders of Release on Recognizance and Orders of Supervision. Though migrants usually complied with these orders, ICE's ability to redetain those who failed to do so was limited. To address this shortcoming, ICE and the former INS at times instituted intensive reporting requirements. Some variations of this strategy involved appearing at a designated location in-person, while others consisted of telephonic reporting. The most promising versions do more than simply track a migrant's presence; they also provide support services that increase a migrant's likelihood of compliance with the conditions of release. An early ATD pilot project commissioned by the former INS did this remarkably well. Created and operated by the Vera Institute of Justice in the New York City area from 1997 to 2000, the Appearance and Assistance Program (AAP) combined tracking protocols with assistance obtaining legal and interpretation services, housing, transportation, and other social services, all overseen by a case manager assigned to each migrant. Roughly 90 percent of program participants satisfied the conditions of their release, including appearing for immigration court hearings. Importantly, the AAP was designed to move migrants out of immigration detention. Program participants were carefully screened to determine what combination of support services would best equip them to comply with their release conditions.

As with so much else, the AAP lost favor within Congress and the former INS after the tragic events of September 11, 2001. The INS and later ICE discarded much of the AAP's focus on providing assistance to migrants to increase the likelihood that they would comply with release conditions, including appearing for court dates, and instead turned their attention to monitoring migrants. In 2004, ICE launched the Intensive Supervision Appearance Program (ISAP) and Electronic Monitoring Device (EMD) program. ISAP's principal feature was close supervision by case specialists employed by Behavioral Interventions, Incorporated (BI Incorporated). Unlike the AAP's case managers, ISAP case specialists provided little to no assistance obtaining the support migrants need to increase compliance with release conditions. Instead, case specialists utilized an array of tools to monitor migrants: electronic bracelets, home visits, and in-person reporting to designated offices.[42] The EMD had a similar focus on monitoring migrants, but relied almost exclusively on technological innovations. One version consisted largely of telephonic reporting while another used radio frequency monitoring of electronic bracelets.[43] The agency later rolled out a third program, Enhanced Supervision Reporting (ESR), that resembled ISAP only offered less intensive supervision.[44]

Though each program offered a different level of monitoring, placement in one of these was not primarily directed by the risk of absconding or endangering the community. Instead, according to former ICE official Dora Schriro, "In practice . . . assignment to a program is determined in part by residency. ISAP and ESR are available to aliens who live within a 50- to 85-mile radius of the 24 field offices. EM is offered to aliens who live in other locations to the extent that funds are available."[45]

Responding to congressional directives to consolidate its nondetention security programs, in 2008 ICE contracted with BI Incorporated, now a subsidiary of the nation's second largest private prison corporation GEO Group, to operate the second generation of the Intensive Supervision Assistance Program (ISAP II).[46] ISAP II provides two levels of supervision: a technology-only option and a more involved program that ICE and BI Incorporated refer to as "full-service." The technology-only option involves electronic monitoring. The full-service model uses electronic monitoring, the possibility of telephonic reporting, unannounced home visits,

42. Memorandum from Wesley J. Lee, Acting Director, U.S. Immigr. & Customs Enforcement, to all Field Office Directors, *Eligibility Criteria for Enrollment into the Intensive Supervision Appearance Program (ISAP) and the Electronic Monitoring Device (EMD) Program* 2 (May 11, 2005), http://www.ice.gov/doclib/foia/dro_policy_memos/dropolicymemoeligibilityfordroisapandemdprograms.pdf.
43. *Id.* at 1–2.
44. SCHRIRO, *supra* note 10, at 20.
45. *Id.*
46. BI Incorporated, *Immigration Services*, http://bi.com/immigration.

and scheduled office visits.[47] Both offer multiple levels of supervision involving in-person visits to ISAP offices as well as unscheduled home visits by case specialists. In general, more intensive supervision occurs when migrants are in the midst of the immigration court process, but becomes less intensive during the appellate process.[48] Together, these technologically sophisticated tools and frequent reporting requirements allow ICE to keep track of nondetained migrants much more closely than previously possible. Where it fails, advocates claim, is in adequately supporting migrants to increase the likelihood that they will appear for court dates and satisfy other conditions of participation.[49]

Though ICE refers to ISAP II as an alternative to detention, it and the other post-September 11 initiatives are better described as alternative forms of custody. The ATD label implies that the program applies to individuals who in the past would have been detained but who are allowed to return to their ordinary lives albeit with the security measures needed to adequately ensure their appearance in court and curtail their ability to endanger the public. ISAP II, in contrast, has the opposite effect: it increases ICE's security capacity at little cost by tracking people who in the past would not have been subject to nearly such restrictive controls. Indeed, since 2008 when ICE launched ISAP II, the immigration detention population has continued to grow.

Despite these concerns and frequent criticisms that anything other than detention is impractical, ICE's existing ATD programs are cost-effective and boast very high compliance rates. Costs for the two ISAP II options differ, but both pale in comparison to detention. According to ICE, it spends approximately $119 per day per detention bed.[50] The technology-only alternative costs $0.30 per day per program participant. The more

---

47. U.S. Dep't of Homeland Security, *Immigr. & Customs Enforcement: Salaries and Expenses, Fiscal Year 2015 Congressional Budget Justification* [hereinafter ICE Expenses] 60, http://www.dhs.gov/sites/default/files/publications/DHS-Congressional-Budget-Justification-FY2015.pdf.

48. RUTGERS SCHOOL OF LAW-NEWARK IMMIGRANT RIGHTS CLINIC, FREED BUT NOT FREE: A REPORT EXAMINING THE CURRENT USE OF ALTERNATIVES TO IMMIGRATION DETENTION appx. F (2012), http://www.law.newark.rutgers.edu/files/FreedbutnotFree.pdf.

49. *Id.* at 8–9.

50. ICE Expenses , *supra* note 46, at 40.

involved full-service option costs \$8.49 per day per person. On average, ICE spends \$4.73 per day per migrant enrolled in an ATD plan.[51] Such low costs have apparently not affected ISAP II's success at ensuring that migrants appear for proceedings as required. In fiscal year 2010, 93.8 percent of ATD enrollees complied with the program criteria.[52] Despite the low costs and high success rates, ICE has yet to substantially scale up its reliance on ATD options. The agency receives enough funding to enroll roughly 22,000 people per day in ISAP II.[53]

Further Reading

MARK DOW, AMERICAN GULAG (2004).

César Cuauhtémoc García Hernández, *Due Process and Immigrant Detainee Prison Transfers: Moving LPRs to Isolated Prisons Violates Their Right to Counsel*, 21 BERKELEY LA RAZA L.J. 17 (2011).

DORA SCHRIRO, IMMIGRATION DETENTION OVERVIEW AND RECOMMENDATIONS (2009), http://www.ice.gov/doclib/about/offices/odpp/pdf/ice-detention-rpt.pdf.

U.S. Dep't of Homeland Security, *Immigration and Customs Enforcement, Performance-Based National Detention Standards 2011*, https://www.ice.gov/detention-standards/2011/.

---

51. *Id.* at 62.
52. *Id.* at 44.
53. *Id.* at 60.

CHAPTER 10

State Involvement in Crimmigration Law Enforcement

Just as the federal government and some states have turned to their penal codes to criminalize immigration-related activity, they have also harnessed their law enforcement powers to target migrants for criminal prosecution or possible removal. The previous two chapters discussed various ways in which the federal government enforces crimmigration law. This chapter, in turn, focuses our attention on the states, including cities and counties. Though a handful of states have led the way, every state is now involved in crimmigration law enforcement thanks to the federal government's role as a central repository of criminal history data. Consequently, this chapter is as much about laws and policies enacted by states, cities, and counties as it is about the federal government's role in encouraging, facilitating, and, some would say, forcing them to help DHS fulfill its immigration law enforcement mission. With such a diverse country and as much political divergence as there is across regions, it should come as no surprise that not all communities have followed the same course. Many states, cities, and counties have adopted laws and policies that limit migrants' potential exposure to crimmigration problems. Accordingly, this chapter discusses key migrant-friendly developments throughout.

Secure Communities

Unlike state and local efforts to criminalize immigration-related conduct using substantive criminal law statutes, crimmigration law enforcement has greatly expanded because of the interdependent nature of law enforcement in the United States. All jurisdictions in the United States have an interest collaborating to stop or investigate crime. As a result, law enforcement officers at all levels of government have long shared identification information with one another. The federal government has operated some form of criminal records clearinghouse since at least 1930. Today's principal criminal records database, the National Crime Information Center (NCIC), is operated by the Federal Bureau of Investigation and is used by roughly 90,000 law enforcement agencies, including DHS, literally millions of times each day to learn more about the people they encounter during their ordinary policing activities. To access the NCIC system, law enforcement officers must submit a suspect's fingerprint data to the FBI's Integrated Automated Fingerprint Identification System (IAFIS) that contains records on over 100 million people.[1]

The Secure Communities program built off this interdependent, intergovernmental foundation by pairing criminal history checks with immigration status checks. As a preliminary matter, it relied on the fingerprint data it received from state and local law enforcement officials upon booking a suspect into custody. Once the criminal history check was completed, the FBI forwarded the fingerprint data it received from the state or local police officer to DHS, which sifted through its own database for a possible match. The DHS database—named the Automated Biometric Identification System, but usually referred to simply as IDENT—tracks immigration history. Despite having come online in 1994, the IDENT database is quite large. By late 2013, IDENT held records on approximately 150 million subjects and was growing at a rate of ten million entries per

---

1. Anil Kalhan, *Immigration Policing and Federalism Through the Lens of Technology, Surveillance, and Privacy*, 74 OHIO STATE L.J. 1105, 1123–24 (2013).

year.[2] The end result is that an ordinary traffic stop or other minor police encounter could lead to an inquiry into a person's criminal and immigration history. If the IDENT search matches the fingerprints to an existing record, ICE's Law Enforcement Support Center is notified. Officials there, in turn, attempt to verify the individual's immigration status. Legal scholar Anil Kalhan explains the rest of the process: "If this review yields a match, LESC notifies the originating law enforcement agency and the relevant ICE field office, which decides, based on enforcement priorities and other factors, whether to interview the individual or issue a detainer requesting that the agency hold the individual."[3]

Secure Communities was launched in 2008 in fourteen jurisdictions. Five years later it had been implemented in every jurisdiction in the United States. None had the option of not participating. According to ICE, the federal government can do as it wishes with the fingerprint data it receives from state and local law enforcement officers. Police officials can, of course, choose not to send fingerprint data to the FBI. It is highly unlikely and borders on the unthinkable that any state, city, or county police force would exercise that option, however, because doing that would prevent them from accessing the NCIC and IAFIS data upon which every law enforcement agency relies to investigate crime.

Several communities voiced strong opposition to the program. The governors of California, Illinois, Massachusetts, and New York, plus city and county officials in some of the nation's largest metropolitan areas, expressed their dismay with Secure Communities, arguing that it frequently resulted in ICE apprehending and removing migrants without a criminal history or without a history of violence. They claimed that this damaged police relations with community members who perceived local police as cooperating with ICE.

Despite the federal government's insistence that Secure Communities was a lawful and effective way of identifying potentially removable individuals, opposition proved too strong. On November 20, 2014, Secretary of Homeland Security Jeh Johnson announced that the department would

2. *Id.* at 1127.
3. *Id.* at 1128.

end the program. Secure Communities, he wrote, "has become a symbol for general hostility toward the enforcement of our immigration laws," thus it was time for the initiative to end.[4]

Priority Enforcement Program

Though DHS began to wind down the controversial Secure Communities program at the end of 2014, it did not alter its commitment to the central feature of its crimmigration enforcement tactics: robust communication between local police and immigration officials. Indeed, in the same memorandum in which he announced Secure Communities' discontinuation, Secretary Johnson wrote that it would be replaced by a new enforcement initiative titled the "Priority Enforcement Program." Like Secure Communities, the PEP would continue to rely on fingerprint data obtained by local police officers and forwarded to the FBI.[5] PEP differs from Secure Communities, however, in that it adopts a new set of enforcement priorities also announced in November 2014. Under PEP, ICE officials should seek custody of individuals convicted of terrorism or espionage; an offense linked to gang activity; a felony in the convicting jurisdiction unless the individual's immigration status was "an essential element" of the offense; an aggravated felony; at least three misdemeanors that don't use immigration status as an element; a misdemeanor involving domestic violence; sexual abuse or exploitation; burglary; unlawful possession or use of a firearm; drug distribution or drug trafficking; driving under the influence; or any offense for which the person served at least ninety days in custody.[6] At the time of this writing, PEP was too new to know how it was actually being implemented.

4. Jeh Charles Johnson, Secretary, U.S. Dep't of Homeland Security, Memorandum for Thomas S. Winkowski, Acting Director, ICE, *Secure Communities* (Nov. 20, 2014) [Johnson Secure Communities Memo], available at http://www.dhs.gov/sites/default/files/publications/14_1120_memo_secure_communities.pdf.

5. *Id.*

6. Jeh Charles Johnson, Secretary, U.S. Dep't of Homeland Security, Memorandum for Thomas S. Winkowski, Acting Director, ICE, *Policies for the Apprehension, Detention and Removal of Undocumented Immigrants* (Nov. 20, 2014), available at http://www.dhs.gov/sites/default/files/publications/14_1120_memo_prosecutorial_discretion.pdf.

287(g) Program

Another initiative through which state and local policing resources are utilized to augment ICE's investigative power is the 287(g) program. Named after the INA section that authorizes this collaboration, the 287(g) program is unique among partnership programs because it explicitly authorizes by statute state and local officers to enforce federal immigration law. For this to happen, ICE and the state or local law enforcement agency must enter into a memorandum of agreement that specifies the scope of authority delegated to local police officers, training requirements, supervision protocols, and more.[7]

At one time, ICE operated three types of 287(g) agreements: the task force model, jail enforcement model, and "hybrid" model. Today it only operates the jail enforcement model. The jail enforcement model authorizes police officers to question people who are booked into police custody about their immigration status. As of April 2015, thirty-four law enforcement agencies in seventeen states had active jail enforcement model agreements with ICE.[8]

Like Secure Communities, the 287(g) program has been widely criticized as overbroad. In addition, critics frequently claimed that ICE insufficiently regulated conduct by local police officers operating under a § 287(g) agreement. A 2009 report by the Government Accountability Office buttressed these claims when it concluded that the program's objectives were unclear and ICE failed to provide consistent supervision of local police officers.[9] Most prominently, the Justice Department concluded that the Maricopa County Sheriff's Office in Arizona had regularly engaged in racial profiling and other discriminatory conduct against Latinos under the auspices of its § 287(g) agreement, leading DHS to terminate the

---

7. For an example of a model 287(g) agreement, visit http://www.ice.gov/doclib/detention-reform/pdf/287g_moa.pdf.

8. U.S. Dep't of Homeland Security, Immigr. & Customs Enforcement, *287(g) Results and Participating Entities*, http://www.ice.gov/news/library/factsheets/287g.htm#signed-moa (last visited April 16, 2015).

9. Richard M. Stana, *Immigration Enforcement: Better Controls Needed Over Program Authorizing State and Local Enforcement of Federal Immigration Laws* 10 (2009), http://www.gao.gov/new.items/d09109.pdf.

agreement.[10] ICE implemented a series of measures in response to such criticisms, including adding a provision to its model memorandum of agreement instructing participating agencies to implement § 287(g) in light of ICE's stated prioritization of migrants convicted of crimes.

Immigration Detainers

To ensure that individuals identified through Secure Communities, § 287(g), or other means as potentially removable are taken into ICE custody, ICE makes ready use of immigration detainers (sometimes referred to as "immigration holds"). A detainer is nothing more than a request by ICE— issued on Form I-247—to a local law enforcement agency that it maintain custody of a person for up to 48 hours (excluding weekends and holidays) after the conclusion of the criminal basis for detention.[11] For many years, ICE issued hundreds of thousands of detainers annually without regard to what crime the detained individual was convicted of violating or even if the person was convicted. It appears that a large number of these were issued against people with no criminal history. Indeed, only 50 percent of people subject to a detainer between October 2011 and September 2013 had any criminal conviction.[12]

Despite their centrality to ICE's modern enforcement practices, detainers are of questionable legality. The INA mentions detainers only once, and that provision allows for a very different type of detainer practice than what ICE currently does. Section 287(d) provides:

> In the case of an alien who is arrested by *a Federal, State, or local law enforcement official* for a violation of any law *relating to controlled substances*, if the *official* (or another official)—(1) has reason to believe that the alien may not have been lawfully admitted to the United States or otherwise is not lawfully present in the United

10. U.S. Dep't of Homeland Security, *Statement by Secretary Napolitano on DOJ's Findings of Discriminatory Policing in Maricopa County*, Press Release (Dec. 15, 2011), http://www.dhs.gov/news/2011/12/15/secretary-napolitano-dojs-findings-discriminatory-policing-maricopa-county.

11. *Galarza v. Szalczyk*, 745 F.3d 634, 642 (3d Cir. 2014).

12. Transactional Records Access Clearinghouse, *Targeting of ICE Detainers Varies Widely by State and by Facility* (Feb. 11, 2014), http://trac.syr.edu/immigration/reports/343/#f1.

States, (2) expeditiously informs an appropriate officer or employee
of the Service authorized and designated by the Attorney General
of the arrest and of facts concerning the status of the alien, and
(3) requests the Service to determine promptly whether or not to issue
a detainer to detain the alien, the officer or employee of the Service
shall promptly determine whether or not to issue such a detainer.
(emphasis added)

First, this language clearly indicates that Congress authorized detainers
against people arrested of a controlled substance violation; it did not authorize detainers against people arrested for any other type of crime. Second, the
text suggests that the detainer must be requested by the arresting agency. In
sharp contrast, a regulation adopted by the agency allows numerous immigration officers to issue a detainer "at any time."[13] ICE relies heavily on this
regulatory authority despite its obvious departure from the statutory text.

An additional question about the detainer practice focuses on whether a
detainer is a request or order that the arresting law enforcement agency hold
onto someone. The INA does not touch on this subject so it is of little help. For
many years ICE gave mixed signals about its position and many law enforcement agencies treated detainers as commands rather than requests. Nonetheless, the regulation governing detainers explicitly describes a detainer as
a "request" by ICE to the arresting agency to inform it prior to releasing
a person subject to a detainer, but it does not state whether the arresting
agency is required to hold a person subject to a detainer in the first place.[14]
Courts have stepped in to fill this void. In *Galarza v. Szalczyk*, the Third
Circuit unequivocally announced that "detainers are not mandatory."[15] Less
than a month later a federal magistrate court came to the same conclusion.[16]

Judicial conclusions that detainers are not mandatory are hugely important. If detainers are not mandatory, then, as a matter of law, law enforcement agencies that keep a person in custody in order to comply with
the detainer do so at their choosing. The Fourth Amendment, of course,

13. 8 C.F.R. § 287.7(a).
14. *Id.*
15. 745 F.3d 634, 642 (3d Cir. 2014).
16. Miranda-Olivares v. Clackamas County, 2014 WL 1414305, *8 (D. Or. Apr. 11, 2014).

does not allow government actors to choose to deprive a person, even a migrant, of her liberty through arrest without probable cause that the detained individual engaged in criminal activity. As the Court explained in *County of Riverside v. McLaughlin*, "the Fourth Amendment permits a reasonable postponement of a probable cause determination while the police cope with the everyday problems of processing suspects through an overly burdened criminal justice system. But flexibility has its limits. . . . A State has no legitimate interest in detaining for extended periods individuals who have been arrested without probable cause."[17] The Court went on to make it quite clear that in most circumstances a person arrested without a warrant issued by a neutral magistrate and supported by probable cause must be brought before a judge for a probable cause hearing within forty-eight hours of arrest.[18]

Immigration detainers seemingly clash with these bedrock Fourth Amendment principles. As legal scholar Christopher N. Lasch points out, neither a warrant issued by a judge nor probable cause are required for a detainer to issue.[19] Indeed, many, if not most, detainers are issued after ICE has done no more than initiate an investigation into whether a person is possibly removable. Launching an investigation obviously does not require probable cause. Similarly, arresting someone solely to conduct an investigation is not constitutionally permissible precisely because it lacks probable cause.[20] Even the other common reasons for issuing a detainer— because a Notice to Appear pursuant to INA § 239(a)(1)(C) or administrative arrest warrant pursuant to INA § 236(a) exists—lack a probable cause requirement altogether or might use a probable cause requirement that is less exacting than applicable in the traditional criminal context, respectively (for more on the probable cause requirement applicable to administrative warrants, see chapter 4).[21] Because the detainer regulation,

---

17. 500 U.S. 44, 55 (1991).

18. *Id.* at 56.

19. *See* Christopher N. Lasch, *Federal Immigration Detainers After* Arizona v. United States, 46 Loyola L.A. L. Rev. 629, 696–98 (2013).

20. Brown v. Illinois, 422 U.S. 590, 605 (1975).

21. Lasch, *supra* note 19, at 697–98; Jennifer M. Chacón, *A Diversion of Attention? Immigration Courts and the Adjudication of Fourth and Fifth Amendment Rights*, 59 Duke L.J. 1563, 1608–09 (2010).

8 C.F.R. § 287.7(d), relies on these justifications to issue a detainer, it explicitly contravenes traditional understandings of the Fourth Amendment.[22] In Lasch's words, "the Fourth Amendment requires any person subjected to a warrantless arrest be brought before a neutral magistrate for a probable cause determination within forty-eight hours—*including* weekends and holidays—absent a showing of extraordinary circumstances," a requirement that the detainer regulation ignores.

Because the possibility that someone might be removable from the United States is not enough to establish the probable cause necessary to prolong their detention after the criminal law justification ends, the choice to abide by a detainer request brings with it the possibility of liability for violating a detainee's Fourth Amendment right to be free from arbitrary arrest. Fearing this possibility, in the aftermath of the Third Circuit and federal magistrate's decisions concluding that detainers are mere requests numerous law enforcement agencies announced that they would no longer honor detainers. Within months, DHS also changed its detainer practice. Rather than send requests for detention, ICE now sends requests for notification, what Secretary Johnson described as "requests that state or local law enforcement notify ICE of a pending release during the time that person is otherwise in custody under state or local authority."[23] By shifting from requests for detention to requests for notification of release, ICE's new detainer practice likely avoids the constitutional concerns of its prior policy.

It does little, however, to alter the impact that detainers have on migrants. As before, detainers will continue to rely on local police work. Only now, ICE will have a little less time to decide whether to take into its custody a person detained by police officers. Instead of waiting until the criminal process ends, ICE officers will have to decide while the individual is subject to criminal detention. In reality, this is likely to mean that ICE now has two business days less than before to take hold of someone. Once it decides to do so, the civil immigration detention and removal process will unfold as before.

---

22. Lasch, *supra* note 19, at 698.
23. Johnson Secure Communities Memo, *supra* note 4.

Independent Investigations

In addition to the substantial amount of assistance that state and local law enforcement agencies provide the federal government, states, cities, and counties periodically launch their own investigations into immigration law. The legality of these often depends on the specifics of the law enforcement actions, but there are two broad categories of independent state or local actions that have developed in the case law: actions to enforce federal immigration law, and actions by state or local officers to enforce state immigration-related crimes.

States and localities appear to have some leeway to arrest migrants for violating federal immigration crimes, though the limits on this authority are murky and fraught with peril for the government entities. The Supreme Court has long taken the view that state police officers can enforce federal crimes if state law empowers them to do so, unless Congress has enacted a statute prohibiting this.[24] Though the Court referenced this position in its 2012 decision concerning Arizona's S.B. 1070 (for a detailed discussion of that decision, see chapter 7), it explicitly did not address this view's merits.[25] The courts of appeals, meanwhile, have adopted differing approaches, best exemplified by decisions of the Ninth and Tenth Circuits. In *Gonzales v. City of Peoria*, the Ninth Circuit held "that federal law does not preclude local enforcement of the criminal provisions of the [INA]," but then suggested that for this to be permissible, state law must expressly authorize state officers to enforce federal criminal laws.[26] The Tenth Circuit took a broader view in *United States v. Santana-Garcia* when it held that, "presum[ing] no state or local law to the contrary," "state and local police officers ha[ve] implicit authority within their respective jurisdictions 'to investigate and make arrests for violations of federal law, including immigration laws.'"[27]

These are not irrelevant differences. A statute allowing state officials to enforce misdemeanors of any kind, including federal misdemeanors,

---

24. United States v. Di Re, 332 U.S. 581, 589 (1948); *see* Miller v. United States, 357 U.S. 301, 305 (1958); Marsh v. United States, 29 F.2d 172, 173–74 (2d Cir. 1928).

25. Arizona v. United States, 132 S. Ct. 2492, 2509–10 (2012).

26. 722 F.2d 468, 475 (9th Cir. 1983), *overruled on other grounds by* Hodgers-Durgin v. de la Vina, 199 F.3d 1037 (9th Cir. 1999).

27. 264 F.3d 1188, 1194 (10th Cir. 2001).

would likely satisfy the Ninth Circuit and Tenth Circuit's tests, while statutory silence would satisfy the Tenth Circuit but not the Ninth Circuit. In most situations, it is likely that state law says nothing about local and state officials' power to investigate and arrest people suspected of committing federal crimes. Instead, the permissibility of state or local enforcement of federal immigration crimes turns on interpretations of broadly worded statutes or common law doctrine regarding law enforcement practices generally. The Ninth Circuit, for example, hinged its analysis on a state statute authorizing officers to arrest anyone for whom they have probable cause to believe committed a misdemeanor.[28] Other statutes authorizing general law enforcement practices would likely be interpreted to prohibit enforcement of federal crimes because they provide narrower warrantless arrest powers. New Mexico's general statute empowering peace officers to investigate crimes explicitly limits their authority to "the criminal laws of the state."[29] Similarly, Florida's warrantless arrest statute authorizes arrests for felonies or misdemeanors "committed . . . in the presence of the officer."[30] Because the Supreme Court appears to view illegal entry as an offense that begins and ends at the moment of entry,[31] whereas the Eleventh Circuit, in which Florida sits, views illegal reentry as a continuing offense,[32] it is likely that Florida's warrantless arrest statute would not allow state or local officers to arrest a migrant for illegal entry but might allow arrest for illegal reentry.

Though these positions adopt different presumptions, they nonetheless expect that any enforcement of federal immigration crimes by state or local police officers will comply with the Fourth Amendment's requirements of reasonable belief to detain or probable cause to arrest. Importantly, simply knowing that a migrant is in the country without authorization is insufficient to establish reasonable suspicion or probable cause of illegal entry or illegal reentry because many people whose presence is unauthorized entered with the government's permission and did

---

28. *Gonzales,* 722 F.2d at 476–77.
29. N.M. Stat. Ann. § 29-1-1.
30. Fla. Stat. Ann. § 901.15(1).
31. United States v. Cores, 356 U.S. 405, 408 n.6 (1958); *see* INS v. Lopez-Mendoza, 468 U.S. 1032, 1057 (1984) (White, J., dissenting).
32. United States v. Castrillon-Gonzalez, 77 F.3d 403, 406 (11th Cir. 1996).

not leave. Likewise, as a federal district court explained, "The fact that
a law enforcement officer suspects, or even knows, that a vehicle passenger is not legally present in the country does not in and of itself provide reasonable suspicion that the passenger was or is being 'smuggled.'
Moreover, a passenger's lack of legal status, standing alone, is in no way
probative as to whether the driver is transporting the passenger for profit
or commercial purpose."[33]

Crucially, even if state or local police officers properly arrest a migrant, they have no power to initiate a criminal prosecution for a federal
immigration crime. This decision, if it is to be taken, is left to United
States Attorneys. The federal government therefore always plays an essential role in enforcing federal immigration crimes.

In other instances, state or local officials avoid relying on federal law by
tapping state criminal laws to prosecute migrants. As detailed in chapter 7,
there is a wide range of state crimes that apply only to migrants or that
apply to migrants in some unique fashion. Using these criminal statutes,
state and local officials can avoid turning power over to federal prosecutors to choose whether and how to pursue a possible criminal conviction.
When states and localities focus on state-law powers to target migrants,
they occasionally do so with excessive zeal and insufficient regard to constitutional limitations. An effort to identify unauthorized migrants living
in Weld County, Colorado, illustrates this point. Working together, the
county sheriff and district attorney in 2009 launched "Operation Number Games" in an effort to identify people working with a social security
number that did not belong to them. In carrying out "Operation Number
Games," sheriff's deputies seized thousands of confidential tax return files
from a local tax preparation business with a reputation for serving the
tax needs of the local migrant population. After sifting through the seized
files, local prosecutors charged dozens of people with identity theft or
criminal impersonation, both state crimes. The Colorado Supreme Court
eventually concluded that the prosecutions could not move forward with
evidence obtained through the tax preparation business's files because

33. Ortega-Melendres v. Arpaio, 836 F. Supp. 2d 959, 973, 975 (D. Ariz. 2011), *affd.
by* 695 F.3d 990 (9th Cir. 2012).

law enforcement officials overstepped constitutional bounds. The Fourth Amendment, the Court held, does not allow for such broad searches. For the government to intrude upon a person's reasonable expectation of privacy in confidential tax information, police officers must provide specific facts to conclude that there is probable cause that the person is believed to have committed a crime.[34]

Jurisdictions contemplating law enforcement actions that approach the blurry boundary between constitutionally permissible and impermissible conduct should consider possible costs. Police departments have occasionally been held liable for investigating immigration crimes in violation of the Fourth Amendment. Similarly, a number of city and county governments have faced liability for keeping a person incarcerated pursuant to an immigration detainer.[35] New York City, for example, settled one wrongfully confined man's lawsuit for $145,000.[36] To be sure, constitutional violations committed in the course of investigating criminal activity tend not to result in liability for the government agency or officer due to a variety of immunity doctrines.[37]

Divergent Prosecutorial Policies

Just as state and local law enforcement agencies take different views toward investigating immigration law activity, they also take different approaches to penalizing migrants who get caught up in the criminal justice system. In a study of forty-two county prosecutors' offices, legal scholar Ingrid V. Eagly identified three distinct formal policies used to guide plea-bargaining. Some offices allow prosecutors to consider potential adverse

---

34. *See* People v. Gutierrez, 222 P.3d 925, 929 (Colo. 2009).

35. *See, e.g.,* Galarza v. Szalczyk, 745 F.3d 634 (3d Cir. 2014); Miranda-Olivares v. Clackamas County, 2014 WL 1414305 (D. Or. Apr. 11, 2014); American Civil Liberties Union, Press Release, *Colorado Sheriff to Pay $30K to Woman Held on Immigration Detainer* (June 19, 2014), https://www.aclu.org/immigrants-rights/colorado-sheriff-pay-30k-woman-held-immigration-detainer (noting a $30,000 settlement Araphoe County, Colorado agreed to pay).

36. *Stipulation and Order of Settlement and Discontinuance,* Harvey v. City of New York, No. 07-cv-0343 (E.D.N.Y. June 12, 2009), http://www.legalactioncenter.org/sites/default/files/docs/lac/Harvey%20v.%20City%20of%20NY%20Stip%20Dismissal%20and%20Settlement.pdf.

37. *See, e.g., Miranda-Olivares,* 2014 WL 1414305 at *12 (noting county's immunity for false imprisonment claim under state tort law).

immigration consequences the defendant faces, others bar prosecutors from extending certain types of pleas to unauthorized migrants, and a couple prohibit prosecutors from considering immigration status or adverse immigration consequences.[38] Prosecutors in Los Angeles County, for example, deliberately seek to neutralize immigration status and possible immigration consequences by not seeking to enhance punishment by capitalizing on a defendant's immigration status while simultaneously taking immigration (and other) consequences into account during plea negotiations.[39] Harris County—in which Houston is located—takes a starkly contrasting approach. It treats unauthorized defendants more punitively than others by, among other things, imposing a high minimum bond solely due to immigration status and prohibiting prosecutors from agreeing to probation as part of a plea deal.[40] Most counties, however, lack any formal policy, leaving decisionmaking to informal processes based on an assortment of considerations.[41] This divergence means that attorneys need to become familiar with local practices. At the same time, it illustrates the impact that internal policies have on migrants and suggests the important role that advocates can play by focusing on prosecutorial practices.

Sanctuary Policies

In stark contrast to the harsh tactics states and localities sometimes employ against migrants described above, at times states, cities, and counties adopt inclusionary policies. Frequently referred to as "sanctuary" policies, these can take significantly different forms, though they all seek to shelter migrants from immigration law enforcement. Most commonly, sanctuary policies prohibit discrimination on the basis of citizenship status, enforcement of immigration laws generally, enforcement of civil immigration laws only, governmental inquiries about citizenship status, notification of federal immigration officials, or a combination of

38. Ingrid V. Eagly, *Criminal Justice for Noncitizens: An Analysis of Variation in Local Enforcement*, 88 NYU L. Rev. 1126, 1154 (2013).
39. *Id.* at 1157–69.
40. *Id.* at 1174–76.
41. *Id.* at 1153.

these.[42] Through an internal policy decision known as Special Order 40, the Los Angeles Police Department, for example, has bound itself since 1979 from "initiat[ing] police action with the objective of discovering the alien status of a person."[43] Much more recently, the city of Durango, Colorado, adopted a resolution prohibiting use of city funds "to identify, apprehend or deport any non-citizen residents on the sole basis of immigration status."[44] The City and County of San Francisco, meanwhile, prohibits using "funds or resources to assist in the enforcement of federal immigration law or to gather or disseminate information regarding the immigration status of individuals," though it goes on to exempt information regarding people who have been arrested or convicted of certain crimes.[45]

No matter the specific details of a sanctuary policy or the method through which it was promulgated, all must contend with Congress's desire to limit their existence. Since 1996, Congress has barred all government entities from prohibiting any government official "from sending to, or receiving from, the Immigration and Naturalization Service information regarding the citizenship or immigration status, lawful or unlawful, of any individual" (sometimes described as "don't tell" measures) via two identical statutory provisions.[46] This limitation only applies to disclosures of immigration information by government entities to federal immigration officials.[47] Congress was quite clear that at least one of these two provisions was "designed to prevent any State or local law, ordinance, executive order, policy, constitutional provision, or decision of any Federal or State court that prohibits or in any way restricts any communication between

---

42. Huyen Pham, *The Constitutional Right Not to Cooperate? Local Sovereignty and the Federal Immigration Power*, 74 U. Cin. L. Rev. 1373, 1389 (2006).

43. Los Angeles Police Department, *Office of the Chief of Police, Special Order 40* (Nov. 27, 1979), http://lapdonline.org/get_informed/pdf_view/44798.

44. Durango, Colo, *City Council Resolution No. 2004-40* (July 6, 2004), http://www.durangogov.org/DocumentCenter/View/782.

45. S.F., Cal., Admin. Code § 12H.2-2.1.

46. 8 U.S.C. § 1373(a) (enacted by Illegal Immigration Reform and Immigrant Responsibility Act, Pub. L. 104-208, 110 Stat. 3009-707, § 642 (Sept. 30, 1996)); 8 U.S.C. § 1644 (enacted by Personal Responsibility and Work Opportunity Reconciliation Act of 1996, Pub. L. 104-193, 110 Stat. 2105, § 434 (Aug. 22, 1996)).

47. Day v. Sebelius, 227 F.R.D. 668, 678 (D. Kansas Feb. 24, 2005).

State and local officials and the INS."[48] Though little case law has developed around these congressional restrictions, what does exist suggests
that some sanctuary policies are legally questionable. Considering a challenge that New York City brought to one of these statutory provisions
under the Tenth Amendment, the Second Circuit concluded that Congress
had not overstepped its authority. States and localities, the court held, "do
not retain under the Tenth Amendment an untrammeled right to forbid
all voluntary cooperation by state or local officials with particular federal
programs"—in this case, immigration law enforcement measures.[49]

Despite the Second Circuit's conclusion, many cities and counties continue to provide migrants with some type of safe harbor. This is possible in large part for political reasons: neither the federal government
nor state government in which sanctuary cities are located have much of
an incentive to raise constitutional challenges to these policies. There is
also an important legal reason, however, that helps explain the continued
viability of such policies. Intentionally or not, Congress wrote the federal
statutes that bar states and localities from limiting their employees' voluntary exchange of information with immigration officials narrowly. These
provisions only affect attempts to limit communication. The New York
policy that the Second Circuit determined the federal statutes trumped,
for example, prohibited city employees from "transmit[ing] information
respecting any alien to federal immigration authorities."[50] Critically, the
federal statutes do not affect policies that limit information gathering.
Quite simply, if government employees cannot ask about immigration
status, they cannot pass along immigration information to immigration officials. Likewise, federal law does not affect state or local policies that limit use of public funds for law enforcement tactics targeting
migrants. Without more, this limitation would not prevent cooperation
with immigration officials, but it would certainly make enforcing immigration law much more burdensome for federal officials than if a migrant

---

48. H.R. Rep. No. 104-725, at 383 (1996), *reprinted in* U.S.C.C.A.N. 2649, 2771.
49. City of New York v. United States, 179 F.3d 29, 35 (2nd Cir. 1999) (invalidating
New York City's Executive Order No. 124).
50. *Id.* (quoting New York City's Executive Order No. 124 § 2(a)).

were already in the custody of a state or local police force. Federal law, therefore, prohibits states and localities from enacting "don't tell" policies, but it says nothing about "don't ask" or "don't enforce" policies.

Further Reading

Anil Kalhan, *Immigration Policing and Federalism Through the Lens of Technology, Surveillance, and Privacy*, 74 Ohio State L.J. 1105 (2013).

Christopher N. Lasch, *Federal Immigration Detainers After* Arizona v. United States, 46 Loy. L.A. L. Rev. 629 (2013).

Huyen Pham, *The Constitutional Right Not to Cooperate? Local Sovereignty and the Federal Immigration Power*, 74 U. Cin. L. Rev. 1373 (2006).

Epilogue

In the passage that opens this book, the towering jurist Oliver Wendell Holmes reminds us that law is not static. It is a winding path through history, a dizzying foray into the vagaries of human nature, an adventure in the unpredictability of legislating, a maddening glimpse into the complexities of policing, and a test of faith in the righteousness of judicial interpretation. "The life of the law," he writes, "has not been logic: it has been experience."[1]

Crimmigration law encapsulates Holmes' vision. It is a product of human experience, a testament to the United States' greatest moments and its most visceral fears. The nation's well-earned self-image of welcoming migrants has been dotted by consistent efforts to demonize those same migrants through the power of criminal law. Despite attempts to penalize migration-related activity, legal advocates trained in the promises of equality and justice have resisted the worst excesses of the state's coercive powers.

---

1. OLIVER WENDELL HOLMES, JR., THE COMMON LAW 1 (Dover Publications 1991) (1881).

This book captures the story of life that has birthed crimmigration law in the United States. It tracks the use of immigration law to sanction for a second time migrants who have engaged in criminal activity. It details the criminal justice system's increasing concern about migration, with a special focus on legislators' attempts to raise the stakes of migration. And it explores the many enforcement tentacles that comprise the crimmigration law regime.

For all its detail, this book is necessarily incomplete. Crimmigration law, as Holmes suggests, is alive. And as with all living creatures, it is constantly changing. It will evolve with every day, propelled by perceptions of security or danger, comfort or unfamiliarity. It will move in the direction of further entangling the worlds of criminal law and immigration law if the community from which it has arisen so desires. It will move in the opposite direction—a direction more reflective of law's past—only if the fears of migrant criminality subside. The last three decades suggest that the former is much more likely than the latter.

If crimmigration law's creation and expansion shows anything, however, it is that law is perpetually malleable. Legislators, lawyers, and judges can and will continue to shape crimmigration law's reach. Only time will tell where this infant area of law leads. The only thing certain, as this book has illustrated, is that there will be much room for contestation as some legislators, lawyers, and courts expand crimmigration law, while others push back.

INDEX